Braude's Handbook of Humor for All Occasions

Compiled and Edited by
JACOB M. BRAUDE

Englewood Cliffs, N. J.
PRENTICE-HALL, INC.

ELEVENTH PRINTING.................. JANUARY, 1967

PRINTED IN THE UNITED STATES OF AMERICA

08134–MO

Dedication

*I dedicate this volume
with deep affection
to my dear wife
Adele
who has been my
constant inspiration.*

By the Same Author
and the Same Publisher

SPEAKER'S ENCYCLOPEDIA OF STORIES,
QUOTATIONS AND ANECDOTES

BRAUDE'S SECOND ENCYCLOPEDIA OF STORIES,
QUOTATIONS AND ANECDOTES

NEW TREASURY OF STORIES FOR
EVERY SPEAKING AND WRITING OCCASION

SPEAKER'S ENCYCLOPEDIA OF HUMOR

TABLE OF CONTENTS

HOW YOU CAN USE THIS HANDBOOK

Once when I addressed the St. Louis Rotary Club at one of its regular weekly luncheon meetings, I did what I had always done before and what I have been doing ever since—I asked the chairman how long he thought I should talk. Very graciously, but with a twinkle in his eye, he said, "Judge, we really don't care how long you talk—we all leave at 1:30."

When I rose to speak and repeated what had taken place between the chairman and me, there was a very positive reaction on the part of the audience. It seemed to establish a sympathetic relationship between us which brought me close to them and at the same time made me feel that I had brought them in direct rapport with me. I have been telling the story of that incident ever since, and in almost every case it tends to establish that same relationship with the audience.

On other occasions, just to vary the monotony, I will inform the audience that I have placed upon myself a strict limitation of time, because I have discovered from experience it is dangerous to turn loose a speaker, who ordinarily hands out thirty, sixty, or ninety days, without some sort of check rein.

Most of the pages to follow are made up of the gems of my personal collection of humorous stories. In this foreword, I'd like to make a few suggestions as to how this material may best be used, and I will try to keep it all brief enough so my audience won't get up and leave before I'm finished.

What is a humorous story?

Defining a humorous story is like trying to explain sex: everyone has his own ideas on the subject. What is hilarious to one person may evoke nothing more than a polite chuckle from another. Humor is a very personal thing. Take the boss who returned in high good humor from a luncheon and called his office staff together to tell them a few jokes. All laughed uproariously except one secretary who didn't change her expression. "What's the matter," grumped the boss, "don't you have any sense of humor?" "I don't have to laugh," said the girl, "I'm leaving Friday."

Yet, even though it be decidedly individual, one thing is certain about all humor: used tastefully and with discretion, it can do more to spice up a speech, liven up a social gathering, ease an uncomfortable atmosphere, bail out an awkward situation—and, incidentally, gain for its user a reputation of sincere good fellowship—than any other single accomplishment.

There's a real, genuine art to telling a funny story. But there are also a number of things which must precede the telling. Probably the most important is recognizing humor when you see it.

What makes a story funny? There are tried and true elements of humor, and familiarity with them will probably make you a better storyteller. At least I think it has been so with me. I have been on the lecture platform for many years, speaking at charity benefits, political meetings, church gatherings, teachers' institutes—and on occasions I have talked just because I had something to say and enjoyed saying it, and I have been doing this for over thirty years. During that time, I've used humor in ever-increasing doses, and so far I believe it has been effective. I haven't lost a single audience through applying liberal doses of humor, but perhaps, early in the game I lost a few for want of it.

What makes a story funny?

Over the years, I've found that these elements will appear in almost every humorous story:

Surprise: The unexpected always gives listeners a pleasurable start of surprise. ("That was no lady; that was my wife.")

Distortion: Almost all humor has in it some element of distortion. ("I don't belong to any organized party. I'm a Democrat.")

Incongruity: Human behavior is remarkably and consistently incongruous. Under an amiable spotlight, it makes a wonderful grist mill for humor. (As, for example, the nurse who told her patient:

2

"I hope everything comes out all right," as she wheeled her into the operating room.)

Impropriety: According to Somerset Maugham, "Impropriety is the soul of wit." (As witness the drug manufacturer who advertised: "Wanted, salesman. Employer guarantees job will be profitable for the undertaker.")

Exaggeration: This comes in two sizes: understatement and overstatement—both of which are simply a form of exaggeration. ("All I know is what I read in the newspaper.")

A humorous story should fit other requirements, too. It should be pertinent to the subject under discussion, otherwise it sounds dragged-in and loses much of its impact. It should be in reasonably good taste and offend no one. The safest joke is the one against one's self. It should have some element of originality. By this, I don't mean that you should make up all your own jokes, but that they should have something of you in them—some touch or modification that identifies them with your style or personality. And finally, a joke should be amusing—a rather obvious requirement which I hear violated frequently by speakers and self-confessed raconteurs.

A humorous story is much more effective if it has some purpose. You may recall that one of the greatest storytellers of all time, Abraham Lincoln, seldom told a joke unless he was illustrating a very specific point or emphasizing an idea. This is a good practice for every storyteller to follow.

Amusement, of course, can sometimes be an end unto itself. But if amusement is coupled with some other purpose, then the joke or story really becomes alive. The storyteller who is completely shallow offers all frosting and no cake when he strings one funny story after another; this is no more desirable than his opposite counterpart who never lightens his speech or conversation with wit. The answer is a happy medium. Use humor tastefully, knowingly, and effectively— but not indiscriminately or overwhelmingly.

In order to do this, it is absolutely imperative that you, yourself, be sold on the humorous story. If your heart isn't in it, you'll have trouble selling it to others. But if you give humor the respect and affection it deserves, it can do great and wonderful things for you— both socially and in business. And it can make living a great deal more fun in the process.

George Jean Nathan once wrote: "The man and woman who can laugh at their love, who can kiss with smiles and embrace with chuckles, will outlast in mutual affection all the throat-lumpy, cow-eyed couples of their acquaintance. Nothing lives on so fresh and ever-green as the love with a funnybone."

When should the humorous story be used?

In today's complex society, all of us are constantly being called upon to talk before groups of one kind or another—from sales meetings to P-TA boards to church committees to Saturday night bridge clubs.

Whatever the occasion or the group you are addressing, the humorous story can be used most effectively in four ways:

—At the beginning of a talk, to warm up an audience and get rid of any feeling of formality or austerity. (Orson Welles once opened a talk before a very sparse audience by saying: "I'm a director and producer of plays, motion picture and stage actor, writer and producer. I also write, direct, and act on the radio. I'm a magician and painter. I've published books, and I play the violin and piano." Here he paused and leered at his audience. "Isn't it a pity," he continued, "that there are so many of me and so few of you.")

—To wrap up a talk on a warm note. (Winston Churchill once advised Lord Halifax on ending a speech: "Say what you have to say and when you come to a sentence with a grammatical ending, sit down.")

—As a text on which to hang a specific theme or plea. (If you were advocating caution with the promises of other countries, you might hang your entire talk on the story about the foxes and fowls who once made a truce and agreed to get along together happily and harmoniously with no aggression on either side. As soon as the agreement was signed, all the fowls went happily out into the henyard where the foxes were wont to prowl. One old hen, however, stayed behind. When some of her younger cohorts asked "Why?" she answered: "I know all about the agreement, but there's bound to be some damned fool of a fox who hasn't heard about it.")

4

—To illustrate points, conclusions or ideas in the body of a discussion. (To bulwark the position that it's important that a group or a committee launch a new program, you might point out: "We're like a turtle—not much good until we stick our neck out a little.")

Nothing is more important than appropriateness in deciding whether or not to tell a story. Jokes about old maids would hardly be appropriate before a group of school teachers or jesting about alcoholism to a convention of liquor manufacturers. But nothing is better than a genuine laugh to smooth over rough places in a gathering of people or to save an uncomfortable situation. When a well-known speaker swallowed a bug, then choked and sputtered in the midst of a semi-serious presentation, the situation might well have been awkward. But he saved it—and even turned it to his own advantage—by saying, when he had regained his composure: "Serves him right. He should have watched where he was going."

I once made the worst possible of all speaking errors by effusing over a town in which I was speaking and then calling it by the wrong name. I was immediately corrected by someone in the audience. "I know," I told him. "I just wanted to see if you were alert." That line got a laugh, and as for me, I got out of a sticky situation.

Should the public address system fail, I like to tell my audience about the speaker who suspected the microphone wasn't working properly and asked a gentleman in the back row if he could hear. "No," was the reply, whereupon a man in the front row stood up and shouted: "I can hear fine. How about changing places with me."

All of these situations could easily and completely break the rapport between speaker and audience. But by the judicious use of humor, one is able to produce just the opposite result.

Finding the story

Where do you go to find a sure laugh-getter in order to be the life of the party—or the speaking platform? There are three principal sources.

The most common, most easily accessible, and at the same time the most treacherous, is your memory. Good storytellers usually have a sizeable mental file of humor tucked away in their subconscious, from which to pull out the proper story for any and every occasion. Much of the apparent ad-libbing you hear from professional comedians or citizens having a reputation for turning a funny story isn't ad-libbing at all—it's simply a prodigious memory at work, disgorging the right story at the right time. Such a memory can be cultivated. One fairly effective method is to implant a story firmly in your mind by telling it to the next half-dozen people you see after you've first heard it. If you're not completely sick of it by that time, it will probably stick with you—ready to be called on at the appropriate time. As Irvin S. Cobb has pointed out: "A good storyteller is a person who has a good memory and hopes other people haven't."

But to those who haven't the time to work at memorizing, or haven't the elephant-like facility to stockpile stories into a mental cache, two other courses are open. The first one takes some reasonably earnest effort; I know, because I've worked at it for many years. This is a card file of stories, carefully indexed and crossindexed by subject matter. To set up and maintain such a file requires only a few odd moments each day, a sharp pair of scissors, a paste-pot, some index cards, a file box, and "an enormous amount of research." Someone has aptly said that if you steal from one, that's plagiarism; if you steal from a hundred, that's research. With this must be coupled a squirrel-like propensity for hoarding. The stories which follow on the pages of this book are relatively few of the many thousands of humorous flotsam and jetsam which I have collected for almost a half-century. You can easily start the same sort of collection yourself—and make it as extensive as you like. If you do, be sure to keep it functional by categorizing the material meticulously. Only in this way can it be of maximum use to you.

The other major source is comprised of the anthologies of humor —some good, some poor, some indifferent. Such books are readymade files of funny stories; they are not, however, frequently indexed to help you find the right story for the right occasion as quickly as possible. Here, most of the spade work has been done by someone else. All you have to do is find the stories to illustrate your specific points, and then choose the one or two you want to use.

In seeking out your stories, however, beware of two major pitfalls. First of all, don't try to pry and strain and force a story into a situation if it doesn't fit, simply because you just heard it and thought

6

it to be hilariously funny. Under those circumstances, it probably won't be funny at all in the retelling.

And secondly, be careful about expecting written or pictured stories which were real laugh-getters to provoke the same results when told. Many written stories and most picture gags do not lend themselves very well to oral expression. If you attempt to make the transposition, try also to adapt the story to telling rather than to reading.

Preparing the story

Now that we have an idea as to what humor is, and have our fingers on a number of sources of funny stories, how do we prepare them for the telling?

If you think no preparation is necessary, then you're probably considered a first-class "square" as a storyteller in your business as well as your social circles.

The first and most important thing about preparing a story is to make it clearly and distinctly your own. Everyone has a speaking style—just as writers have distinctive writing styles. You should never attempt to tell a story that cannot be adapted to your speaking style. This sometimes necessitates taking liberties with a story. A minister would hardly tell a story in the same manner as a bartender; yet the same story might well illustrate a pertinent point for each of these gentlemen. Each, of course, would have to adapt it to his own style before telling it.

The speaker who makes no effort to convert a body of material to his own style is much in the position of the preacher who had to appear before his congregation without sufficient time to prepare his sermon. He started out, "This morning we will have to rely on the Lord for guidance and read our sermon from the Bible. Tonight I will come better prepared."

You can also gain impact from a story by turning it into a personal narrative—either connected with someone in your audience or with yourself. The use of the first or second person is much more effective in putting across a joke than the impersonal third person. The late comedian, Bob Burns, was an outstanding example of how to personalize jokes. His narratives always had personality; yours can, too.

Then you should tell the type of stories you most enjoy telling. Your own feeling about a story is infectious. If you don't *really* like it, you can hardly expect your audience to like it. So when you're deciding whether or not to tell a particular story, make sure you like it yourself.

Here are a few other hints in preparing your story; if somehow or other you can work in the audience, by all means do so—and if you can build them up in the process, so much the better. And be sure to *learn your story*. Nothing can be more deadly or devastating than the self-satisfied raconteur who stops midway through his story on the way to its climax, and then tries frantically to recall the punch line. This isn't the way to get ahead through humor—no matter what sort of an audience you may be addressing. As for myself, before I tell a story to any group, I rehearse it—many times. When I finally tell it, I know it. I strongly recommend this same procedure to you.

Actually, a good storyteller is in much the same position as the rookie paratrooper who came to his sergeant and asked for a transfer. "How come?" asked the sergeant.

"I just don't like parachute jumping," answered the rookie.

"But why?" persisted the sergeant.

"Well," answered the recruit, "I guess I don't like to practice at anything where I have to be perfect the first time."

Some "Do's" in telling a story

Now that we have selected and prepared the story, we're ready for the business of telling it. It's impossible to be specific in telling someone else how to tell a funny story. But there *are* some helpful general hints that I like to call my ten commandments for effective storytelling.

1. Enjoy the story thoroughly yourself—and thereby get all of the original freshness and punch out of it.

2. Follow the proper, logical sequence in telling the story. Confusion is not helpful to an audience from whom you are seeking a laugh.

3. Keep it simple—in the terms used, in number of characters, in length, in pace.

4. Personalize it as much as possible.

5. Try to make the wit sound spontaneous—never forced.

6. Use humor sparingly enough in a semi-serious discussion so that it glitters when it appears, while at the same time it spices up the point under discussion.

7. Construct your story in such a way that it concludes rather abruptly with some climactic word or phrase. Then for heaven's sake, quit. Don't "step on your laugh" with anticlimactic prattle.

8. Try to build laughs throughout the story. This won't detract from your punch line. On the contrary, it will sharpen it by putting the audience in a receptive mood for the climax of the story.

9. Use the collective insult—an increasingly popular laugh-getting device these days—with great care. It can be used effectively if used good-naturedly and without animus. But it can also ruffle some feathers if not used tactfully. Fortunately, it's human nature for an individual to figure that the speaker is talking about everyone but him when a collective insult is offered—which is why speakers get away with it. But if you try this technique, be sure to stay within areas of recognized strength and superiority. Thus you can insult the athletic prowess of a group of All-Americans or the musical knowledge of an organization of composers. But use this device with extreme caution.

10. Finally, above all else, be yourself. In the human scheme of things, some people are better storytellers than others. Your objective should be to get the most out of the talents you possess. Trying to be something you aren't doesn't serve this end. An easy, natural amiability—which doesn't attempt to tackle material beyond its depth—will tell and sell a story better than well-practiced and carefully-calculated sham.

And some "Don'ts"

Learning what *not* to do is every bit as important in storytelling as knowing the positive side. Here are some things I strongly recommend avoiding if you want to bring off a successful bit of spoken humor:

1. Don't announce that a funny story is now coming up. Try to slip into it easily and effortlessly, and be in the midst of it before your listeners are aware of what is going on.

9

2. Don't use material that is so foreign to the experience of the audience as to be virtually meaningless.

3. Try never to tell a story in which you yourself "played the hero." If you're the butt of the joke, well and good. But there is seldom anything funny to an audience in a speaker telling how he scored a personal triumph.

4. Never tell a story that makes you uncomfortable, or of which you're the slightest bit ashamed. The speaker who has to resort to off-color stories to make a point is seldom invited to speak again. BUT—if you decide, for some compelling reason, to tell a doubtful story, then tell it confidently and not apologetically.

5. It is best not to laugh at your own jokes—at least not sufficiently so that you get in the way of your story.

6. Don't tell a story to death. Just give your audience enough to make the punch line very clear.

7. Never, never tell a story that will offend anyone who might be listening. If even one person in a group might be offended, the other listeners will resent your use of such material. It just isn't worth the risk; consequently, you should take great care not to step on any individual sensibilities.

8. It is best never to repeat a story before the same group unless you can satisfactorily explain away the need for so doing.

9. Don't oversell an upcoming joke; it may not be as funny to your audience as it was to you.

10. Avoid dialects unless you are peculiarly suited to telling this sort of joke, or unless dialect is absolutely necessary to put over your point. Most people do not tell dialect stories well, although many of them think they are adept at doing so. On the whole, the scales are tipped decidedly against dialect jokes for the run-of-the-mill storyteller. In addition to the fact that they are oftentimes offensive to someone, it takes exceptional skill to tell them correctly. Try to assess your own abilities in this direction with a reasonable amount of objectivity before you embark on a dialect story. If there's a question of good taste, or if you doubt your dialect abilities, by all means leave that sort of story strictly alone.

11. Avoid profanity; it is very seldom funny.

Now, having disposed of all these rules and regulations, let me go back to the point at which we started: the greatest asset in telling a humorous story is an appreciative sense of humor. If you have none, I feel sorry for you, because you're missing the greatest asset with which God has endowed us for meeting the everyday problems of life.

Sinclair Lewis once wrote: "There are two insults which no human will endure: the assertion that he hasn't a sense of humor; and the doubly impertinent assertion that he has never known trouble." So if, happily, you are able to have a laugh at yourself and the world around you once in a while, then the foregoing thoughts may be helpful to you.

In all the foregoing my intentions are to be helpful—like the kind-hearted elephant who assisted the indigent hen in hatching her eggs by sitting on them for her. Or the sweet old home-front lady who knitted a pair of socks for a soldier. He put them on gratefully on a cold day near the front, then limped for two tortured hours of marching. When the column finally rested, he pulled off his shoes, peeled the sock off his aching foot, and found a wad of paper rolled into the toe. Opening it, he read a note saying: "God bless your tired feet."

Unlike these well-intentioned people, I hope that the collection of humor to follow and my suggestions for making the best use of these confections will offer utility as well as good intentions.

And even if you never use them at all—if, praise be, you're never asked to speak to anyone, anywhere, I think you'll enjoy reading them. I still do, after having looked at them many thousands of times.

One final thing. I have provided this volume with a set of three indexes which I hope will be helpful. There is no use trying to recall a story or trying to tell it if you can't put your finger on it when you need it. The several indexes should be very helpful in this regard. In addition to the general index which lists the subject items as well as all names and personalities referred to in the text, this volume is unique in that it contains, in addition, two special indexes; one for Special Occasions and the other for Special Groups, and under each of these I have selected some items which could properly be used when addressing such groups or speaking on such occasions.

HUMOR

SECTION

Advertising

1. *Hard-boiled sales manager:* "Show me a single order that advertising ever put on our books."

Salesman: "I will, just as soon as you show me one load of hay that was ever put in the barn by the sun."

2. A man who owned a house on Chicago's fashionable Lake Shore Drive decided he was tired of it and called upon a real estate broker to offer it for sale in his behalf.

In the following Sunday's *Chicago Tribune* he read the ad which the broker had worked up for him. It sounded so good that he re-read it to himself. Then he called up the broker, to whom he said: "I've decided not to sell." "What made you change your mind?" asked the realtor. "That ad of yours," he replied. "It convinced me that this was the kind of house I've been looking for all my life."

3. A bulletin board outside a church announced Sunday services— "Do you know what hell is?" Underneath was printed in small letters—"Come and hear our organist."

4. John Wanamaker's first advertising man refused to tell anything but the literal truth in his ads. The buyer of neckties sent for him one day and asked him to get up an ad along these lines: "You can have these beautiful neckties for 25¢, reduced from $1." The ad man looked at the ties, felt them, then asked, "Are they any good?"

The buyer said, "No, they're not."

The ad man went back to his office and wrote this ad:

> "THEY'RE NOT AS GOOD AS THEY LOOK,
> BUT THEY'RE GOOD ENOUGH—25¢."

Wanamaker was buying cheap ties for three weeks to supply the demand.

5. One of the insurance organization's stenographers persisted in falling asleep at her desk. The situation being what it was, the cashier felt he should talk it over with the office manager before discharging her.

ADVERTISING

The manager was definitely perturbed. "But we can't let her go," he moaned. "You know we'd never be able to get another girl to take her place." Then a possible solution to the problem dawned upon him.

"I'll tell you what," he suggested. "Print a placard to hang on her when she's sleeping at her desk. Say on it: 'When you are adequately covered by insurance, you, too, will sleep this way.'"

6. Not long ago a patron of a restaurant in Chicago summoned his waiter and delivered himself as follows:

"I want to know the meaning of this. Look at this piece of beef. See its size. Last evening I was served with a portion twice the size of this."

"Where did you sit?" asked the waiter.

"What has that to do with it? I believe I sat by the window."

"In that case," smiled the waiter, "the explanation is simple. We always serve customers by the window large portions. It's good advertising for the place."

7. The Reverend Earl Devanny (a Protestant pastor with an Irish-sounding name), of Woodbridge, New Jersey, advertised a sermon entitled "What Heaven Is Like, and How To Get In."

This drew only a moderate congregation. So the minister thought hard and advertised another sermon for the following Sunday. The title was: "What Hell Is Like, and How To Get In."

This time the response was so overwhelming that the church was filled to overflowing.

8. The managing editor of a well-known publication once asked a man, "Did you ever have your hat blown off?"

"Yes," said the merchant.

"What blew it off?"

"The wind."

"Did you ever see the wind?"

"No."

"Well, advertising is like the wind—an invisible force. You can't see it but you can and will see the results, just as you saw your hat go rolling down the street."

9. "Advertising costs me a lot of money."

16

"Why, I never saw your goods advertised."

"They aren't. But my wife reads other people's ads."

10. Ignace Paderewski, the talented Polish pianist, arrived in a small western town about noon one day and decided to take a walk in the afternoon. While strolling along he heard a piano, and following the sound, came to a house on which was a sign reading:

MISS JONES. PIANO LESSONS 25¢ AN HOUR

Pausing to listen, he heard the young woman trying to play one of Chopin's nocturnes, and not succeeding very well.

Paderewski walked up to the house and knocked. Miss Jones came to the door and recognized him at once. Delighted, she invited him in and he sat down and played the nocturne as only Paderewski could, afterwards spending an hour in correcting her mistakes. Miss Jones thanked him and he departed.

Some months afterwards he returned to the same town, and again took the same walk.

He soon came to the home of Miss Jones, and looking at the sign, he read:

MISS JONES. PIANO LESSONS $1.00 AN HOUR.
(PUPIL OF PADEREWSKI).

11. "To what do you owe your advanced age and good health?" asked the stranger.

"Can't say yet," said the old man, "but there's several of those testimonial fellers dickering with me."

Advice

12. Two battered old hulks of humanity were sitting together on a park bench. One of them leaned over and said to his neighbor, "I'm a man who never took advice from anybody."

"Shake, pal," said the other, "I'm the man who followed everybody's advice."

13. When General Mark Clark was asked what was the best advice he ever received, he answered: "To marry the girl I did."

"Who gave you that advice, General?" his questioner asked.

The General smiled. "She did."

17

ADVICE

14. *Young Man* (buying an engagement ring): Will you please engrave it "From Henry to Clara"?

Jeweler: Take my advice, and just have "From Henry."

15. A man and his two sons were leading a donkey to town to sell him. They had not gone far when they met a group of girls returning from town. "Look!" cried one, "did you ever see such fools. There they have a donkey to ride and what are they doing, leading him." So the father put his sons on the donkey and proceeded on the way. At length they came upon a group of men talking in earnest. "There!" said one of them. "That proves exactly what I was saying, no one pays any respect to old age these days. Look at those two young men riding while their poor old father walks."

The father stopped the donkey and told his sons to dismount so he could take their place, and in this manner they proceeded along the way until they met a group of women and children.

"Shame on you," they cried, "how can you ride when your sons can hardly keep up with you?" The good father, wishing to please, hoisted his sons up behind him on the donkey.

Just as they were entering town, a citizen called out to them: "I have a good mind to report you to the animal society for overloading that poor beast—you big hulks should be carrying that poor donkey instead of him carrying you."

The father and his sons dismounted and tied the donkey's legs together, and with a pole across their shoulders, carried the donkey on into town.

Just as they were crossing over a stream of water, a group of townsfolk started laughing at them. The poor animal, frightened by the uproar, struggled to free himself. In the midst of the turmoil, the donkey slipped off the pole and over the side into the water and was drowned. *Moral:* Try to please all and you will please none.

16. Willie arrived home with two black eyes.

"Fighting again!" said his mother. "Didn't I tell you that when you are angry you should count a hundred before you do anything?"

"Yes, I know," replied Willie, "but the other boy's mother told him to count only to fifty."

17. *Motto:* "Keep your nose to the grindstone, your shoulder to

18

the wheel, and your eye on the ball. Now try to work in that position."

Age

18. "How old are you?" asked a caller.

"Well," said little Billie, "when I'm home I'm five, when I'm in school I'm six, and when I'm on a streetcar I'm four."

19. "Your age, please?" asked the census taker.

"Well," said the woman, "let me figure it out. I was 18 when I married and my husband was 30. He is now 60, or twice as old as he was then, so I am now 36."

20. A young man foolishly twitted a much older man on his age. The older man looked at him and said: "Young man, an ass is older at twenty than a man at sixty."

21. A young man was deeply in love with a beautiful girl. One day she told him that the next day would be her birthday, and he laughingly said that he would send her a bunch of roses, one for each year of her life.

That evening he wrote to his florist, ordering twenty-four roses to be sent to the young lady on the first delivery the following day.

The proprietor of the flower shop, looking over the mail in the morning, saw the order and said to his salesman:

"Tom, here's an order from young Mr. Higgins for twenty-four roses. He's a mighty good customer; let's give him a break and put in an extra dozen."

And the young man never did find out what made the young lady so angry with him.

22. *Traffic officer:* "As soon as I saw you coming around the curve, I said to myself, 'Forty-five at least.'"

Woman driver: "Well, you're way off. It's this hat that makes me look so old."

23. *Ruth:* "How old are you?"

Goldie: "I just turned twenty-three."

Ruth: "I get it. Thirty-two."

AGING

24. *Judge:* "Your age, madam?"
Lady witness: "Thirty years."
Judge: "You may have difficulty proving that."
Lady witness: "You will find it difficult to prove the contrary. The church that had the record of my birth burned down in 1920."

25. A doctor asked a woman patient her age.
"I never tell anyone my age," she answered coyly, "but, as a matter of fact, I've just reached twenty-one."
"Indeed," said the doctor, "what detained you?"

26. *Joe:* "Did you ever see a company of women silent?"
Bloe: "Yes, I have."
Joe: "When?"
Bloe: "When the chairman asked the oldest lady to speak up."

27. *Visitor:* "And how old are you, my little man?"
Little Man: "Well, it's like this. The latest aptitude test shows my psychological age to be 12; my moral age, 4; my anatomical age, 7; and my physiological age, 6. I suppose, however, you want to know my chronological age; that's 8."

28. Little Bobby was called from his play to meet a visitor.
"How old are you, little man?" he was asked.
"I'm at the awkward age," he replied.
"Really?" asked the visitor. "What do you mean by the awkward age?"
"Too old to cry and too young to swear."

Aging

29. You really are getting old when your work is less fun and your fun is more work.

30. A nice old gentleman of 75 got a perfect score on a medical check-up, and the physician asked him how he kept in such good condition.
"Well, sir," he replied, "when I was married some 50 years ago, my wife and I agreed that if I lost my temper she would remain silent, and if she lost her temper I would leave the house. I attribute my good health to the well-known advantages of an outdoor life!"

20

31. Fresh from the back-country, the youngster at the recruiting officer's desk was being subjected to routine questioning. Birthday? No, he didn't know when that was, but—he brightened—he knew how old he was; he was 32. The officer was skeptical. How did he know? Maw had told him once how old he was and he added a year at plowing time ever since.

"Well," queried the officer, "did you add a year at spring plowing or at fall plowing?"

"Dog-gone it," exclaimed the would-be sailor, "that explains it. I thought I was getting old too derned fast!"

32. Uncle Zeze, the town character, was 80 years old.

"Don't you hate to grow old?" he was asked.

"Heck, no," was his answer. "If I wasn't old I'd be dead."

33. "Your wife used to be terribly nervous. Now she is cool and composed as a cucumber. What cured her?"

"The doctor did. He told her that her kind of nervousness was the usual symptom of advancing age."

34. Mr. and Mrs. Victor Borge met Sonja Heine, the skating queen, at a party. "My," Mrs. Borge said later, "she certainly looks young?"

"Why not?" Victor commented. "She's been on ice all her life."

Ancestry

35. "Well, I've got nothing to complain about," said the slightly disheveled young man as he listened to another slightly disheveled young man describe his ejection from a dance hall in a tough neighborhood. "They treated me all right."

"They did?"

"Yes, they threw me out the back door but when I told the bouncer that I came from a very good family he picked me up gently, brushed me off, and escorted me back into the dance hall. Then he threw me out the front door."

36. "I have a very distasteful job," complained the genealogist. "I have been employed by Mrs. Richey to look up her family tree, and it will be my unpleasant duty to inform her that one of her ancestors was electrocuted at Sing Sing."

"Why worry about that? Just tell her the man occupied the chair of applied electricity at one of our public institutions."

37. Two men were discussing the Darwin theory of evolution one morning as they rode their train to work. As they talked, a man sitting behind them pricked up his ears and finally leaned over from his seat.

"Do you men really believe in that Darwinian theory?" he asked curtly.

"Yes," quickly retorted one of the men, "and I am inclined to go farther than Darwin did."

"What do you mean by that?" snapped the man in the seat behind.

"Well, sir," smiled the first, "I believe that some members of *your* species have started on the return trip."

38. Isadora Duncan, the great dancer, once wrote to George Bernard Shaw and suggested, or so the wits say: "We two ought to have a child, so it could inherit my beauty and your brains."

Shaw reportedly wrote back: "Madam, I am flattered—but suppose it turned out to have my beauty and your brains?"

39. Signor Marconi, inventor of wireless telegraphy, was once interviewed in Washington, and spoke in praise of American democracy.

"Over here," he said, "you respect a man for what he is himself —not for what his family is—and thus you remind one of the gardener in Bologna who helped me with my first wireless apparatus.

"As we worked together on the apparatus a young count joined us one day, and while he watched us work he boasted of his lineage.

"The gardener, after listening a long while, smiled and said:

" 'If you come from an ancient family, it's so much the worse for you, sir; for, as we gardeners say, the older the seed the worse the crop.' "

40. "That sergeant! I've never heard a man talk so fast in all my life."

"Why shouldn't he? His father was a tobacco auctioneer and his mother was a woman."

Antiques

41. An antique collector passing through a small village stopped to watch an old man chopping wood with an ancient ax. "That's a mighty old ax you have there," he remarked.

"Yup," said the villager, "it once belonged to George Washington."

"Not really!" gasped the collector. "It has certainly stood up well."

"Of course," admitted the old man, "it's had three new handles and two new heads."

42. An architect was having a difficult time with a prospective home builder. "But can't you give *some* idea," he pleaded, "of the general type of house you want to build?"

"Well—" replied the man hesitantly, "all I know is it must go with an antique doorknob my wife bought in Vermont."

43. *Bridesmaid:* "She's the angriest bride-to-be I've ever seen. I just can't imagine why; the newspapers carried a complete account of her wedding plans."

Maid of Honor: "That's true—they even included the fact that the groom is a well-known collector of antiques."

44. *Customer:* "What! Five hundred dollars for that antique? Why, I priced it last week and you said three hundred and fifty."

Dealer: "Yes, I know; but the cost of labor and materials has gone up so!"

Apology

45. Greatly excited, a man hurried into the office of a country editor and exclaimed, "That notice of my death in your paper is a lie, sir, a lie. I'll horsewhip you in public if you don't correct it and apologize in your next issue."

The next issue of the paper contained the following announcement:

"We regret to announce that the paragraph in our last issue which stated that Colonel Wimpole is dead is not true."

46. An incorrigible youngster was hauled before the principal for having told his teacher to go to that four-letter place where they have no snow.

The principal explained to him that such language could not be tolerated, but that if he would apologize to his teacher, she might give him another chance.

The boy was too stubborn to back down completely. Finally, however, between sniffles, he managed to make some concession: "Miss Peters," he said, "you don't need to go there now."

Appreciation

47. "Little pictures leave me cold; it's the grand, big canvases that I like."

"You're an art critic, I take it?"

"Not I; I'm a frame maker."

48. *Stranger:* "Good morning, doctor, I just dropped in to tell you how much I benefited from your treatment."

Doctor: "But you're not one of my patients."

Stranger: "I know. But my uncle was and I'm his heir."

Arithmetic

49. The teacher was hearing the youthful class in mathematics.

"No," she said, "in order to subtract, things have to be in the same denomination. For instance, we couldn't take three pears from four peaches, nor eight horses from ten cats. Do you understand?"

There was assent from the majority of the pupils but one little boy in the rear raised his hand inquiringly.

"Well, Bobby," asked the teacher, "what is it?"

"Please, teacher," he said, "couldn't you take three quarts of milk from two cows?"

50. Spring vacation was near and the teacher was trying to give her class an impression of fractions which would last until school resumed. She told them they could think of fractions at home as well as in school and gave such examples as "half a sandwich," "a quarter of a pie" and "tenth part of a dollar."

At that point one little boy caught on and proudly contributed, "My father came home last night with a fifth."

51. "Put down," the little fellow said, reading from a book, "ten pounds of sugar at twenty cents a pound, and four pounds of coffee at eighty cents a pound, and two pounds of butter at seventy-two cents a pound, and two bars of soap at fifteen cents each."

"I've got them down," said the grocer, looking up from his pad.

"How much does it come to?" the lad asked.

The grocer totalled the column.

"Six dollars and ninety-four cents," he announced.

"And if I were to give you a ten-dollar bill how much change would I get?"

"Three dollars and six cents," said the grocer impatiently. "Come son, let's get going. I'm in a hurry."

"Oh, I didn't want to buy them," said the boy as he quickly disappeared through the door. "That's our arithmetic lesson for tomorrow and I needed help with it."

52. "If there were four flies on a table and I killed one, how many would be left?" asked the teacher.

"One," answered the bright little girl—"the dead one."

53. A pretty girl taking public-service examinations had this problem put to her: If a man buys an article for $12.25 and sells it for $9.75, does he gain or lose by the transaction?

The young thing pondered deeply, then answered: "He gains on the cents but loses on the dollars."

54. *Son:* "But, Dad, I don't want to study arithmetic."

Father: "What, a son of mine doesn't want to grow up to be able to figure out baseball scores and batting averages?"

Art

55. *Critic:* "It's an elegant statue, all right, but isn't that an odd position for a general to assume?"

Sculptor: "Perhaps it is. You see, I was halfway finished when the committee decided that it couldn't afford a horse for him."

56. *Visitor to art exhibit:* "Why did they hang this picture?"

Friend: "It must be because they couldn't find the artist!"

57. When Grant Wood painted scenes of his native Iowa, he would usually take artistic license, painting the villages and fields the way he wished they looked rather than as they were. Once, when he got through painting a neighbor's farm, having again improved something here and there, he showed the finished product to the farmer, who looked at it and remarked: "Yep, looks just like it—and thanks for cutting the weeds."

58. The French artist, Dufy, had completed a somewhat idealized portrait for an important client. "But," protested the patron, "it doesn't look like me!"

"Well, then," responded the imperturbable Dufy, "try to look like your portrait."

Attention

59. "You lied to me," said the farmer to a salesman who had sold him a mule. "I handled that mule like a baby, and yet I can't get him to do a single lick of work."

"Let's go out and have a look at him," said the salesman.

They went to the farm. The mule was standing hitched to a plow. He wouldn't budge. The salesman picked up a heavy stick and broke it over the mule's head. "Now try him," he said.

"Giddap," said the farmer and the mule started off.

"I don't understand this," the farmer said. "I'm sure that you told me I'd have to treat this mule gently."

"You do," said the salesman. "But first you have to get his attention."

60. "See that boy over there annoying Mary?"
"Why, he isn't even looking at her."
"Yes, and that's just what's annoying her."

Auction

61. A man finally bought a parrot at an auction after some very spirited bidding.

"I suppose the bird talks," he said to the auctioneer.

"Talks?" was the reply. "He's been bidding against you for the past half hour."

26

62. "And this," said a house owner, pointing to an oil-portrait, "is one of my ancestors."

"Yes," replied his visitor. "You know, he came very nearly being mine. I bid up to fifty pounds for that picture at an auction, but I couldn't afford any more."

Authorship

63. Announcements of the professor's new book and his wife's new baby appeared almost simultaneously. The professor, when he was congratulated by a friend upon "this proud event in your family," naturally thought of that achievement which had cost him the greater effort and modestly replied:

"Well, I couldn't have done it without the help of two graduate students."

64. It was P. G. Wodehouse who dedicated one of his books to his wife and daughter like this:

"Without whose unfailing help and advice this book could have been written in half the time."

65. An idealistic lady complained to the writer of popular novels that nothing he had written would live.

"Perhaps not," said the realist, "but when it's a question of me or my writings living, I always sacrifice my writings."

66. An aspiring author sent a manuscript to an editor with a letter in which he stated, "The characters in this story are purely fictional and bear no resemblance to any person, living or dead."

A few days later he received his manuscript with the penciled notation: "That's what's wrong with it."

67. A struggling author had called on a publisher about a manuscript he had submitted.

"This is quite well-written, but my firm only publishes works by writers with well-known names," said the publisher.

"Splendid," said the author. "My name's Smith."

68. Seven times a persistent young playwright brought to Charles Frohman an impossible farce, slightly rewritten after each submission, and seven times the celebrated producer rejected it.

"Once and for all, the play won't do!" Frohman stormed. "There is no need showing it to me again!"

"But isn't there some way you can put it on the stage?" the playwright pleaded.

Frohman reflected a moment. "There is one way," he admitted, "but you wouldn't care for it."

"Oh, I'd submit to anything to get my play on the stage!" the eager playwright declared.

"Very well, then," said Frohman. "We'll just grind it up and use it as a snowstorm."

69. Russel Crouse, the noted author and playwright, once told a group of authors that the best rejection slip he ever heard of was the one which read: "I'm returning this paper—someone wrote on it." It was signed by the editor.

70. Asked if he had known Mark Twain, the white-bearded proprietor of a roadside stand in Hannibal, Missouri, where the great humorist had spent his boyhood days, replied:

"Sure, I knew him," was the prompt and indignant reply. "And I know just as many stories as he did, too. Only difference is, he writ 'em down."

71. The teacher had assigned her class to write a composition on the funniest thing they had ever seen. Almost immediately after the assignment, she noticed that Johnny was folding his paper. So she asked him to bring his essay forward if he had finished. He did so, and here is what the teacher read: "The funniest thing I ever saw was too funny for words."

72. *Author:* "Here is the manuscript I offered you last year."
Editor: "What's the idea of bringing this thing back when I rejected it last year?"
Author: "Well, you see, you've had a year's experience since then."

73. "So you got your poem printed?"
"Yes," replied the author. "I sent the first stanza to the editor of the Correspondence Column with the inquiry, 'Can anyone give me the rest of this poem?' Then I sent in the complete poem over another name."

Automobile

74. "If your wife wants to learn to drive the car, don't stand in her way!"

75. *Used car dealer* (driving up a hill): "This is the opportunity of a lifetime."

Customer: "Yes, I can hear it knocking."

76. "I've been watching that mechanic for the last 15 minutes. There's a man who really knows his business. He didn't spill a drop of oil on the ground. He put the hood down gently, fastened it securely, and left no fingerprints on it. He wiped his hands on a clean tissue before opening the door, spread a clean cloth over the upholstery, meshed the gears noiselessly, and drove carefully out into the street."

"Yeah, that's his own car."

77. A man stopped at a small town garage and told the mechanic, "Whenever I hit eighty, there's a terrible knocking in the engine."

The mechanic gave the vehicle a prolonged and thorough examination, and after much testing, wiped the grease from his hands and drawled, "I don't see nothin' wrong, mister. It must be the good Lord a-warnin' you."

Bachelorhood

78. An old man was talking to a bachelor and asked him why he did not marry. The bachelor parried the question by telling about different young women he had known, finding some fault with each one. But it appeared that all of them had succeeded in getting married.

"You are in danger of getting left," said the old man to him. "You had better hurry up before it's too late."

"Oh," said the bachelor, "there are just as many good fish left in the sea."

"That may be true," replied the old man, "but the bait—isn't there danger of the bait becoming stale?"

79. "Is Dan a confirmed bachelor?"

"He is now. He sent his picture to a Lonely Hearts Club and they sent it back with a note saying, "We're not that lonely.""

80. *Miss Joyce:* "I know he's rich, but isn't he too old to be considered eligible?"
Miss Royce: "My dear, he's too eligible to be considered old."

Baldness

81. Two ladies were discussing what they would wear to the country club dance.
"We're supposed to wear something to match our husband's hair, so I'm going to wear black," said Mrs. Johnson.
"What will you wear?"
"Goodness," gasped her companion, "I don't think I'll go."

82. Women need never expect to be men's equals until they can sport a large bald spot on the top of their heads and still think they're handsome.

83. *Jack:* "Have any of your childhood dreams been realized?"
Mac: "One of them. When my mother used to comb my hair I always used to wish I didn't have any."

84. Junior and his mother, looking through the family album, came to a picture of a handsome young man with a mustache.
"Who's that?" asked Junior.
"Why, that's your father," said the mother proudly.
"Yeah?" said Junior skeptically. "Then who's that bald-headed guy that's living with us?"

85. Dr. Coit, a well known M.E. clergyman of Northern New York, called once on Dr. Buckley, editor of the *Christian Advocate*. In the course of conversation, Dr. Buckley asked: "Say, Coit, do you believe that the hairs of your head are all numbered?" "Why, to be sure I do," replied Dr. Coit. "Does not the Bible tell us that they are?" "Well, then," said Dr. Buckley, with a twinkle in his eye as he glanced up to the bald head of his companion, "if I were you I would get some of the back numbers."

Banking

86. A group of California bankers once gave a dinner at which were many prosperous Indians of the section. These Indians had not gone in for bank accounts to any extent, and the object of the dinner, of course, was to sound them out. Approaching the richest among them, the host of the dinner remarked, "Chief, you've made lots of money, but never opened an account with us. Why don't you think it over?"

The chief thought it over right then and there. "When I got money," he said in deep, low tones, "you pay me four per cent. When I no got money you charge me eight. I'm tired."

87. *Woman to bank teller:* "Very well, if you insist I've overdrawn, I'll just have to cash it somewhere else."

88. "What is your name, sir?" the bank teller asked politely.
"Don't you see my signature?" snapped the indignant patron.
"Yes, sir. That's what aroused my curiosity."

89. *Teacher:* "Where is the capital of the United States?"
Pupil: "All over Europe!"

90. Mr. Murphy opened an account for his wife at the bank. A few weeks later the cashier asked Murphy to inform her that she had overdrawn.

Murphy told his wife the news, and the following morning she handed her husband a letter to deliver to the cashier.

The cashier opened the letter, grimaced, and handed it back to the wondering husband. It was a large sheet of paper, on which was written in block letters the one word, "TELLTALE."

91. One day an Indian came into a bank in Oklahoma and asked about a loan.
"Me want $200."
"And what security have you?"
"Got 200 horses."
This seemed sufficient security and the loan was made.
A short time afterward the Indian came back with $2,200 in

31

cash, paid off the note, and started to leave with the rest of the roll in his pocket.

"Why not let me take care of that money for you?" asked the banker.

Looking the banker straight in the eye, the Indian asked, "How many horses you got?"

92. A grizzled old banker, who pioneered in a small western town, was being interviewed on the subject of his successful career.

"How did you get started in the banking business?" queried the interviewer.

"It was very simple," replied the banker. "I put up a sign reading: BANK. A man came in and gave me $100. Then another came in and handed me $200. By that time my confidence had reached such a point that I decided to put in $50 of my own."

93. *City Banker* (visiting farm): "I suppose that's the hired man."

Farmer: "No, that's the first vice-president in charge of cows."

94. Several men in the smoking room were arguing as to who was the greatest inventor. One contended for Stephenson, who invented the railroad; another for Edison; another for Marconi; and still another for the Wright brothers.

Finally one of them turned to a small man who had been listening but who had said nothing.

"What do you think, Mr. Morrison?"

"Well," came the reply with a knowing smile, "the man who invented interest was nobody's fool."

95. "Did you get my check?" inquired Brown of Jones.

"Yes, twice," replied Jones. "Once from you and once from the bank."

96. A businessman visited his banker and asked: "Are you worried about whether I'll be able to meet my note that comes due next month?"

"Yes, I must admit that I am somewhat concerned," confessed the banker.

"Good," said the client. "That's why I am paying you six per cent."

97. It was during a financial panic that a farmer went to his bank for some money. He was told that the bank was not paying out money but was issuing cashier's checks instead. He could not understand this and insisted on money.

The officers took him in hand, one after another, with little effect. At last the president tried his hand, and after long and minute explanation, some inkling of the situation seemed to be dawning on the farmer's mind. Much encouraged, the president said: "You understand now how it is, don't you, sir?"

"I think I do," admitted the farmer. "It's like this, is it not? When my baby wakes up at night and wants some milk, I give him a milk ticket."

Bankruptcy

98. A man was making application for employment and asked the personnel manager, "Does your company pay my Blue Cross insurance?"

"No, you pay for it; it's deducted from your salary each month," he was informed.

"Last place I worked they paid for it," the applicant said.

"Did they give you a life insurance policy, too?"

"Sure."

"Profit sharing?"

"Sure."

"Two- and three-week vacations?"

"Yes, and they had big bonuses, and gifts for your birthday, and . . ."

"Why did you leave?"

"The company folded."

99. A man called a dozen of his creditors together to tell them that he was about to go into bankruptcy:

"I owe you over a hundred thousand dollars," he said, "and my assets aren't enough to pay 5 cents on the dollar. So I guess it will be impossible for you to get anything—unless you want to cut me up and divide me among you."

Up spoke one of the creditors: "I move we do it. I'd like to have his gall."

Barber

100. The one-armed stranger winced as the barber nicked him again. But the man with the razor chattered on, unnoticing.

"Haven't you been in here before?" he babbled.

"No," said the stranger sadly, "I lost this arm in a sawmill."

101. *Barber:* "Haven't I shaved you before, sir?"

Customer: "No, I got that scar in France."

102. Two youngsters were sitting spellbound in the barber shop watching the barber give a customer a hair singe. As the taper and scissors moved expertly over the man's hair, suddenly one boy turned to the other exclaiming: "Look! He's searching for them with a flame thrower."

103. "Have you got another razor?" asked the man in the chair of his barber.

"Why?" asked the barber.

"Well, I'd like to defend myself if I can," answered the customer.

104. An eastern college professor appeared one day in the faculty dining room with his face cut in several places and patched here and there with adhesive tape. In fact, he looked as though he had been shaved with a hoe.

"What's happened to you?" inquired one of the group.

"I was shaved today by a man who took highest honors at Harvard in scholarship," he replied. "He speaks several languages and by many is considered an outstanding authority on French literature."

"Indeed!" said the friend. "But if he is so learned, how come he's a barber?"

"He isn't," said the professor. "I shaved myself today for the first time."

105. *Barber:* "You say you've been here before? I don't remember your face."

Customer: "I don't doubt that. It's healed now!"

106. The barber was amazed to get a tip from his new customer before he even climbed into the chair.

"You're the first customer to give me a tip before I give him any service," said the barber.

"That's not a tip," was the answer. "That's hush money."

Beauty

107. The pretty restaurant cashier had applied for a vacation.

"I must recuperate," she said. "My beauty is beginning to fade."

"What makes you think so?" asked the proprietor.

"The men are beginning to count their change."

108. "My wife," boasted the husband, with tongue in cheek, "is just as beautiful today as she was when I married her twenty years ago." Then he added, "Of course, it takes her longer."

109. A wealthy American girl was attending a weekend party at a country home in England.

"You American girls haven't such healthy complexions as we English women have," said an English duchess to the girl. "I always wonder why our noblemen take a fancy to your white faces."

"It isn't our white faces that attract them," responded the American girl. "It's our green backs."

110. Lincoln tells the story of how he became possessed of a jackknife.

"In the days when I used to be on the circuit, traveling on horseback from one county court to another, I was once accosted by a stranger, who said:

" 'Excuse me, sir, but I have an article which belongs to you.'

" 'How is that?' I asked, considerably astonished.

"The stranger took a jackknife from his pocket.

" 'This knife,' said he, 'was placed in my hands some years ago, with the injunction that I was to keep it until I found a man homelier-looking than I am myself. I have carried it from that time till this; allow me to say, sir, that you are fairly entitled to the property.' "

It is said that Lincoln later gave this knife to a minister.

111. A city boy and a country lad were walking down a street. Coming toward them was a product of the beauty parlor—permanent wave, scarlet fingernails, drugstore complexion and gaudy lipstick.

"Now what do you think of that?" asked the city boy.

The farm boy looked carefully and observed: "Speaking as a farmer, I should say that it must have been mighty poor soil to require so much top-dressing."

Begging

112. A bum asked for 20 cents for a cup of coffee. The man he accosted said, "I thought coffee was only a dime."

"Yeah, but I've got a date," said the bum.

113. *Lady to Beggar:* "Aren't you ashamed of yourself to stand here begging on the street?"

Beggar: "What do you want, lady; should I open an office?"

114. "My poor man," said the kind old lady to the beggar, "it must be dreadful to be lame. But think how much worse it would be if you were blind."

"You're right, lady," agreed the beggar. "When I was blind I was always getting counterfeit money!"

115. "No, certainly not," said the woman to a man who had knocked at her door and begged for food. "Go away at once or I'll call my husband."

"Your husband isn't home," replied the tramp.

"How do you know he isn't?" asked the woman.

"Because a man that marries a woman the likes of you is only home at mealtime."

116. *Housewife:* "Why should a big, strong man like you be out begging?"

Hobo: "Well, lady, it's the only profession I know in which the gentleman can address a beautiful woman like you without an introduction."

117. *Man* (to panhandler): "Why don't you go to the Settlement House and get a free meal?"

Panhandler: "Gee whiz, don't you ever feel like eating out?"

118. A beggar on the street was regarding enviously the richly dressed man whom he was importuning for aid. "You have no reason to envy me," said the other, "even if I do look prosperous. I have my troubles, too."

"No doubt you have, boss," replied the unfortunate one, humbly, "but the difficulty with me is, I ain't got nothing else."

Behavior

119. A young woman, defending her attendance at some doubtful places of amusement, said, "I think a Christian can go anywhere."

"Certainly," rejoined her friend, "but it reminds me of the time I went with some friends to explore a coal mine. One girl wore a pretty white dress. When someone commented, she said to the old miner who was our guide, 'Can't I wear a white dress into the mine?'

" 'Yes, Mum,' returned the old man, 'there's nothing to keep you from wearing a white frock down there, but there will be considerable to keep you from wearing one back.' "

120. "How did you keep from crying?" someone asked a little girl who had fallen and hurt her knee.

"Oh," she answered, "I just said to myself, 'Stop that,' and made myself mind me."

121. "Good heavens!" cried Whistler as he saw his mother on her knees scrubbing the floor. "Have you gone off your rocker?"

122. One day when nylons were on sale at Marshall Field's, a dignified, middle-aged gentleman decided to get his wife a pair. But he soon found himself being buffeted and stabbed by frantic women. He stood it as long as he could. Then with head lowered and arms flailing, he plowed through the crowd. "You, there!" challenged a shrill voice. "Can't you act like a gentleman?"

"Hell," he replied, still charging forward, "I've been acting like a gentleman for an hour. From now on, I'm acting like a lady."

123. A man from Milwaukee went into the washroom of the Union Station in Chicago, and was surprised to notice how spick and span everything was, and that a number of people seemed to be leaving very quickly. He wondered what had caused all this activity and tension, until he looked up and saw a sign on the wall reading, "You are now on T.V."

BLAME

124. *Mother:* "Well, son, were you a good boy in school today?"
Son: "Sure—how much trouble can you get into standing in a corner all day?"

125. *Minister:* "Should I give you something to strengthen your will-power?"
Parishioner: "No, give me something to weaken my conscience instead."

126. There were guests in the home of four-year-old Jane and all the while they were there she wore her best company manners. But the moment the door closed behind them she became disobedient.

"Why is it," asked her mother, "that you are so naughty now? You were such a lady while our guests were here."

"Well, mother," answered Jane, "you don't use your company silver all the time, do you?"

127. One day, when Al Smith was showing a group of women through his Empire State Building, and they were zooming up the hundred floors in the elevator, one of the women said, "Mr. Smith, if the cable in this elevator should break, would I go up or down?" And Al replied—"Lady, that all depends on the kind of life you've lived."

128. The six-year-old went off to school, looking very grown up in a new blouse and skirt. When she came home, her mother asked if anyone had commented on her new outfit. "Yes, the teacher did," said Jackie. "She said as long as I was dressed like a lady, why didn't I act like one!"

Blame

129. There was an epic weekend at Long Beach, California, in full alcoholic swing when the earthquake came. Chimneys toppled in the street. Water mains were broken. All the guests rushed outside from the party. But one chap was missing.

The heroic host dashed back and there in the bathroom he found his friend, kneedeep in water.

The guest only mumbled—"Honest, Paul, I swear all I did was pull the handle."

130. *Lady:* "Why did you kick your little brother in the stomach?"
Tommy: "Well, it was his fault; he turned around."

131. *Father:* "Yes, my boy, I'm a self-made man."
Son: "Gee, Pop, that's what I admire about you. You always take the blame for everything."

132. *Harry:* "Are you trying to make a monkey out of me?"
Carrie: "Why should I take the credit?"

133. An editor had to admonish his son because of the lad's truancy from school and general lack of diligence.

"You must go every day, study hard, and become a really good scholar," said the father. "Otherwise, you know, you will never follow in my footsteps and become an editor. Knowledge is important. What would you do, for instance, if your magazine came out full of mistakes?"

"Father," said the boy, "I would blame the printer."

And the father went away happily, knowing that he had a successor.

134. "But how on earth did you come to get so completely intoxicated?"

"Well, you see, it's like this, your Honor. I got into bad company. There were four of us. I had a bottle of whiskey—and the other three don't touch the stuff."

135. *Employer:* "For this job we want a responsible man."
Applicant: "That's for me. Everywhere I've worked, when something went wrong, they told me I was responsible."

136. *Woman:* "Can you fix that dent in my fender so my husband won't know I damaged it?"
Garage mechanic: "Nope, but I can fix it so that in a week you can ask him how he dented it."

Boastfulness

137. The braggart was letting everybody know that he could bend a horseshoe with his bare hands. All of a sudden one farmer had enough. "That's nothing," he commented, "my wife can tie up ten miles of telephone wire with her chin."

138. Two salesmen were bragging about the size of their respective firms. One of them boasted that his company spent $3000 a year just for ink which they used in their correspondence.

"That's nothing," replied the other. "We save that amount each year by eliminating the dotting of "i's" and the crossing of "t's."

139. *Father:* "And there, my son, I've told you the story of your daddy and the Great World War."

Son: "Yes, daddy, but what did they need all the other soldiers for?"

Books

140. *Customer:* "Have you a book called, *Man, the Master of Women?*"

Salesgirl: "Fiction counter to the left, sir."

141. *Librarian:* "I trust you found that novel interesting."

Patron: "No, not very, but the letter someone left in it for a bookmark was certainly a lulu!"

142. "When does a book become a classic?" asked the English instructor.

"When people who haven't read it begin to say they have," replied a bright pupil.

143. "I would like a nice book for an invalid," said the little old lady.

"Yes, madam," said the clerk. "Something religious?"

"Er-no," replied the lady, "the doctor told him this morning he was going to get well."

Boredom

144. An American businessman, visiting in Mexico, watched an Indian making pottery vases. He asked the price. "Twenty centavos each."

"And for 100?"

The native thought it over and then answered: "That will be 40 centavos each."

The American thought the Indian was making a mistake in his quotation of the price, so he tried again. "And if I bought 1000 all alike?"

"All alike?" he said. "One thousand? Well, senor, then they would cost you 60 centavos apiece."

"Impossible! Why, you must be insane!"

"It could be," replied the Indian. "But I'd have to make so many, and all alike, and I wouldn't like that. So you see, you would have to pay me well for my work as well as for my boredom."

145. "There are some people who not only keep you from being lonely, but make you wish you were."

146. Dorothy Parker once visited the country estate of some friends for the weekend. It was so boring to her that she almost immediately sent the following telegram to a friend: "Please send me a loaf of bread—and enclose a saw and file."

147. At a particularly dull academic meeting, a fellow guest remarked sympathetically to Einstein, "I'm afraid you're terribly bored by all this." "Oh, no," replied the great Einstein, cheerfully, "on occasions like this I retire to the back of my mind and there I am happy."

Borrowing

148. "Hello," said one voice.
"Hello," came the answer.
"Is that you, John?" asked the first.
"Yes, this is John," came the answer.
"It doesn't sound like you, John."
"Well, this is John speaking all right."
"Are you sure this is John?"
"Sure, this is John."
"Well, listen, John, if you're sure it's you, then lend me fifty dollars, will you?"
"All right," came the answer, "I'll tell him when he comes in."

149. *Father:* "I'm busy. Be short."
Son: "I will. I am."

BUSINESS

150. "Has Jones ever paid back the $10 you loaned him a year ago?"

"Oh, yes; he borrowed $25 more from me last week and only took $15."

151. *Small Johnny:* "How much am I worth?"

Papa: "You are worth a million dollars to me, my son."

Small Johnny: "Well, would you mind advancing me a quarter on account?"

Business

152. Everybody who has a hobby that is losing money wants to call it a business; but everyone who has one that is making money wants to call it a recreation.

153. A hardware merchant became curious when, week after week, a certain farmer came in and bought several hammers. Finally he asked why.

"Oh," said the farmer, "I sell them to folks in my neighborhood for a dollar apiece."

"But, man," protested the dealer, "that doesn't make sense. You're paying me $1.25 each for the hammers."

"I know, I know," conceded the farmer, "but it beats farming!"

154. A man was admiring his new suit. His friend asked him what was so wonderful about it. He said, "The wool is from Australia, the buttons from California, the thread from Japan, and the lining from New York." On being asked what was so wonderful about that, he replied, "Isn't it wonderful that so many people can make a living from a suit that I haven't paid for?"

155. *Teacher:* "What is capital punishment?"

Pupil (whose father is a big businessman): "It's when the government sets up business in competition with you, and then takes all your profits with taxes in order to make up its losses."

156. David Starr Jordan, trying to advise a difficult young man on choosing a career, finally asked in despair: "Isn't there anything on earth you'd like to be?"

42

"Why, yes," the young man drawled, "I'd like to be a retired businessman."

157. When Marshall Field III was a small child, he displayed some of the cautious shrewdness which made his grandfather the greatest merchant prince in America.

Being left alone in a hotel lobby for half an hour, young Marshall approached an old lady and asked if she could crack nuts.

"No, dear," replied the old lady. "I lost all my teeth years ago."

"Then," said Master Field, extending both hands full of pecans, "please hold these while I go and get some more pecans."

158. A company was conducting a survey among its stockholders and asked one of them how she knew that the company was successful and that the management was doing a good job. Her reply was almost a classic. She said, "When I get the annual report, I look at the total assets and the total liabilities. If they are the same, I know that everything is all right."

159. During a British election campaign, a Conservative candidate was addressing a meeting when a Socialist candidate heckled him by shouting: "Why have we the finest generation of children ever known in this country?"

Immediately from the speaker came the reply: "Because they were produced by private enterprise."

160. Seated in a hotel lobby was a party of businessmen attending a convention. Among them was a man who announced himself as a mind reader.

"I will bet ten dollars with any man in this group," he said, "that I can tell him what he is thinking about."

"I'll take that bet," said one of the businessmen.

The mind reader gazed intently into his eyes for a few seconds, and then announced:

"You are thinking of going to the city, buying $10,000 worth of goods, then going home, declaring yourself a bankrupt, and settling with your creditors at ten cents on the dollar."

The merchant did not answer, but reached into his pocket and handed over the ten dollars.

"Ah," said the mind reader, "then I read your mind correctly."

"Not at all," said the businessman. "But the idea is easily worth the ten dollars."

161. "Got any Krunchy Flakes?" asked the customer of the clerk in the grocery store.

"Yes, sir," responded the clerk. "How many boxes would you like?"

"Are they any good?"

"The best breakfast food on the market," replied the clerk with all assurance.

"Are you certain of that?"

"Yes, sir. I have them for breakfast every morning. How many boxes, please?"

"None."

"None?"

"That's right. You may recall that you wrote the company complaining about them, but I'm glad you changed your mind. I happen to be the President of Krunchy Flakes, Incorporated."

Card-playing

162. Turning to the best player of the bridge foursome, the novice asked, "How would you have played that last hand of mine?"

"Under an assumed name," was the prompt answer.

163. Four men were playing bridge. One of them made a bad misplay. After the hand had been played, his partner asked:

"Did you lead that card from strength or from weakness?"

"From neither," the other man answered, "from ignorance."

164. Four card sharps got together on a train. A tense, hard-fought game ensued. Suddenly the dealer tossed his cards down and said: "This game is crooked."

"What makes you think so?" asked the card sharp on his left.

"That guy," pointing to the player across the table, "is not playing the hand I dealt him."

165. The wife plays a snappy game of bridge, while the husband boasts of knowing no rules. However, one evening, in an exuberant mood, he bid and made a grand slam, doubled and redoubled. Gleefully, he turned to his wife: "And you thought I couldn't do it!"

"Well, dear," she countered, "you *couldn't* have, if you'd played it right!"

166. They sat there holding hands—a deathly silence prevailed. She had a feeling—yes, something told her—that he would ask the all-important question.

She braced herself for the words that she knew would surely come, and with appealing eyes she turned her face towards him.

"Why did you trump my ace?" he thundered.

167. Strolling through the card room of a businessmen's club, a member was surprised to see three men and a dog playing poker. Pausing to watch, he commented on the extraordinary performance of the dog.

"He's not so smart," the dog's owner said in disgust. "Every time he gets a good hand he wags his tail."

168. Arriving home earlier than usual, he found his wife in the arms of his best friend.

"I love your wife, and she loves me," said the surprised friend. "Tell you what I'll do, I'll play you a game of cards for her. If I win, you divorce her, and if you win, I promise never to see her again. O.K.? How about making it gin rummy?"

"That's all right with me," agreed the husband, "and how about a penny a point to make the game a bit interesting?"

169. A young surgeon received a telephone call from a colleague who invited him to make a fourth hand at bridge.

"Going out, dear?" asked his wife suspiciously.

"I'm afraid so," was the brave reply. "It's a very important case. In fact, there are three doctors there already."

170. "Did you hear the one about the bridge expert being the father of twins?"

"Yeah, looks like his wife doubled his bid."

171. To her husband, arriving home at 2 a.m., she snapped: "I suppose you've been holding a sick friend's hand all night!"

"If I had been holding *his* hand, dear, I'd have made enough money to buy you a mink coat."

45

Cause and Effect

172. Two young ladies were discussing a young man.

"Oh, he's so tender!" said the one who happened to be his sweetheart.

"Perhaps that's because he's in hot water so much," suggested the other.

173. Two Iowa farmers had been in the habit of meeting each other every week or so for a great many years while on their way to market.

Their conversation was usually very brief and confined to something like this:

"Good morning, Lemuel."

"Good morning, Silas."

"Nice day, Lem."

"Sure is, Si."

"Well, good day, Lem."

"So long, Si."

This remained the pattern of their dialogue over the years, unless the state of the weather made necessary some minor adjustment.

One particular day the conversation changed. In addition to the foregoing mutual exchange of greetings, Lem opened with the following additional colloquy: "Say, Si, what did you give your horse when he had the colic?"

"I gave my horse turpentine when he had the colic," came the direct reply.

"Thanks, Si," and with that they parted as usual.

The following week they met again and Lem said: "What did you say you gave your horse when he had the colic?" Si answered: "I gave my horse turpentine when he had the colic."

"Well, I gave my horse turpentine too, and he died."

"So did mine. Good day, Lem."

"So long, Si."

174. George Bernard Shaw, tall and slender, was once told by G. K. Chesterton who was noted for his rotundity:

"To look at you, Shaw, a person would think there was a famine in England."

46

To which Shaw sarcastically retorted: "Yes, and to look at you, he'd think you were the cause of it."

175. *Missionary:* "Why do you look at me so intently?"
Cannibal: "I'm the food inspector."

176. The cloak room attendant gave an old gentleman his overcoat. The gentleman asked: "How do you know this is mine?" "I don't know," said the attendant. "Then why did you give it to me?" said the old gentleman. "Because you gave it to me," responded the attendant.

177. "Smith," said the restaurant manager to a waiter, "why did that man at table number five leave so abruptly?"
"I don't know," replied the waiter. "He asked for sausages, and I told him we were all out of them, but if he could wait a few minutes, I'd get the cook to make some. I went to the kitchen, and as I set down a tray of dishes, I stepped on the dog's tail and he let out a wild yelp. Then when I came back into the dining room, the man was on his way out the front door."

178. The gentleman behind the desk received the stranger with a smile, bade him be seated, and said, "Have a cigar?"
"Don't mind if I do," said the visitor. And then sensing something unusual in the atmosphere, he added, "Is this a special occasion?"
"I'll say it is," was the reply. "I've got an addition to the family."
"Really?" said the stranger. "Congratulations!"
He put a match to the cigar, puffed on it a few times, and then observed, "About the fifth child, I presume."

Caution

179. *Magda:* "If you could have two wishes, what would they be?"
Zza-Zza: "Well, I'd wish for a husband."
Magda: "That's one wish; what's the other?"
Zza-Zza: "The other I'd save until I saw how he turned out."

180. "Remember," warned the minister to his friend who was about to sign a television contract, "the big print giveth and the small print taketh away."

47

181. *Teacher:* "What is the difference between caution and cowardice?"

Pupil: "Caution is when you're afraid and cowardice is when the other fellow is afraid."

Childbirth

182. The young father-to-be, registering his wife in the maternity ward, asked anxiously, "Darling, are you positive that you want to go through with this?"

183. *Investigator:* "Are you a natural-born citizen of the United States?"

Anxious witness: "N-no, sir. I'm a Caesarean."

Children

184. Child psychologists say the modern child treats his parents with awe. This confirms our own observation. It's always, "Aw, why can't I have the car?" or "Aw, why can't I have a bigger allowance?"

185. In a school in one of Chicago's poorer districts, a questionnaire was sent home with a new pupil, requesting information regarding the home environment, number of brothers and sisters, father's occupation, etc. The next day she returned with a scrap of paper on which was the following: "We have 18 children. My husband can also do plumbing and carpentry work."

186. During the beginning of an earthquake, a couple sent their small son to an uncle who lived out of the danger zone. A few days later, they received a telegram reading: "Am returning your boy. Please send earthquake instead."

Choice

187. In a Belfast home without a maid and seldom with a guest, the young son was very anxious to help his mother when his father appeared with two dinner guests.

When the dinner was nearly over, the child went to the kitchen and proudly carried in the first piece of pie, giving it to his father, who passed it to a guest. The boy came in with a second piece and gave it to his father, who gave it to the other guest. That was too much for the youngster, and he piped up: "It's no use, dad! The pieces are all the same size."

188. *Doctor:* "The best thing for you to do is to give up drinking and smoking, get up early every morning, and go to bed early every night."

Patient: "What's the second best?"

Church attendance

189. Striving to impress upon young Gordy the importance of attending church regularly, Mother pointed to a picture of the Pilgrims going to church.

"See," she said, "they went to church every Sunday."

Gordy looked at the picture, noting the guns carried by the men, and replied, "Gee whiz, mom, I'd go every day in the week if I could shoot Indians on the way!"

190. "Well," said the tavern keeper to an old customer, "I see you've been over to the revival meeting and given the evangelist your last nickel. Now you'll have to walk home."

"Yes," remarked the other in a rather pleased tone of voice, "and many a time I've given you my last nickel and couldn't walk home."

191. "Doctor, I should like to join your church. I enjoy the singing and the preaching immensely." "That is very kind of you to say," was the reply, "but what part of church work would you like?" "No —no—no; that is not my thought, but just to attend church and enjoy it." "If that is so," replied the preacher, "I would suggest your joining the Church of the Heavenly Rest."

192. A minister met an unregenerate acquaintance on the street and inquired, during their brief conversation, "Just what do you have against coming to church?"

"Plenty!" snarled the sinner. "The first time I went, they threw water in my face, and the second time they tied me to a woman I've had to support ever since."

"I see," said the minister quietly, "and the next time they'll throw dirt on you."

193. "You seem to have a very small congregation in this church," said one girl to another.

"Yes," agreed her friend, "so small sometimes that every time the clergyman says 'dearly beloved' you feel as if you'd received a proposal."

194. *Son:* "Did you go to Sunday School when you were a little boy?"

Father: "Why, certainly. I never missed a Sunday."

Son: "See, mother? It won't do me any good either."

195. Annoyed by poor attendance at his Sunday morning services, a minister in England drove around his parish one Sunday morning, blowing his car horn to wake everybody up.

196. *Bulletin board outside a church:* "Wanted: Men, Women, and Children to sit in slightly used pews Sunday mornings, 11 to 12 o'clock."

Circumstantial evidence

197. An English lady, self-appointed supervisor of village morals, accused a workman of having reverted to drink because "with her own eyes" she had seen his wheelbarrow standing outside a public house. The accused made no defense, but that evening placed his wheelbarrow outside her door and left it there all night.

College

198. "Well, son, how were your marks in college this year?"

"Underwater."

"What do you mean 'underwater'?"

"All below 'C' level."

199. College has been defined as a fountain of knowledge where students gather to drink.

200. Two fathers at the club were discussing the daughters in their respective families.

"What do you think," said one. "Should I send my daughter to college or not?"

"Well, I'll tell you my experience. It may help you to decide. It cost me a thousand dollars a year to send Penelope to college, and it took her four years to capture a husband. I spent three hundred to send Alice to the beach for three weeks, and she came home married. I recommend the beach."

201. A rich old aunt was paying her nephew's college expenses and her visitor asked if it was expensive.

"Well," said the aunt, "some of the languages run pretty high. My check this month covered $10 for chemistry, $20 for Latin, and $250 for Scotch."

202. The dean of women at a large coeducational college recently began an important announcement to the student body as follows:

"The president of the college and I have decided to stop necking on the campus."

203. A young man who had just received his college degree rushed out and said: "Here I am, world; I have an A.B.!"

And the world replied: "Sit down, son, and I'll teach you the rest of the alphabet."

204. *Sophomore:* "Dad, do you know that you're a lucky man?"
Father: "How is that?"
Sophomore: "You won't have to buy new books for me this year. I'm taking last year's work over again."

205. The father, passing through his son's college town late one evening, thought he would pay his son a surprise visit. Arriving at the son's fraternity house, he rapped on the door but was unable to rouse anybody. Then from a second floor window came a sleepy voice.

"Whaddyah want?"

"Does Steve Jones live here?" said the father.

"Yeah," replied the voice. "Bring him in."

206. *Father:* "How can you say that dating at college keeps you young?"
Son: "Well, I started dating two years ago as a freshman, and I'm still a freshman."

51

COLLEGE

207. A photographer was taking a picture of a man and his college-boy son. The photographer suggested that the boy stand with his hand on his father's shoulder.

"It would be more appropriate," said the long-suffering parent, "if he stood with his hand in my pocket."

208. One day, an Eastern University professor visited the expanding campus of the University of California at Los Angeles. He watched construction work on half a dozen new buildings. He inspected new laboratories and attended summer classes in modern study rooms. He walked across miles of eucalyptus-lined lawns and athletic fields with one of the deans. He was impressed.

"My," he said, "just how many students do you have here?"

"Let me see," the dean answered thoughtfully, "I'd say about one in a hundred."

209. A professor was delivering the last lecture of the semester. He told his students that he expected them to devote all their time to preparation for the final examination. "The examination papers are now in the hands of the printer," he concluded. "Now, is there any question you would like answered?"

Silence prevailed for a moment; then a voice piped up from the rear of the room: "Yes, who's the printer?"

210. "What do you expect to get out of college?" was the question asked by an inquisitive professor.

To which one extremely rich young lad replied, "I won't have to buy my bonds from a stranger."

211. *Visitor:* "Can you tell me where the science building is?"
Freshman: I'm sorry, but I'm just here on an athletic scholarship."

212. One of the questions propounded in the examination was: "Give in detail the process for making bichloride of mercury."

In answer to this question the pupil wisely (so he thought) wrote: "God made all things, even bichloride of mercury."

Imagine his chagrin when he received his corrected paper and read: "God gets the credit. You don't."

213. *Professor:* "What three words are used most among college students?"

Student: "I don't know."
Professor: "That's correct."

214. Two college presidents were discussing retirement plans.
"I'd like to be superintendent of an orphan asylum," said the first. "No visits from parents."
"My plan is better," said the second prexy. "I want to be warden of a penitentiary. No alumni reunions."

Communism

215. Thieves who once broke into the Kremlin were said to have stolen the complete results of the next election.

216. Asked the first Russian: "What was the nationality of Adam and Eve?"
"There's no doubt that they were Soviet citizens," replied the second.
"They had nothing to wear, nothing to eat but an apple, and lived in paradise."

217. A Russian U.N. delegate was shown a copy of a Sears Roebuck catalogue. "Do you mean to tell me," he said, "that in America all these things are available to the masses?"
"Available, heck," exclaimed an American, "in America we have to *beg* people to buy them."

218. Two strangers stood on a Bucharest street corner admiring an automobile, parked at the curb.
"My, that's handsome," said the first. "The Russians certainly know how to make an automobile."
"That's not Russian," the second man answered, "don't you recognize an American car when you see one?"
"Of course I do; I knew it was an American car, but I had no idea who *you* were!"

219. A certain Moscow comrade stood in so well with the party that he was granted a permit allowing him to buy a railroad ticket without having to stand in line. One day he went to the station and presented his precious permit.
"Get in that line over there," he was told.

"But," protested the privileged one, "this permit allows me to buy a ticket without standing in line!"

"I know that," rejoined the station agent, "and that is the line for people that don't have to stand in line to buy tickets."

220. A Communist politician, the Red Boss of a small Balkan state, was bitterly disappointed when nobody would use the newly-issued postage stamps bearing his portrait. The Moscow-appointed dictator questioned a postmaster, who explained that the fault lay with the stamps not sticking.

Seizing one, the politician licked it and affixed it to an envelope. "Look," he declared. "It sticks perfectly. Now why aren't they on every envelope?"

The patient postmaster hedged a little, then murmured: "Well, comrade, you may as well know the truth. The people keep spitting on the wrong side."

221. Stalin one day was giving Mao Tse Tung instructions in practical communism.

"Comrade," he said, "how would you make a cat eat chili pepper?"

"There are two ways," said Mao. "I could force it down him, or I could stuff a fish with the pepper and give the fish to the cat."

"Wrong," replied Stalin. "It's not compatible with our ideology. The first method is coercion, the second deception. You know we never coerce or deceive the people."

"Then how would you do it?" asked the confused Mao.

"I would rub the pepper on the cat's tail. When this started to smart, the cat would turn around and lick its tail, thus eating the pepper voluntarily."

222. A Russian about to be sentenced to Siberia had this to say to the court: "If the United States is such a terrible place, why not send me there instead of sending me to Siberia?"

Competition

223. A man's pants do not compete with his vest. Each has its own area to cover.

224. A settlement worker met one of her cases on the street. "What are you doing now?" she asked.

"Selling fly paper."

"But it's winter. What's the idea of selling fly paper in winter?"

"Well," said the case, "I figured there would be no competition."

Compromise

225. "I'll meet you halfway," said the wife during an argument. "I'll admit I'm right if you admit you're wrong."

226. His wife kept nagging him all year long for a trip to the Thousand Islands, so her husband compromised by taking her 1,000 times to Coney Island.

227. It's a wise wife who asks for something she knows her husband can't afford, so that she can compromise on what she really wants.

228. "Daddy, will you buy me a drum?" asked the little boy of his father.

"I should say not," answered the head of the household. "It's altogether too noisy."

"Suppose," compromised the lad, "I only play it when you're asleep."

Conscience

229. Conscience: that something which prompts a man to tell his wife before someone else does.

230. An enterprising merchant was trying to get his prospective customer to stock up on his product. In his zeal, he tried to bribe the merchant with a bottle of whiskey.

"Oh, no," said the storekeeper, "my conscience would not allow me to accept a gift."

"Suppose I sell it to you for a nickel," responded the salesman.

"In that case I'll take two," replied the merchant.

231. "My what a beautiful umbrella you have. Did you just get it?"

"Yes, I did and here's how I got it. I was walking home this afternoon and it started to rain. I stepped into a doorway, intending to wait for the rain to stop. I was getting rather impatient, for there was no indication of any let-up, when I noticed a young man walking towards me with a large umbrella. Hoping I might get to walk along under it with him, I called, 'Where are you going with that umbrella?' With that, he dropped this umbrella and ran. That's how I got it."

232. Sir Arthur Conan Doyle of Sherlock Holmes fame once sent a telegram to each of 12 friends, all of whom were noted for their virtue. The message was worded: "FLY AT ONCE; ALL IS DISCOVERED." Within 24 hours, all 12 had left the country.

Courage

233. Some listeners were peppering the writer and big-game hunter, Ernest Hemingway, with questions, following a dramatic account of his adventures in Africa.

"Is it true," asked one, "that wild beasts in the jungle won't harm you if you carry a torch?"

"That all depends . . ." replied Hemingway ". . . on how fast you carry it."

234. A hillbilly came to town carrying a jug of liquor in one hand and a shotgun in the other. He stopped a man on the street, saying to him, "Here, friend, take a drink outa my jug."

The man protested saying he never drank.

The hillbilly leveled his shotgun at the stranger and commanded: "Drink!"

The stranger drank, shuddered, shook, shivered, and coughed. "Gad, that's awful stuff you've got there."

"Ain't it, though?" replied the hillbilly. "Now you hold the gun to me while I take a swig."

Courtship

235. *Guest at wedding reception:* "Are you the bridegroom?"
Young man: "No, ma'am, I was eliminated in the semi-finals."

236. *George:* "You should see the new altar in our church."
Mary: "Boy, lead me to it."

237. "Honey," said the young man, "if you will marry me I'll put in electricity, get some modern kitchen things, paint the house inside out, and buy a milking machine."

"Henry," sighed the wise young lady, "suppose you do all those things—and ask me again."

238. *Flo:* "I thought you said you'd be deaf to any proposal from him?"

Jo: "Yes, I did (looking at the gorgeous diamond in the engagement ring), but I didn't say I'd be stone-deaf."

239. "At her request you gave up drinking?"
"Yes."

"And you stopped smoking for the same reason?"
"I did."

"And it was for her that you gave up dancing, gambling, and billiards?"

"That's correct."

"Then why didn't you marry her?"

"Well, after all that reforming, I decided I could do better."

240. "I broke my engagement," the girl confided to her friend. "My feelings are changed completely from what they were when I accepted him."

"But why do you still wear the ring?" asked the friend.

"Oh," replied the girl in surprise, "my feelings toward the ring are just the same."

Cover-up

241. When a worried-looking man in a florist shop asked for potted geraniums, the clerk, out of geraniums, suggested chrysanthemums.

"No, they won't do," replied the man. "I promised my wife I'd water her geraniums while she was away."

242. "Thanks very much," said the minister. "I must call this afternoon and thank your mother for those eight beautiful apples."

"Please, sir," said Tommy, "do you mind thanking her for 12?"

243. Architects cover their mistakes with ivy, doctors with sod, and brides with mayonnaise.

CREDIT

244. *Teacher:* "Johnny, what is the term 'etc.' used for?"
Little Johnny: "I guess it's to make people think we know a lot more than we do."

Credit

245. A customer sent the following note to his grocer:
"Please send six dozen eggs: if good, I will send check."
The grocer, however, was not doing any business on such risky terms, so he replied;
"Send check: if good, I will send six dozen eggs."

246. A man had barely paid off the mortgage on his house when he mortgaged it again to buy a new car. Then he sought out a loan broker to borrow money on the car so he could build a garage.
"If I do make you the loan," asked the broker, "how will you manage to buy gas for the car?"
"It seems to me," the man replied with great dignity, "that a fellow who owns his own house, car, and garage should be able to get credit for gas."

247. Some years ago a harness dealer had a customer who picked out a fancy saddle for his pony and said, "I'll take it. Please charge it."
After the customer had left, the proprietor asked his bookkeeper to charge the customer with the purchase. "To whom?" asked the bookkeeper. "Don't you know him?" replied the proprietor. "No," answered the bookkeeper. "Well," said the proprietor, "only twelve men have ponies in town—send them all a bill." The bookkeeper did.
Three of them paid.

248. "My wife used to buy in three or four stores and her bills were tremendous. Now her bills are smaller," confided one husband to another.
"How does she do it?"
"Now she buys from thirty to forty stores."

249. *Grocer:* "I can't give you any more credit, sir. Your bill is bigger now than it should be."
Customer: "I know it. Make it what it should be and I'll pay it."

Creditor

250. Artist James M. Whistler often lived beyond his means. As a result, he was hounded by creditors. Their presence caused him no distress. Rather, he treated them with the utmost cordiality.

Once, when a persistent creditor called at the artist's home to collect a bill, he was served champagne.

"If you cannot afford to pay your bills," he demanded with some asperity, "how can you afford to drink champagne?"

"Your anger is too hasty, sir," replied Whistler. "I assure you, I haven't paid for this either."

251. "There's a man outside," said the secretary to her boss, "who wants to see you about a bill you owe him. He wouldn't give his name."

"What does he look like?"

"Well, he looks like you had better pay him."

252. *Landlord:* "You didn't pay the rent for last month."
Tenant: "No? Well, I suppose you'll hold me to your agreement?"
"Agreement! What agreement?"
"Why, when I rented you said I must pay in advance or not at all."

253. Mr. Benningham met his tailor one day. "Why don't you send me a bill?" he asked the tailor.

The tailor explained that he never asked a gentleman for money. Mr. Benningham asked what happened if someone did not pay.

"Oh," said the tailor, "after a certain time I conclude he is not a gentleman and then I ask him."

Crime and Punishment

254. "This crime was the work of a master criminal," said the prosecutor, "and was carried out in a skillful, clever manner."

Blushing, the defendant rose to his feet.

"Sir, flattery will get you nowhere. I ain't gonna confess."

255. An accused criminal looked up at Lord Bacon who, as chancellor, was trying his case.

"Your lordship really ought to let me go free. We're kin you know, for my name's Hogg and Hogg's kin to Bacon."

Whereupon Bacon dryly replied, "Not until it's hung!"

256. A convicted murderer was scheduled to die in the electric chair. On the morning of the day of his execution, he was asked by the warden: "Is there anything special you'd like for your breakfast this morning?"

To this the condemned man replied: "Yes, mushrooms. I've always been scared to eat them for fear of being poisoned."

257. "For ten years," the new boarder said, "my habits were as regular as clockwork. I rose on the stroke of six, and half an hour later was at breakfast; at seven I was at work; dined at one, had supper at six, and was in bed at nine-thirty. Ate only plain food, and hadn't a day of illness all the time."

"Dear me!" said a hearer, in sympathetic tones, "and what were you in for?"

Criticism

258. Sir Lewis Morris was complaining to Oscar Wilde about the neglect of his poems by the press.

"It is a complete conspiracy of silence against me," said Morris, "a conspiracy of silence. What do you suggest I do, Oscar?"

"Join it," said Wilde without much hesitation.

259. "What's your candid opinion of my new novel?" asked the author, anxiously.

"It's worthless," was the cruel and blunt reply.

"I know," persisted the author, "but I'd like it just the same."

260. Once, when a young musician's concert was poorly received by the critics, Sibelius patted him gently on the shoulder. "Remember, son," he consoled the young man, "there is no city anywhere in the world where they have erected a statue to a critic."

261. "Good Heavens, man! I saw your obituary in this morning's paper!"

"Yes, I know. I put it in myself. My opera is to be produced to-night, and I want good notices from the critics."

262. *Master of ceremonies:* "This quartette has performed the impossible. They have taken music which it was said would live for years and years—and have killed it in one night."

Curiosity

263. A short time ago a certain man decided to see just how strong a woman's curiosity was. He cut a small "personal" item from the newspaper and left the paper where his wife would be sure to find it. When he returned home the next evening he was surprised to find the domestic atmosphere hanging heavy with thunder clouds. Investigation revealed that his wife had borrowed a neighbor's paper to see what he had clipped. He fumbled in his vest pocket for his clipping and was electrified to find on the opposite side from the "personal" item, this headline:

"Prominent Citizens Figure in Wild Party at Roadhouse. Due to Prominence of Participators, No Names Are Given at This Time."

And now a certain man has no further interest in feminine curiosity!

264. Hiram bought a pink shirt with huge purple dots. In the pocket was a note with a girl's name and address, and a request that the buyer of the shirt send his photograph.

"Ah, romance," mused Hiram, as he addressed the envelope, and mailed a snapshot as requested.

Several days later he received a reply. He hastily tore open the letter, only to read:

"Thanks for the photo. I just wanted to see what kind of a jerk would buy that kind of shirt."

265. A man sitting at his window one evening casually called to his wife: "There goes that woman Frank Harris is so terribly in love with."

With that, his wife in the kitchen dropped a plate she was drying, ran through the door, knocked over a lamp, and looked out the window.

"Where, where?" she cried.

"There," he said, "that woman in the gabardine suit, on the corner."

"Why, you big idiot," she replied, "that's his wife."
"Yes, of course," he answered with a satisfied grin.

266. An attractive young woman had an amazing record in the house-to-house sale of vacuum cleaners. Questioned as to her success, she confessed to an effective stratagem:
"I always make it a point to address my sales talk to the husband —in tones so low that the wife won't want to miss a single word!"

Dancing

267. A worried father hurried to his teen-age son's hospital bedside. The lad had a broken leg and myriad cuts and bruises. "What happened, son?" asked the father. "Did you have an accident coming home from your girl's house?"
"No," the boy groaned.
"Well, how *did* it happen?" persisted the father.
"We were jitterbugging," the boy explained, "when her old man came in. He's deaf and couldn't hear the music—so he threw me out the window!"

268. After a visit to dancing school, one mother advised her small daughter that she should not just dance silently like a totem pole; talking to her partner was also a part of the social picture.
On a later visit the mother saw that each time the music started, the same little boy tore across the floor, bowed to her daughter, and swept her away to the music.
On the way home, her curiosity aroused, the mother asked how it was that the same boy chose her for every dance.
"Oh, him," the child explained, "I'm telling him a continued murder story."

269. Johnny had taken his first dancing lesson. When he returned home his mother asked him how he liked it. "Why mother, it's easy," said Johnny. "All you do is turn around and keep wiping your feet."

270. Of a lackadaisical couple dancing a minuet, Lord Chesterfield once remarked that "they looked as if they were hired to do it, and were doubtful of being paid."

62

Death

271. When Thoreau, the naturalist, was close to death, he was visited by a very pious aunt who asked, "Henry, have you made your peace with God?"

"I didn't know," was Thoreau's answer, "that we had ever quarreled."

272. Shortly after the tragic death of his young son, Samuel Taylor Coleridge had occasion to send a book to a friend who had suffered a similar loss. On the flyleaf he inscribed, "To my friend, in recollection of his son and my son, who, by the grace of God, have the privilege of being boys throughout Eternity."

Debt

273. The celebrated French poet, Saint-Foix, who, in spite of his large income, was always in debt, sat one day in a barber shop waiting to be shaved. He was lathered, and a tradesman entered who happened to be one of the poet's largest creditors. No sooner did he see Saint-Foix than he angrily demanded his money. The poet composedly begged him not to make a scene.

"Won't you wait for the money until I am shaved?"

"Certainly," said the other, pleased at the prospect.

Saint-Foix then made the barber a witness to the agreement, took a towel, wiped the lather from his face, and left the shop. He wore a beard until the end of his days.

274. For some reason, medical men claim that we're taller in the morning than in the evening. We've all noticed that we're shorter around the end of the month.

275. "I'll make you this proposition," said the merchant to his prospective customer. "You pay me $100 for the merchandise now and owe me the rest."

"That's all right with me," replied the customer.

Several months went by and the merchant hadn't received the balance of the money from the customer, so he decided to call upon him.

"How about the balance of the money?" he asked.

"I'm owing it to you," was the reply. "I told you that I would pay you $100 down and owe you the rest. If I pay up then I will have broken our agreement, because then I won't owe it to you any more. And I'm sure you want me to stick to our agreement."

276. In a western town close to a reservation, an Indian paid a debt of $50 to the local supply house. The proprietor thanked him for the money, but the Indian stood with arms folded, waiting, waiting.

Finally the proprietor asked the Indian what he wanted.

"Receipt," he replied.

"What do you want a receipt for?"

The Indian said: "When I go to meet the Great Father, he will want me to show that I paid all my debts before he will let me into the Great Hunting Ground. I don't want to hunt all over Hell trying to find you."

277. "Thankful! What have I to be thankful for? I can't pay my bills."

"Then, man alive, be thankful you aren't one of your creditors."

278. *Geology Professor:* "The geologist thinks nothing of a thousand years."

Student: "Great guns! And I loaned a geologist ten dollars yesterday."

Diagnosis

279. While the diagnosis of the patient, who had eaten and drunk rather generously, was proceeding, the sick man said: "Doctor, do you think the trouble is in my appendix?" "Oh, no," said the doctor, "the trouble is in your table of contents."

280. "Doctor, did you ever make a serious mistake in your diagnosis?"

"Yes, I once treated a patient for indigestion, when she could have afforded an appendectomy."

281. A lady with a pain in her side went to see a physician. He told her she had appendicitis and must have an operation. She disliked this diagnosis so she went to another doctor. He told her she had gall bladder trouble and must have an operation. "Where do you go from here?" inquired a friend.

"Back to the first," she declared. "I'd rather have appendicitis."

282. A man sought medical aid because he had popped eyes and a ringing in the ears. A doctor looked him over and suggested removal of his tonsils. The operation resulted in no improvement, so the patient consulted another doctor who suggested removal of his teeth. The teeth were extracted but still the man's eyes popped and the ringing in his ears continued.

A third doctor told him bluntly, "You've got six months to live." In that event, the doomed man decided he'd treat himself right while he could. He bought a flashy car, hired a liveried chauffeur, had the best tailor in town to make him 30 suits, and decided even his shirts would be made-to-order.

"Okay," said the shirtmaker, "let's get your measurement. Hmm, 34 sleeve, 16 collar—"

"Fifteen," the man said.

"Sixteen collar," the shirtmaker repeated, measuring again.

"But I've always worn a 15 collar," said the man.

"Listen," the shirtmaker said, "I'm warning you. You keep on wearing a 15 collar and your eyes will pop and you'll have a ringing in your ears."

283. The two specialists at the bedside differed in their diagnoses. "My dear colleague," said the first specialist, "it would appear the lady has rheumatism."

The patient looked up and said, "How right you are!"

The second specialist shook his head, "I think it's arthritis."

The patient smiled wanly, "How right you are."

The patient's husband was put out. "You both can't be right."

The patient looked at her husband. "How right you are."

284. "I can't quite diagnose your case," said the doctor. "I think it's drink."

"All right, doctor," the patient gravely replied, "I'll come back some time when you're sober."

285. A doctor was called on by a testy aristocrat. "What's your trouble?" the doctor asked.

"That's what you are supposed to find out," was the reply.

"If you'll be kind enough to wait an hour or two, I'll call in a friend of mine, a veterinarian, who is the only person I know who can make a diagnosis without asking questions!"

286. *Doctor:* "You have acute appendicitis."

Chorus Girl: "Listen, Doc, I came here to be examined, not flattered."

Diplomacy

287. The street corner orator was anti-Irish.

"Show me an Irishman," he yelled, "and I'll show you a coward."

A big Irishman stepped forward inquiring, "What did you say?"

The speaker was frightened but held to his guns and repeated the remark.

"I'm an Irishman," said the big fellow as he clenched his fist.

"And I'm a coward," said the smart-aleck orator, and continued with his speech.

288. Little Mary's mother and father both fancied themselves as violinists. In front of both of them a visitor asked Mary, "Who do you think plays better, your mother or your father?"

"Heifetz," answered Mary clearly demonstrating her qualifications for membership in the diplomatic corps.

289. "Pop," said Edgar, looking up from the book he was reading, "what is meant by 'diplomatic phraseology'?"

"Well," replied the father, "if you were to say to a homely girl, 'Your face would stop a clock,' that would be uncomplimentary and utter stupidity, but if you said to her, 'When I look into your eyes, time stands still,' that would be diplomatic phraseology."

Discipline

290. "If I were the sort of man," said Sir Henry Wood, "who never answered letters, forgot appointments, and didn't know where to lay his hands on things, they would call me an artist. Because I am not, they call me a disciplinarian."

291. A little boy went to school and the teacher asked, "What is

66

your name?" He replied, "Johnny Don't." It seems he had never heard his mother call him anything else and supposed that was his real name.

There are too many parents who bring up their children on too many "don'ts."

Divorce

292. "I think you might as well give your husband a divorce," the judge advised.

"What!" shouted the wife. "I have lived with this bum for 20 years and *now* I should make him happy!"

293. *Lawyer:* "You say you want to get a divorce on the grounds that your husband is careless about his appearance?"

Client: "Yes, he hasn't shown up in almost five years."

294. "My husband has lost all his money on the stock exchange."

"Oh, I do feel sorry for him."

"Yes, so do I. He'll miss me."

295. "Just think of it!" exclaimed the romantic young newly-wed, "a few words mumbled over your head and you're married."

"Yes," agreed the old cynic, "and a few words mumbled in your sleep and you're divorced."

296. "So you want to know if you have grounds for divorce," said the lawyer. "Are you married?"

"Yes."

"Then you have grounds for divorce."

297. "Unmarried?"

"Twice."

Doctor-Patient

298. A doctor was treating a patient for melancholic insomnia. He had tried everything, but the patient continued sleepless—and pessimistic. Finally, he decided on a new remedy.

"Get some good old Barbados rum," he directed. "Cover a lump of sugar in the bottom of a large glass. Fill with hot water and drink slowly. Repeat this every hour."

"But doctor," asked the patient, "will that put me to sleep?"

"No," said the doctor, "but it will make you not mind staying awake."

299. "Are you medical or surgical?" asked one small boy of another in the hospital ward.

"I don't know," replied the youngster.

The questioner was scornful, having been a patient in the hospital for some months. Condescendingly, he undertook to make his meaning plainer for the sake of the lower intelligence of his less quick-witted companion: "Were you sick when you came in, or did they make you sick after you got here?" he inquired.

300. Johnny Patterson, the famous Irish clown, lay critically ill. The doctor, having done all he could, closed his medicine case and prepared to leave.

"I'll see you in the morning, Johnny," he said cheerfully.

Instinctively, the dying clown smirked and gave his eye a professional roll that had helped launch many a quip.

"Sure, doc," he murmured, "but will I see you?"

301. A doctor, wishing to deal tactfully with a quite healthy retired businessman who kept worrying about his heart, threw a friendly arm around the man's shoulders and said in a reassuring voice: "Your heart will last as long as you live." And the businessman was delighted, comforted, and reassured.

302. A man had an attack of pneumonia and a doctor was called in. After an examination, the doctor said, "You are a musician, I think, and play a wind instrument?"

"Yes."

"That explains everything. There's a distinct straining of the lungs, and the larynx is inflamed as though by some abnormal pressure. What instrument do you play?"

"The accordion."

303. *Doctor:* "Look here, don't you know my office hours are from eight to ten in the evening?"

Patient: "Yes, I do, but the dog that bit me didn't."

304. "Did the doctor tell you what you had?"

"No, he took what I had without telling me."

305. A fellow with a bad rash on his hands came into a doctor's office for an examination.

The doctor examined the hands intently; then, with a puzzled look, he got down a large tome from a shelf and spent some time studying a single paragraph. Then he examined the hands carefully again, and buried himself in another medical tome. The process was repeated a third time, after which the doctor gazed thoughtfully out the window for several minutes.

Finally he shot a sharp look over his glasses at the patient.

"Have you ever had this before?" he asked.

"Yes," said the patient.

"Well," said the doctor, "you've got it again."

306. "Medicine won't help you any," the doctor told the elderly patient. "What you need is a complete rest and a change of living. Get away to some quiet country place for a month. Go to bed early, eat more roast beef, drink plenty of good rich milk, and smoke just one cigar a day."

A month later the patient walked into the doctor's office. He looked like a new man and the doctor told him so.

"Yes, Doctor, your advice certainly did the business. I went to bed early and did all the other things you told me. But say, Doctor, that one cigar a day almost killed me at first. It's no joke starting to smoke at my age."

307. The doctor's new secretary, a conscientious girl, was puzzled by an entry in the doctor's notes on an emergency case: "Shot in the lumbar region," it read. After a moment she brightened and, in the interest of clarity, typed into the record: "Shot in the wood."

308. "Well," breathed the young medic as he joined a colleague in the hospital cafeteria, "I certainly performed that last operation in the nick-of-time. Another few hours and the patient would have recovered without it!"

309. The lecturer at a medical college was exhibiting a diagram and said, "The subject here limps because one leg is shorter than the other."

Then he addressed one of his audience: "Now, Mr. Smith, what would you do in such a case?"

DOCTOR-PATIENT

Young Smith pondered deeply before answering. "I imagine, sir, that I should limp, too."

310. *Doctor:* "I'm sorry to tell you that your wife's mind is completely gone."
Husband: "Well, I'm not surprised. She's been giving me a piece of it for twenty years."

311. *Doctor:* "Well, you'll get along all right. Your leg is swollen, but I wouldn't worry about it."
Patient: "No, and if *your* leg was swollen, I wouldn't worry about it, either."

312. *Doctor:* "Your husband must have absolute rest and quiet. Here are some sleeping tablets."
Patient's wife: "When must I give them to him?"
Doctor: "They're for you."

313. "When I'm sick," said the young man, expounding his views on the subject of illness, "I go to see the doctor. For after all, doctors have to live. He writes me out a prescription, which I take to the pharmacist. I pay the druggist willingly, for after all, a pharmacist, too, must live. Then I go home and pour the medicine down the drain. For after all, I have to live."

314. The impatient old duffer finally got tired of sitting in the reception room waiting for his turn to see the doctor.
"I guess I'll go home," he said, "and die a natural death."

315. A certain stomach specialist in one of our big cities has a formula for patients with nervous indigestion.
He asks them, "Do you play golf?"
If they say, "Yes," he tells them to cut it out.
If they say, "No," he tells them to start playing.

316. *Patient:* "I say, doctor, don't you think it would be a good idea if I packed up and went to a place where the climate was warmer?"
Doctor: "Good Lord! Isn't that the very thing I have been trying to prevent?"

317. "Well, I can find nothing organically wrong with you," said the doctor as he started to put his instruments back into his bag. "As you know, many illnesses come from worry. You probably have some business or social problem that you should talk over with a good psychiatrist. I had a case very similar to yours only a few weeks ago. The man had a $5000 promissory note to meet in a few days. He didn't see how he was going to be able to get the money with which to discharge his obligation and, in consequence, worried himself into a state of nervous exhaustion."

"And did you cure him?" asked the patient hopefully.

"Yes, I did," said the doctor. "I told him he must stop worrying; that life was too short to make oneself sick over a scrap of paper. Now he's back to his normal self again and has stopped worrying entirely."

"You said it, man," muttered the patient dejectedly. "I'm the one who loaned him the $5000."

318. *Doctor:* "Wait a minute, I didn't tell you to say ah-h-h."
Patient: "I know you didn't. I just saw the nurse."

319. *Patient:* "Doctor, is it true that sleeping outdoors will cure insomnia?"
Doctor: "Perfectly true. But sleeping indoors will do the same thing."

320. A harried business executive went to his physician to get a prescription for sleeping pills, only to find that he was allergic to sedatives.

"What about some of this twilight sleep I've read about?" he asked the doctor.

"Oh, that's only for labor," was the reply.

"Good heavens!" exclaimed the executive, "haven't you anything for management?"

321. The doctor was taken to the patient's room but came down in a few minutes and asked for a screw driver. Five minutes later he was back and asked for a can opener. Soon after he returned and demanded a chisel and hammer. The distraught husband couldn't stand it any longer. "Please, Doc, what's wrong with my wife?"

"Don't know yet," the doc answered. "Can't get my bag open."

DOCTOR-PATIENT

322. *Excited Wife:* "Doctor, do hurry! My husband is at death's door!"

Cooperative doctor: "Don't you worry, lady. I'll pull him through."

323. "Doc," he said, "if there's anything wrong with me, don't give me a long scientific name. Say it so I can understand it."

"Very well," the doctor agreed, "you're lazy."

"Thanks, Doc, now give me the scientific name so I can tell my boss."

324. *Patient:* "Since we have known each other for a long time, Doctor, I do not intend to insult you by paying my bill, but I have left you a handsome legacy in my will."

Doctor: "That's fine. By the way, let me have that prescription I just gave you. I want to make a slight change in it."

325. A man who went to his doctor's consulting room was somewhat surprised when the nurse told him to step into the next room and remove his clothes.

"But, nurse," he started in a hoarse whisper, "it's my throat."

"Please do as I tell you," snapped the nurse, "or I shall be forced to cancel your appointment."

So, shrugging his shoulders, he went into the next room and there sat a young fellow who was looking very uncomfortable and quite naked except for a large parcel he held across his knees.

"Doesn't that beat everything," said the man, removing his coat. "I come in here with a sore throat, and I have to take my clothes off."

"What are you grumbling about?" was the reply. "I just came along to deliver this parcel."

326. *Patient* (coming out of an anesthetic): "Why are all the blinds down, Doctor?"

Doctor: "Well, there's a fire across the alley and I didn't want you to wake up and think the operation was a failure."

327. *Doctor* (after examining the patient): "I don't like the looks of your husband, Mrs. Kildare."

72

Mrs. Kildare: "I don't either, Doctor, but he's so kind to the children."

328. After the physician checked the patient over, he asked, "Have you been living a normal life?"

"Yes, Doctor."

"Well, you're going to have to cut it out for awhile."

329. *Patient:* "Doctor, isn't it somewhat out of your way to visit me here?"

Doctor: "Not too bad. I have another patient nearby, and in that way I can kill two birds with one stone."

330. *Wife:* "I want the truth. Is there no hope for my husband?"

Doctor: "Madam, I'm afraid that he can't recover, but to make sure, I'm going to call in another doctor."

331. One busy morning it took some time for the doctor to see all of the patients in his waiting room. He apologized to an elderly man for the long delay.

"I didn't mind the wait so much, Doctor," came the reply, "but I thought that you would prefer treating my ailment in its earlier stage."

332. "How is your doctor son getting along in his practice?"

"Excellently—he has made enough money so he can occasionally tell a patient there is nothing wrong with him."

333. The doctor was questioning the nurse about her latest patient. "Have you kept a chart of his progress?" he asked.

"No," said the nurse, "but I can show you my diary."

334. An eminent specialist who devoted much of his time to charity work in clinics was surprised to have a bewhiskered old gentleman ushered into his Park Avenue consultation room one day.

"Remember me, Doctor?" asked the man. "You treated me over at the clinic. Well, I've been left a little money and I guess I can afford my own doctor now."

"But what made you come to me?" the physician wanted to know. "I wasn't the only doctor who treated you at the clinic."

"I know," the old man said quietly, "but you were the only one who helped me with my coat."

Drunkenness

335. The wonderful love of a beautiful maid—
The love of a staunch, true man—
The love of a baby unafraid—
Have existed since life began.
But the greatest love—the love of loves—
Even greater than that of a mother—
Is the passionate, tender, and infinite love,
Of one drunken bum for another.
            —Author Unknown

336. At the police station the indignant drunk demanded, "What I want to know is what I was brought in for."

"You were brought in for drinking," the sergeant replied.

"Well, that's different," the drunk continued, "When do we get started?"

337. "Look, dear, how picturesque! The Smiths are taking in a Yule log."

"Yule log, my eye. That's Smith."

338. A drunk was walking along the street, one foot on the curbstone, the other in the gutter. An officer stopped the man. "Why are you walking that way?" he demanded. "You must be drunk!"

"Drunk, am I? So that's it!" exclaimed the little fellow. "Thank God! I thought I was lame."

339. A disreputable character in court had just admitted being drunk.

"Did you have to drink the whole bottle at one sitting?" demanded his Honor.

"Couldn't help it, Judge," answered the drunk, "I lost the cork."

340. In Brighton, Colorado, a drunk, obviously in no condition to take the wheel, was getting into his automobile when a sheriff's deputy halted him and asked: "You're not going to drive that car, are you?"

"Certainly I'm going to drive," the man replied. "I'm in no condition to walk."

341. A drunk in the Empire State Building stepped into an elevator shaft and dropped thirty stories to the basement. When he landed, he shook his fist and exclaimed, "I said up, not down."

342. A pink elephant, a green rat, and a yellow snake walked into a cocktail bar.

"You're a little early, boys," said the bartender. "He's not here yet."

343. A New York publisher who was a teetotaler dropped into the office just before press time, and found the assistant managing editor in charge.

"Where's Jones?" he asked, naming the managing editor.

"On one of those periodical binges of his," said the assistant.

"Where's the city editor?"

"Drunk as a lord down at Jack's place."

"The make-up editor wasn't on duty when I came through the composing room. Where's he?"

"Oh, he's in a Turkish bath over in Brooklyn getting a hang-over boiled out."

The proprietor collapsed in a chair, shaking his head sadly.

"Well," he said, "for a man who never touches a drop, I seem to suffer more from the effects of drunkenness than any man in this town."

344. The drunk sitting at the bar was adjacent to a man and his wife. Suddenly the drunk came forth with a resounding burp.

"How dare you belch before my wife," thundered the husband.

With that the drunk unsteadily got off the bar stool and making a sweeping bow said, "A thousand pardons, sir . . . I did not know it was the madam's turn."

345. Watching a drunk try without success to unlock the door to his house, a policeman asked if he could handle the key for him.

"No thanks," the man replied, "I can hold the key—you hold the house."

346. Two drunks were walking down a railroad track. Said the first one, "These long stairs sure do get me."

"It's not the stairs," replied the second. "It's these low banisters."

DRUNKENNESS

347. "It is alcohol, and alcohol alone, that is responsible for your present position," said the judge.

"Thank you, your Honor, for sayin' that. You're the first person that has not said that it was all my fault."

348. The local drunk in a small town staggered out of a bar. Gazing around in a befuddled manner, he spotted the town's only taxicab in front of the bar, and climbed in. "Take me to Charley's Place, driver," he said.

"Buddy, you're in front of Charley's Place now," replied the driver.

"O.K., Mac!" said the drunk as he staggered out of the cab. "But the next time, don't drive so blamed fast!"

349. A minister, returning home late one night from a sick call, noticed one of his parishioners staggering down the street.

"Let me help you to the door," said the minister, guiding the inebriated member of his flock gently home.

At the door the besotted man pleaded with the minister to come into the house with him. But the minister demurred on the grounds that it was too late.

"Pleash, Rev'ren'," the man begged. "Jusht for a minute. I want the wife to see who I been out with tonight."

350. "Are you positive that the defendant was drunk?" asked the Judge.

"No doubt," growled the officer.

"Why are you so certain?"

"Well," replied the officer, "I saw him put a penny in the patrol box on Fourth Street, then look up at the clock on the Presbyterian Church, and shout: 'Hurray! I've lost fourteen pounds!'"

351. *Employer:* "Mr. Jones, you disappoint me. I was told you were seen at the company party intoxicated and pushing a wheelbarrow."

Jones: "Why, yes, but I thought you approved."

Employer: "Of course not. Why should I approve?"

Jones: "Because you were riding in the wheelbarrow."

352. "Sometimes," said Mrs. Thorndale to the new maid, "it will be necessary for you to help me upstairs."

"I understand, ma'am," replied the girl, "I drink a bit myself."

353. "What did your wife say when you came in drunk last night?"

"Nothing. And I was going to have those front teeth pulled anyway."

354. A drunk who had wandered into a cemetery at night, and then had stumbled into an open grave, was screaming for help at the top of his voice. Hearing his cries in the darkness, another drunk staggered over to the grave to investigate.

"Help, help!" hollered the first drunk, "get me out. It's cold down here."

"It sure is, buddy," replied the second drunk, walking away, "too bad they forgot to cover you up."

355. Two drunks sat on the curb, meditating.

Said one to the other: "Watsch yer wife shay when you shtay out late like thish?"

"Ain't got no wife," replied the other.

"Then watsch the idea of shtaying out sho late?"

356. The inebriated husband tip-toed up the stairs. He patched up the scars of the brawl with adhesive tape and then climbed into bed, smiling at the thought that he had put one more good one over on his wife.

Came morning. He opened his eyes and there stood his angry wife.

"You were drunk last night," she declared with fire in her eyes.

"Why, darling, I was nothing of the sort."

"Well, if you weren't, then who put all the adhesive tape on the bathroom mirror?"

Economy

357. The wife of a young engineer, off on a job in Iceland, knitted him a warm jacket which she air-mailed with the following letter:

"Postage costs so much for every little ounce that I have cut off the buttons. Love and kisses.

"P.S. The buttons are in the right-hand pocket."

358. The daughter was concerned about the amount of money her boy friend was spending on her each time he took her out.

EDUCATION

"Mother," she said, "what is the best way to stop Jerry from spending too much money on me?"

"Marry him!"

Education

359. At a meeting, a self-made man got up and talked at length about how thankful he was that he had never come in contact with the pernicious influence of any schools, colleges, or universities. He admittedly had no education and was proud of it.

When he had finished the chairman inquired, "Do I understand you to say that you are thankful for your ignorance?"

"You can put it that way if you like," was the answer. "Why?"

"Oh," said the chairman, "I just wanted to point out that you have a great deal to be thankful for."

360. Upon due reflection, a rural school teacher decided to give full credit to a pupil for his answer to an arithmetic problem.

The question: "If your father sold fifteen hundred bushels of grain for $2 per bushel, what would he get?"

The answer: "A new car."

361. "Jones never completed his education, did he?"

"No, he lived and died a bachelor."

362. The clerk in Wahr's Book Store in Ann Arbor told the University of Michigan student, "Here's a book that will do half your work for you."

"That's great," said the student. "Give me two of them."

363. The bright young high school graduate applied for his first full-time job in the railroad car department. He read the application blank which asked, "What machines can you operate?"

The youth studied hard, then wrote, "Slot and pinball."

364. Two first graders were standing outside of school one morning. "Do you think," asked one, "that thermonuclear projectiles will pierce the heat barrier?"

"No," said the second, "once a force enters the substratosphere . . ."

Then the bell rang. Said the first: "There goes the bell. Darn it, now we've gotta go in and string beads."

365. *Teacher:* "Which hand is the Statue of Liberty holding over her head?"
Smart Kid: "The one with the torch."

366. Tired after a busy day, a distinguished congressman in Washington handed the menu back to the waiter and said: "Just bring me a good meal."

A good meal was served and the congressman gave the waiter a generous tip. "Thank yo', suh," the waiter said, "an' if you' got any friends what can't read you' jes' send 'em to me."

Efficiency

367. Driving into a Laguna Beach, California, service station, a motorist asked for ten gallons of gas. Three servicemen hopped to work smartly—cleaning windshield, checking tires and water, etc. The driver paid his bill and drove off.

A few minutes later he returned and asked: "Did any of you put gas in my car?" The three attendants went into a huddle—then confessed nobody had.

368. *Efficiency expert:* "Smith, what do you do here?"
Smith: "Nothing."
Efficiency expert: "Brown, what do you do here?"
Brown: "Nothing."
Efficiency expert: "Hmmmm—duplication."

Embarrassment

369. The most embarrassing moment in the life of Jane Wyman happened when she was entertaining very special guests. After looking over all the appointments carefully, she put a note on the guest towels, "If you use these I will murder you." It was meant for her husband. In the excitement she forgot to remove the note. After the guests had departed, the towels were discovered still in perfect order, as well as the note itself.

370. Some years ago, one of the bright young men who represented Standard Oil in China returned to America for a vacation, in the course of which he met and married a lovely girl from his home town.

"You'll just love Shanghai," he assured her again and again on the way out, "particularly my Number One Boy, Ling. You won't have to lift a finger. Ling runs the household."

They arrived in Shanghai, the bride met Ling, and approved. The next morning her husband kissed her good-bye before reporting back on the job. "Sleep as long as you like, darling," he told her. "Ling will take care of everything."

A few hours later she awoke again, to find herself being shaken ever so gently by the Number One Boy. "Time to get dressed and go home now, Missy," he said.

371. *She:* "That's the fifth time you've gone back for ice cream and cake. Doesn't it embarrass you?"

He: "Why should it? I keep telling them I'm getting it for you."

372. "Are you troubled much by your children telling lies?" asked one mother of another.

"Not so much," replied her friend, "as by their telling the truth at inappropriate times."

Employment

373. "You say you want a job in this office? Well, what can you do?"

"Nothing."

"I'm sorry, but you should have applied sooner. All those high-salaried positions were taken long ago."

374. *Boss:* "What are you doing here? I thought I fired you two weeks ago."

Office Boy: "I know. I just came back to see if you were still in business."

375. "I'm Mr. Brown's wife," said a brunette, introducing herself to a blonde at a party.

"I'm his secretary," said the blonde.

"Oh," said the brunette, arching her eyebrows slightly, "were you?"

80

376. "Why were you discharged by your last employer?"

"I was overly ambitious."

"Explain, please."

"I wanted to take work home with me."

"Who was your last employer?"

"The First National Trust and Savings Bank."

377. "Why did you leave your last position?"

"Illness. The boss got sick of me."

378. "See here, Jones," complained the boss, "how is it you never get to work on time any more?"

"Well, boss," replied Jones, "you see it's like this. You've drilled me so darn well never to watch the clock here at the office that I've lost the habit of watching it at home."

379. *Employe:* "I have been here 10 years doing three men's work for one man's pay. Now I want a raise."

Employer: "Well, I can't give you a raise, but if you'll tell me who the other two men are, I'll fire them."

380. Klumseigh obtained a job as shipping clerk in a retail china shop. On his third day he smashed a big vase. On pay day he was called into the manager's office and told that half his wages would be deducted each week until the vase was paid for.

"How much was the vase worth?" asked the anxious employe.

"About three hundred dollars," replied the manager.

"Hurray!" shouted Klumseigh. "It looks as if I've got a steady job at last!"

381. The autocrat of the office had one of his more brow-beaten employes on the carpet: "Jones, I understand you've been going over my head!"

The timid employe murmured that he hadn't said anything to anyone as far as he knew.

"Ha!" snarled the boss. "Isn't it true that you've been praying for a raise?"

382. *Visitor:* "How many people work here?"

Employer: "Oh, about one in every ten!"

383. The boss called one of his clerks into his private office. "I have noticed, Smith," he began, "that you, of all my clerks, seem to put your whole life and soul into your work. No detail is too small to escape your attention. No hours are too long for you."

Smith glowed with pride and anticipation of promotion and a raise in salary.

"And so, Smith," continued his employer, "I am forced much against my will to let you go. It is just such men as you who go out and start rival businesses."

384. "Do you think you know all about how to run a grocery store?"

"No, sir, I do not."

"Well, I'll try you. You talk like you've had experience."

385. *New boss:* "Have you any letters of reference?"

New employe: "Sure, read this."

New boss: "To whom it may concern: John Jones worked for us one week, and we were satisfied."

386. *Personnel Manager:* "How long did you work in the other place?"

Job applicant: "Fifty-five years."

Personnel Manager: "How old are you?"

Applicant: "Forty-five years."

Personnel Manager: "How could you work 55 years when you are only 45 years old?"

Applicant: "Over time."

387. When Eddie, the slow-moving and inefficient clerk in a small-town store, was not in evidence one morning, a customer asked, "Where is Eddie? He ain't sick, is he?"

"Nope, he ain't," replied the proprietor. "He just ain't workin' here no more."

"That so?" responded the villager. "Got anybody in mind for the vacancy?"

"Nope. Eddie didn't leave no vacancy."

388. The housewife was interviewing an applicant for a job on her household staff.

"Do you know how to serve company?" she asked.

"Yes, ma'am; both ways," was the reply.

"Just what do you mean 'both ways'?"

"So's they'll come back or so's they won't."

389. An employer had spent a great deal of money to insure that his men should work under the best conditions. "Now, whenever I enter the workshop," he said, "I want to see every man cheerfully performing his task, and therefore I invite you to place in this box any further suggestions as to how that can be brought about."

A week later the box was opened; it contained only one slip of paper, on which was written: "Don't wear rubber heels."

390. *Character on the streetcar:* "I don't have anything to worry about. My wife takes care of my money, and my mother-in-law tends to my business. All I need to do is work."

391. *Sign at a factory gate:* "Anyone who likes work can have a whale of a good time here."

392. *Personnel Manager:* "We can pay you seventy dollars a week now and seventy-five dollars a week in six months."

Applicant: "Thank you, sir. I'll drop back in six months."

393. "Just what have you done for the good of humanity which might help me in pronouncing sentence?" asked the judge of the convicted pickpocket who stood before him.

"Well, your Honor," replied the offender, "I've kept three or four detectives and policemen working regularly."

394. A girl applied for a job as a stenographer, and was given a test in spelling.

"How do you spell Mississippi?" she was asked.

"The river or the state?"

395. *Vocational adviser to young man:* "Your vocational aptitude test indicated your best opportunities lie in a field where your father holds an influential position."

396. "Gentlemen," said the sourfaced boss, "I've called you in to announce a big sales contest which I am starting immediately and which I will personally supervise." There was an excited murmur from the assembled salesmen, and an eager voice from the rear called out: "What does the winner get?" "He gets," announced the boss, "to keep his job!"

397. A lady was choosing between two applicants for a position as gardener while her mother-in-law, seated on the porch behind the men, pointed frantically towards the less prepossessing. Supposing that the old lady had some personal knowledge of the applicant, she engaged him. "Did he ever work for you?" she asked, when the two were alone.

"No," replied the old lady, "I never saw or heard of either of them."

"Then why did you point to him? The other had the better face."

"Face!" returned the old lady briskly. "When you pick a man out for work, go by his overalls. If they are patched on the knee, you want him. If they are patched on the seat, you don't."

Etiquette

398. A New Hampshire farmer had been urged to attend the funeral of his neighbor's third wife. "But I'm not goin'," he announced to his own wife.

"Goodness sakes, why not?" she asked.

"Well, Mary, I'm beginnin' to feel kinda awkward about goin' so often without anything of the sort to ask him back to."

399. The wife had been watching the new neighbors down the street. She reported to her hubby: "They seem a most devoted couple. Every time he leaves, she comes out on the porch and he hugs and kisses her. Why don't you do that?"

"Me?" cried the hubby in amazement. "Goodness! I haven't even been introduced to her yet."

400. Tommy had been invited to dinner at the house of some particular people, and his mother, who was not to accompany him, was anxious about his table behavior. She gave him elaborate instructions before leaving home, and on his return made special inquiries.

"Oh, I got on all right," Tommy assured her, "at least I—I only did one thing wrong, and I couldn't help it, and I got out of that fine."

"What did you do, Tommy?"

"Oh, I was cutting my meat and it slipped off the plate on to the floor."

"Oh, my dear boy!" cried his mother in distress. "What on earth did you do then?"

"Oh, I just said, sort o' careless, 'That's always the way with tough meat,' and went on with my dinner."

401. *Convict:* "How long are you in for?"
New cellmate: "Ninety-nine years. How long you in for?"
Convict: "Seventy-five."
New cellmate: "Then you take the bunk nearest the door; you're getting out first."

402. A little girl went to see the president of the bank, and explained that her girls' club was raising money, and would he please contribute.

The banker laid a dollar and a dime on his desk and said, "Take whichever you want."

The little girl picked up the dime and said, "My mother always taught me to take the smallest piece." However, picking up the dollar bill also, she added, "But so I won't lose this dime, I'll take this piece of paper to wrap it up in."

403. A young lad had returned from a birthday party. His mother, apprehensive lest his appetite should have overcome his manners, asked, "Are you sure you didn't ask your hostess for a second piece of cake?"

"Oh, no, mother. I only asked her for the recipe so you could bake a cake like it, and she insisted on giving me two more pieces."

404. The following note was received by a rural school teacher from the mother of one of her pupils:

"Dear teacher: My boy is getting all peeked and thin. He says he can't get no blood out of his vittles from you always nagging at him about his manners. Now I want to tell you my kids don't need any teacher to learn them manners. If you had ever et at our house and knowed how refined their pa is you would be ashamed. I have lived with their pa for 20 years and never once have I seed that man put his knife in the butter without licking it first. I don't want to have to complain to you again."

Example

405. The teacher was trying to popularize arithmetic by bringing home the examples to the pupils.

Teacher: "Now, Junior, if you had $5 in one pocket and $7.50 in the other, what would you say you had?"

Junior: "The wrong pants."

406. The ball team had hit a terrific batting slump. The coach called a special batting-practice session one morning. Disgusted by the ineptness of his crew, he finally grabbed a bat and charged out, snorting, "Here, you dopes! I'll show you something!" He ordered the pitcher to let 'em come in, but fast.

But the coach, it developed, was sadly out of practice. After seven or eight futile swipes, he flung the bat aside. "Now," he said, "that's the sort of thing you guys have been doing. I want you to get in there and start to slug the ball!"

Explanation

407. The young fellow turned to the man next to him on the bus and asked if he'd tell him the time.

"Tell you the time?" the man replied. "I should say not! Why, if I told you the time, I'd probably ask you to get off with me and have a drink—you seem like such a nice young fellow. If we had a drink, I'd probably follow it up with an invitation to dinner. When we got home, you'd most likely be attracted by my young daughter. You'd probably want to marry her, and she'd most likely agree. And if you think I'd like a son-in-law who can't afford a watch of his own, you're crazy! So why should I tell you the time?"

408. "Gladys," exclaimed her mother, more in sorrow than in anger, "you're a very, very vain little girl. You are always looking at yourself in the mirror. You don't see me looking in the mirror all the time, do you?"

"No, Mother, I don't," acknowledged the child, "but then you don't have to—you can see me without looking in the mirror."

409. The mental patient walked up to the new superintendent at the State Hospital. "We like you much better than we did the last fellow," he said.

The new official beamed all over. "And would you mind telling me why?" he asked.

"Oh, you seem so more like one of us. "

410. *Sunday School Teacher:* "Now, why was it that Mary and Joseph took Jesus with them to Jerusalem?"

Mary (aged four): "I guess they didn't have a sitter."

Extravagance

411. *Wife to harassed husband:* "Why are you complaining? That checking account is my only extravagance!"

412. A husband and wife were having a spirited discussion about who was the more extravagant.

"You accuse me of reckless extravagance," said he scornfully. "When did I ever make a useless expenditure?"

"Well," replied she naively, "there's that fire-extinguisher you bought last year. We never used it once, not once."

Fame

413. The popular movie comedian Joe E. Brown, relates that in the course of his tours in the Pacific Theater of War during the late conflict, he was one day thrilled by the prospect of being photographed with General Douglas MacArthur.

When the two men had finally been brought together for the picture, Brown could not help exclaiming, "What an honor!"

Whereupon the General explained: "This picture is for my little son, Joe. He wants his dad photographed with a celebrity."

414. A small boy whose hobby was collecting autographs, once approached former President Herbert Hoover with a request for his signature. Mr. Hoover, a lover of boys and a great friend of youth, responded promptly to the request.

"And would you mind signing four more times?" the youngster importuned.

"Why do you want four more?" asked the ex-President.

"Because it takes five Hoovers to get one Babe Ruth!" was the prompt and honest response.

415. Long on egotism but short on cash, the young actor was trying to talk his impatient landlord into waiting for the rent.

"In a few years," he said, "people will point to this apartment and say, 'Smith, the famous actor, once lived in there.' "

"If I don't get my rent tonight," said the landlord, "they'll be able to say it tomorrow."

Family

416. "How do you like your new baby sister, Tommy?"

"Oh, she's all right, I guess. But just like Pop says, there are lots of things we needed worse."

417. "John," said the wife, "I'm ashamed of the way we live. Mother pays our rent. Aunt Martha buys our clothes, and my sister sends us money for food. I don't like to complain, but I'm sorry we can't do better than that."

"You should be," replied the husband indignantly. "You've got two uncles that don't send us a dime!"

418. During a bad electrical storm, mother thought her young son would be frightened, so she tiptoed into his room to comfort him.

The boy opened his eyes and mumbled: "What's Daddy doing with the television set now?"

Farming

419. A book agent came to sell one of the combination farmer-merchant-bankers of southeast Arkansas a set of books on scientific agriculture. The old man thumbed through them.

"No, I don't want to buy them."

"You ought to buy them, sir. If you had these books you could farm twice as good as you do now."

"Hell, son," he replied, "I don't farm half as good as I know how now."

420. A farmer was explaining to a townsman how it happened that all the costs of food had gone up.

"When a farmer has to know the botanical name of what he grows, the entomological name of the insects which try to destroy it, and the pharmaceutical name of the stuff used to spray it, somebody's got to pay for it."

421. A free-advice seeking woman asked a farmer what would be good to plant in a spot that gets very little rain due to overhanging eaves, has too much late afternoon sun, has clay soil, and is on a rocky ledge. "Lady," he answered, "how about a nice flagpole?"

422. *Farmer* (carrying a milk pail, approaches a cow): "Well, Bessie, what will it be—milk or hamburger?"

Fashion

423. A beautiful Hollywood actress was trying on a dress in the studio wardrobe department. "I don't like that color," commented the designer. "Now if you'd wear a dress to match those stockings, you'd be a sensation."

"I certainly would," replied the actress. "I'm not wearing stockings."

424. "Did you give your wife some of the money you won?"

"Sure thing! I told her to buy some decent clothes—but she said, 'I've worn decent clothes all my life; now I'm going to dress like other women.' "

425. A staid gentleman was upset by the dress of modern girls at a rodeo.

"Just look at that young person with the short hair and the blue jeans," he remarked to a bystander. "Is it a boy or a girl?"

"It's a girl; she's my daughter!"

"Oh, please forgive me, sir. I had no idea you were her father!"

"I'm not. I'm her mother!"

426. *Tall girl:* "Have you a skirt that will make me look shorter?"

Saleswoman: "No, but we have a skirt that will make everyone else look longer."

427. "That blonde looked quite tempting in the biblical gown she was wearing last evening."

"What do you mean, biblical gown?"

"Well, you know, sort of 'low and behold.' "

Father-Son

428. *Dad to lad:* "Well, son, you're right. This old report card of mine you found in the attic isn't any better than yours. I guess the only fair thing to do is give you what my father gave me."

429. Endeavoring to rest after an exhausting day, poor father was being bedeviled by an endless stream of unanswerable questions from little Willie.

"What do you do all day down at your office, Daddy?"

"Nothing!" shouted the father.

After a thoughtful pause, Willie asked, "Daddy, how do you know when you are through?"

430. *Father:* Johnny, don't you know the difference between right and wrong?"

Johnny: "Sure!"

Father: "But you always do wrong."

Johnny: "Well, that shows it isn't guesswork."

431. "My father always proposed a toast before he disciplined me."

"That's funny! What was it?"

"Bottoms up, son!"

432. A father was scolding his six-year-old for having told an extra-big fib. "I never told lies when I was your age," he said sadly.

The lad allowed a moment to pass and then, rather brightly, asked: "How old were you when you started, Dad?"

433. A little six-year-old boy came to his father with the inevitable question, "Where did I come from?" The father had been expecting to hear the question at some time and was fully prepared. When he finished his thorough and factual explanation an hour later, he asked his son, "Why did you want to know where you came from?"

The boy answered, "My boy friend, Johnny, comes from Toledo, and I wanted to know where I came from."

434. Dan and Peter were helping their dad to shift the furniture. Dan was sweating, carrying a wardrobe uphill, when his dad called out: "I thought Peter was helping you to move that!"

"So he is. He's inside, carrying the coat-hangers."

435. When Kipling was a boy he went on a voyage on a sailing vessel with his father. The father was suddenly awakened one day by a sailor, who said to him in great alarm, "Your son has climbed out on the yardarm, and is hanging on by his hands. If he should let go, he would be drowned." The elder Kipling knew what kind of a boy Rudyard was, and said, quietly, "But he won't let go." And the father turned over and went to sleep again.

Fishing

436. Brown's fishing venture had been a flop, and on his way home he entered the local fish market. When the dealer asked what he wanted, Brown said, "Just stand over there and throw me five of the biggest trout you have."

"Throw 'em? What for?" asked the dealer in amazement.

"So I can tell the wife I caught them," replied Brown. "I may be a poor fisherman, but I'm no liar."

437. Uncle Joe Cannon, the unforgettable Speaker of the House of Representatives, was once telling Chauncey Depew about a fish he had almost caught. "About the size of a whale, wasn't it?" suggested Depew. "I was baiting with whales," was Uncle Joe's reply.

438. A man had been out fishing, and was describing to a friend the exact size of the fish he caught. "It was fully so long," he asserted, spreading his hands apart. "I never saw such a fish."

"Probably not," remarked his friend.

439. "Surely you don't believe your husband's story about fishing," the catty neighbor said. "I notice he didn't bring any fish back."

"That's what makes me believe he was fishing."

440. *First Fisherman:* "It's getting late and we haven't caught a single fish."

Second Fisherman: "Let's let two more big ones get away and then go home."

FISHING

441. Two ardent disciples of Izaak Walton went fishing. After a while one said to the other:

"Had any luck?"

"No," was the reply. "I can't get the cork out."

442. *Man* (showing snapshot of himself with a fish to neighbor): "But my daughter caught the really big fish on our vacation—a young man 22 years old!"

443. A little boy was taken on a fishing trip by his father, along with some other fishermen, and at the close of the day, when they were all seated around the campfire, the youngster listened to all the "tall" tales of the big catches told by the men. When they retired, he whispered to his father:

"Say, Dad, is it true that George Washington never told a lie?"

"Yes, my son, but why?"

"Well, I was just thinking, he must never have gone fishing."

444. "I notice that in telling about the fish you caught, you vary the size of it for different listeners."

"Yes, I never tell a man more than I think he will believe."

445. President Cleveland, while talking to a friend about one of his many fishing expeditions, used to tell the following story:

"It is remarkable," said the President, "how mean some people are. I had with me on one of my trips several countrymen who were evidently familiar with my reputation as a fisherman. Before starting out on the trip one of them made the following suggestion: 'Mr. President,' said he, 'let's agree that the first one who catches a fish must treat the crowd.'

"I assented to this, and we started. Now, don't you know, those two fellows both had a bite and were too mean to pull them up."

"I supposed you lost, then," remarked the friend.

"Oh, no," replied the President. "I didn't have any bait on my hook."

446. One over-enthusiastic fisherman was haled into court and charged with catching 18 more black bass than the law allows. "Guilty or not guilty?" asked the judge.

"Guilty," the young man admitted.

92

"Ten dollars and costs," announced the judge.

The defendant paid the fine, then asked cheerfully, "And, now, Your Honor, may I have several typewritten copies of the court record made to take back and show my friends?"

447. *Warden:* "You can't catch fish here without a permit."
Fisherman: "I'm doing very well with just a worm, thank you."

448. Two fellows, fishing on a Sunday morning, were feeling pretty guilty. Said one to the other: "I suppose we should have stayed home and gone to church."

To which the second angler replied lazily, "Heck, I couldn't have gone to church anyway. My wife's sick in bed."

449. "Did you fish with flies?" asked a friend of the returned vacationer.

"Fish with flies!" exclaimed the vacationer. "I hope to tell you we did. We fished, camped, dined, and slept with them."

450. *Sweet young thing* (on her first fishing trip): "How much did that red and green thing cost?"

Boy friend: "You mean the float? Oh, about fifteen cents, I guess."

Sweet young thing: "Then that's what I owe you—mine just sank."

451. A boy, who instead of going to school had gone fishing, on his way home met one of his school chums. Seeing that the boy was carrying a fishing pole, the chum asked:

"Catch anything?"

"No," replied the boy, "I ain't been home yet."

452. It was a very hot afternoon and much too uncomfortable for work. The lazy farmer decided to go fishing, but had trouble getting his wife to agree to allow him to take the day off.

"Mary, I think I'll go fishing this afternoon."

"Oh, no, you won't," she said. "You've got to go and dig those potatoes today."

Knowing her only too well, he did not argue with her. Quietly he started off for the potato patch. In a short time, however, he returned and said to her, "Mary, look what I found while digging for the potatoes." And he produced a coin, all discolored and tarnished.

93

FORGETFULNESS

She polished it on her apron and discovered it was a real honest-to-goodness quarter. And into her pocket it went.

The farmer went back to his work and soon he was back again. This time he had half a dollar.

"John," she said, "I really think it is too fine an afternoon for you to be digging those potatoes. Suppose you go out and do your fishing; I'll finish digging the potatoes myself."

And with that, off he went with his fishing tackle, while she proceeded to the potato patch. Needless to say she dug all afternoon and found no more coins.

453. After several hours of luckless fishing, the little girl suddenly threw down her pole and cried, "I quit."

"What's the matter?" asked her father.

"Nothing," said the child, "except that I can't seem to get waited on."

Forgetfulness

454. "You bad boy," cried the exasperated mother. "Didn't you promise me you wouldn't bite your baby sister again?"

"Yes, I did," shamefully admitted the little brother, "but I forgot not to."

455. At a big gathering in Hollywood, a celebrity-seeker approached Groucho Marx with an excited "Remember me, Groucho?"

"I never forget a face," replied the funny man, "but in your case I'll make an exception."

Frankness

456. *Officer:* "Are you happy now that you're in the Navy?"
Boot: "Yes, sir."
Officer: "What were you before you got into the Navy?"
Boot: "Much happier."

457. A young lady called one day on Rubinstein, the great pianist, who had consented to listen to her playing.

"What do you think I should do now?" she asked when she had finished.

"Get married," was Rubinstein's answer.

458. As the three ladies picked up the menus, each put on a pair of glasses.

"Of course, I really need mine only for close reading," remarked the first.

"I only wear mine when the light is poor," explained the second.

The third was much franker. "I rarely wear mine," she declared, "except when I want to see!"

459. The application blank for a new driver's license carried the following question: "Have you ever been arrested?" The applicant put down "No."

The next question was, "State why?" The applicant put down: "Never been caught."

Friendship

460. "Be nice to your friends. If it wasn't for them, you'd be a total stranger."

461. An elderly colored woman, who is one of the best-liked persons in her community, was asked: "What's your formula for making and keeping friends?"

"We-el, honey, dey's jes' one daily rule I follows," she replied. "I'se allus mighty careful to stop and taste mah words 'fore I lets 'em pass mah teeth."

Fund-raising

462. A small boy swallowed a coin, which greatly alarmed his mother.

"Quick, quick, send for the doctor," she appealed to her husband.

"No, I think we ought to send for the minister," replied the child's father.

"The minister? Why, you don't think the child is going to die, do you?" exclaimed the mother.

"Oh, no," replied the husband, "but you know our minister. He can get money out of anybody!"

463. Benjamin Franklin, who, among other things, was one of the best money raisers of his generation, once set forth his principles for the guidance of a campaign committee:

"First," he said, "call upon those who you know will give something; next apply to those of whom you are uncertain; and finally, to those you are sure will give nothing, for in some of these you may be mistaken."

464. When Dean McGeorge Bundy rose to make the principal address at a Harvard alumni dinner, he prefaced his speech by saying: "I am happy to see so many smiling faces among those we are about to impoverish." He then launched into a serious discussion of a drive to raise $82,500,000 for Harvard University.

Genius

465. *Tommy:* "Dad, it says here that a certain man was a financial genius. What does that mean?"

Father: "That he could earn money faster than his family could spend it."

466. Alexander Hamilton once said, "Men give me credit for some genius. All the genius I have lies in this: when I have a subject in hand, I study it profoundly. Day and night it is before me. My mind becomes pervaded with it. Then the effort which I have made is what people are pleased to call the fruit of genius. It is the fruit of labor and thought."

467. Upon finishing a highly praised concert, Beethoven was surrounded by friends and admirers who could not say enough for his piano magic. One particularly enthusiastic woman remarked: "Oh, sir, if God had only given me that gift of genius."

Beethoven replied, "It is not genius, madam. Nor magic. All you have to do is practice on your piano eight hours a day for forty years and you'll be as good as I am."

Gift

468. *Wife* (to husband on Christmas morning): "You angel! Just what I need to exchange for just what I wanted."

469. A movie producer was telling a friend about giving his girl friend a string of pearls for her birthday. "Why," said the friend, "don't you give her something practical—like an automobile?"

The producer smiled and replied, "Did you ever hear of a phony automobile?"

470. Looking for an inexpensive gift for a friend, a tightwad entered a gift shop, but found everything too expensive.

Pricing a glass vase that had been broken, he found that he could buy it for almost nothing. He asked the store to send it, hoping his friend would think it had been broken in transit.

In due time he received an acknowledgment: "Thanks for the vase," it read, "and it was so thoughtful of you to wrap each piece separately."

471. Wanting to surprise his girl on her birthday with her favorite perfume, but not knowing the name of it, an ardent Belfast lover hit upon a scheme. He took her French poodle out for a walk, and headed for the perfume counter of an exclusive gift shop.

Enlisting an assistant's help, he started testing. Stoppers from eight or nine bottles of perfume were waved under the animal's nose. No response.

But on the next stopper the dog frantically wagged his tail and jumped into the assistant's arms.

472. For a camera bug's birthday, a woman decided to present her friend with fifty flash bulbs. She knew very little about cameras, and before wrapping each bulb in gold paper, she carefully tested it in her husband's camera. She was delighted that every bulb "worked," and happily sent them off to her friend—who still hasn't the heart to tell her the facts about cameras.

473. A bride-to-be was showing her wedding list to a friend. After reading the names, her friend looked puzzled.

"What's the matter?" asked the bride-to-be.

"Isn't it rather strange," queried the friend, "that you have only put down the names of married couples?"

"Yes, that was Don's idea. Don't you think it's rather clever? He says that way the presents will be all clear profit."

474. Don't promise to buy your wife a diamond locket for Christmas unless you mean it. If you do, there'll be only the jeweler to pay; whereas, if you don't, there'll be the devil.

Giving

475. The businessman had just handed his youthful visitor a dollar, for which he received an "associate membership" card in the local boys' club.

"Now that I am a member," the businessman said, "just what are my rights and privileges?"

After thinking the matter over carefully, the boy replied, "Well, it gives you the right to contribute again next year."

476. Mark Twain used to tell the story of two women who ardently desired to see Sarah Bernhardt during her last great American tour; but after much consideration, they decided it would be sinful to spend twenty dollars—the price of two tickets—on one night's entertainment. Not to benefit by their own self-denial, they decided to give the twenty dollars to an old couple whom they knew to be in great need. And the old couple immediately went and bought two tickets to see the divine Sarah!

477. "Dear," the little woman reported, "a man came yesterday gathering contributions for the old clothes drive."

"Did you give him anything?" the husband inquired.

"Yes, Henry," she replied. "I gave him that ten-year-old suit of yours and that dress I bought last month."

478. Mrs. Busybody was pumping the local doctor about the demise of the town's richest man. "You knew him well," she cooed. "How much wealth did he leave?" With a tip of his hat, the old doctor replied, "All of it, madam, all of it."

479. "What sort of fellow is he?"

"Well, it's like this. After a beggar has touched him for a dime, he'll tell you he has just given a little dinner to an acquaintance of his."

480. A mother chided her small daughter, returning from a visit to a pleasant lady up the street, her arms loaded with childish plunder. "Oh, it's all right," the child insisted. "She likes me. I'm somebody she can give things to."

Golf

481. "Do you play golf?"
"No, but I can't give it up."

482. Isn't it great to get out on the old golf course again and lie in the sun?

483. "Well, you said I had to choose, didn't you?" demanded the husband, in bed with his golf clubs.

484. *Golfer:* "Caddy, why do you keep looking at your watch?"
Caddy: "It ain't a watch, sir, it's a compass."

485. A woman entered the sporting goods department of a large store and told the salesman, "I'd like a low handicap, please."
"A low handicap?" the man repeated, puzzled.
"Why, yes," she said, "for my husband's birthday. He's always wishing he had one."

486. *Nurse:* "Whom are they operating on today?"
Orderly: "A fellow who had a golf ball knocked down his throat at the links."
"And who is the man waiting so nervously in the hall? A relative?"
"No, that's the golfer. He's waiting for his ball."

487. *Golfer* (to member ahead): "Pardon, but would you mind if I played through? I've just heard that my wife has been taken seriously ill."

488. A complacent golfer teed his ball, looked down the fairway to the green and boasted, "That's good for one long drive and a putt." He swung and moved his ball a few feet off the tee. Stepping forward, the diplomatic caddy handed him a club and said, "And now for one hell of a putt."

489. At a home-talent golf tournament the club secretary caught one of the members driving off about a foot in front of the teeing mark.
"Here!" he cried, indignantly. "You can't do that. You're disqualified!"

"What for?" demanded the golfer.

"Why, you just drove off in front of the mark."

The player looked at the secretary coldly. "Go back to the club-house," he said tersely, "I'm playing my third stroke."

490. Two women were returning from their first attempt at bowl-ing. The husband of one, an inveterate golfer, asked with a raised eyebrow: "How'd you make out?"

"Well," she said, "at least we didn't lose any balls."

491. Caddie: a golfing expert who loses balls for you in one round, so that he can find them for himself in the next.

492. St. Peter and St. Thomas were playing golf one heavenly afternoon, and St. Peter's first drive was a hole-in-one. St. Thomas stepped to the tee and also scored a hole-in-one.

"All right, now," said St. Peter, "let's cut out the miracles and play golf."

493. A wife, to whom golf was a total mystery, never could under-stand why her husband insisted on tiring himself by walking so far every time he played.

One day, she went with him to see what the game was all about. She followed him until he landed in a bunker. There he floundered about for some time in the sand.

The lady seated herself on top of the bunker, took out her knit-ting, and said complacently: "There, I knew you could just as well play in one place if you made up your mind to!"

494. *Small girl, as golfer in sand trap pauses for breath:* "He's stopped beating it, Mummy. I think it must be dead."

495. "Well, what do you think of my game?" said the enthu-siastic golfer to his friend.

"Oh, it's all right," replied the frank friend, "but I still prefer golf."

496. *Irate golfer:* "You must be the world's worst caddie!"
Caddie: "Hardly. That would be too much of a coincidence."

497. One of the most quoted mistakes in newspaper history was written by a California sportswriter. Covering a women's golf tournament several years ago, he wrote a paragraph which came out in the paper this way:

"At this point the gallery deserted the defending champion to watch Miss Blank, whose shorts were dropping on the green with astonishing regularity."

498. *Golf pro:* "Now just go through the motions without hitting the ball."

Beginner: "That's precisely the trouble I'm trying to overcome."

499. *First golfer:* "Shall we play again next Saturday?"

Second golfer: "Well, I was going to get married on Saturday, but I can put it off."

500. A young broker, after a particularly brutal session in a sand trap, sought to relieve the uncomfortable silence by cheerily declaring to his caddy: "Funny game, golf." The boy morosely replied: " 'Tain't meant to be."

501. The school teacher was taking her first golf lesson. "Is the word spelled 'put' or 'putt'?" she asked the instructor.

" 'Putt' is correct," he replied. " 'Put' means to place a thing where you want it. 'Putt' means merely a vain attempt to do the same thing."

502. A pair of dub golfers were on the first tee. The first fairway was bordered by rows of trees. One of the dubs sliced so that the ball struck one of the trees and, without moving from his stance, he caught the ball on the rebound. Bewildered, he asked his friend, "What shall I do now?" Without hesitation a suggestion was made: "Tee it up, hit it again, and then put your hands in your pockets."

503. One Saturday afternoon, the locker room boy answering the telephone heard a female voice say, "Is my husband there?"

The boy promptly answered, "No, ma'am."

"How can you say he isn't there before I even tell you who I am?"

"Don't make no difference, lady. They ain't never nobody's husband here."

504. The portly, overdressed golfer joined his foursome on the first tee. Noting that he had two caddies, one of the players asked, "How come the two boys?"

"Well, you see," said the duffer, "I nearly always have to send one back for laughing."

505. On the completion of an irrigation project in India, the American engineer who had bossed the job was offered a tremendous sum of money as a bonus. When it was politely refused, the Maharajah who had made the offer tried again, this time with a hatful of priceless gems. But the American still said "No," explaining that the contract price was more than adequate for the work done. But still the potentate persisted, and the American finally relented to the point of agreeing to accept some token gift.

"I am a golf enthusiast," he said. "So if you want to give me something, I'd like very much to have three matched golf clubs."

Months went by. The American engineer had long since returned home, and had all but forgotten the proposed gift. Then one day a cablegram arrived from the Maharajah reading as follows: "Have finally been able to buy three Golf Clubs in your country. Sorry they don't quite match. Only two of them have swimming pools."

506. "Why, I distinctly *heard* you take six strokes in those woods," said the score keeper of the foursome.

"Only three," came the disarming reply. "The other three were echoes."

507. *First golfer:* That was a lovely drive you made.
Second golfer: Which one?
First golfer: Why, the one when you hit the ball.

508. A golfing clergyman had been beaten badly by a parishioner, some thirty years his senior. He returned to the clubhouse, disappointed and disgruntled.

"Cheer up," said his opponent. "Remember, you win at the finish. You'll probably be burying me someday."

"Yes, but even then," said the preacher, "it will be your hole."

509. *Judge:* "Do you understand the nature of an oath?"
Boy: "Do I? Ain't I your caddy?"

510. *Explorer:* "We were surrounded by savages. They uttered awful cries and beat their clubs upon the ground."
Weary listener: "Golfers, probably."

102

511. The golfer, rushing his wife to the hospital, didn't get there in time, and the baby was born on the institution's front lawn. Later when he received the bill, one of the items listed was "Use of Delivery Room, $25." He paid for everything except this and wrote a letter to the hospital, explaining that his wife had never even been in the delivery room. The hospital's administrator, also a golfer, read the letter and sent a new bill reading, "Greens Fee, $25."

512. "Really, I can't play golf," said the dumb blonde. "I don't even know how to hold the caddie."

513. The marble tournament was in full swing. One little boy had missed an easy shot, and let slip a real cuss word.

"Henry!" called the preacher from the spectator's bench, "what do little boys who swear when they are playing marbles turn into?"

"Golfers," little Henry replied.

514. *Judge:* "How did the trouble start?"
Defendant: "Well, judge, she asked me to play a round, and I didn't know she was a golfer."

Gossip

515. An old man invested in one of those new hearing aids that are practically invisible, and he was assured by the salesman that he could return it if it didn't prove twice as effective as the cumbersome device he had been using for a number of years. He returned in a few days to express his great satisfaction with the new device.

"I'll bet your family likes it too," hazarded the clerk. "Oh, they don't even know I've got it," chuckled the old gent. "And do you know what, I'm having a perfectly grand time with it! Just in the past two days, I've changed my will twice!"

516. *Mistress:* "Marie, when you wait on the table tonight for my guests, please don't spill anything."
Servant: "Don't you worry, ma'am; I never talk much."

517. If you tell a man anything, it goes in one ear and out the other. And if you tell a woman anything, it goes in both ears and out of her mouth.

Gratitude

518. The husband returned home from a trip unexpectedly to find his little boy crying. "Daddy," he said, "there's a bogeyman upstairs in mama's closet!"

"That's silly. You're old enough to know better. Come on upstairs and I'll show you.

He opened the closet door and there was his best friend, Sam. "So!" stormed the husband. "It's you! I feed you, buy all your clothes, lend you my car and money, and how do you repay me? By hiding in my wife's closet and scaring the wits out of my little boy!"

519. "Doctor," asked the woman patient, "why am I seized with these restless longings for the glamorous and faraway?"

"My dear lady," replied the doctor, "they are the usual symptoms of too much comfort in the home and too much ingratitude in the heart."

520. *Diner:* "Waiter, didn't you hear me say 'Well done'?"

Waiter (ignoring pale pink steak): "Yes, sir. Thank you, sir. It's seldom we get any thanks."

Honesty

521. One of two women riding on a bus suddenly realized she hadn't paid her fare.

"I'll go right up and pay it," she declared.

"Why bother?" her friend replied. "You got away with it—so what?"

"I've found that honesty always pays," the other said virtuously, and went up to pay the driver.

"See, I told you honesty pays!" she said when she returned. "I handed the driver a quarter and he gave me change for 50 cents."

522. Two boxing managers were discussing the forthcoming fight. "At the end of the second round," said one, "your man will hit mine and he will go down for the count."

"No, no," protested the other. "Not in the second round; in the seventh or eighth. We mustn't cheat the public."

523. "I am going away for a few days, Bridget," said the lady of the house to her servant girl, "and I am going to leave with you all my keys, those to my closets as well as those to my chests and jewel boxes. I know that they will be safe with you, but, of course, I expect you not to touch them."

When the mistress returned, the girl said to her, "Madam, I'm going to leave you."

"Why, Bridget?"

"Because you don't trust me."

"How can you say that, when I left you with all my keys?"

"That you did, ma'am; but not one of them fits."

524. *Wife:* "The cleaning woman must have stolen two of our new towels!"

Husband: "Well, some people are like that. Which towels were they?"

Wife: "Oh, you know. The ones we brought back from the hotel in Des Moines."

525. *Sandy:* McPherson's a cheat, and I'm not gonna play golf with him again."

Andy: "Why not, something happen?"

Sandy: "Well, how could he find his lost ball a yard from the green when all the time it was in my pocket?"

Honeymoon

526. The honeymoon is really over when he phones to say he'll be late for dinner . . . and she's already left a note saying it's in the refrigerator.

527. The newlyweds were driving away from the church in the limousine. The groom pulled the bride toward him, put his arm around her shoulder, kissed her, and said, "Now, Honey, about that nonsense of you quitting your job . . ."

528. *He:* "If I had a million dollars, do you know where I'd be?"

She: "Why sure, big boy—you'd be on our honeymoon."

529. *Foreman:* "How long do you want to be away on your honeymoon?"

Employe: "Well how long would you suggest?"
Foreman: "How would I know; I haven't seen the bride."

530. "Jack, dear," said the bride, "let us try to make the people believe we've been married a long time."

"All right, honey," replied the recent groom, "but do you think you can carry both suitcases?"

531. A young teacher substituted for a friend who was taking a week's honeymoon. Later, at a party, someone started to introduce the groom to her.

"Oh," he answered alertly, "I know Miss Jones very well. In fact, she substituted for my wife on our honeymoon."

532. In spite of the expense and the loss of time involved, the bridegroom should always accompany the bride on the honeymoon. It may be the last vacation he ever has.

Horse-racing

533. Jimmy Durante bet on a horse at Santa Anita and the nag lost by inches.

"What that horse needed," bragged an ex-jockey, "was my riding."

"What he needed," corrected Durante, "was my nose."

534. *Mother:* "Marie, before you become serious with that boy friend of yours, be sure that he is kind and considerate."

Daughter: "Oh, I'm sure of that, Mother. Why only the other day he told me that he had put his shirt on a horse that was scratched."

535. A fellow who once picked a winning horse by accident, and couldn't give up the habit of trying again, took an afternoon off to go to the races.

"Gosh, I hope I break even," he told his companion as they left the office together. "I sure need the money."

Hospitality

536. Daniel Webster had been shooting in the marshes, and when it grew dark he found that the inn where he was staying was too far away, so he walked on until he came to a farmhouse, by which time he was cold and hungry. It was a very cold night, and the family had gone to bed. Webster pounded on the door, and at last a window opened and a man's voice asked: "Whatd'ya want?" "I want to stay here all night," shouted the weary Webster. "O.K. stay there," said the farmer, slamming the window closed.

537. *Alice:* "We passed your house yesterday."
Sue: "Thanks. We appreciate it."

Hotel

538. A bellboy burst into a Texas hotel room and was reproved by the guest for his lack of manners.

"But didn't you ring?" asked the boy.

"Yes, of course I rang."

"Three times?" asked the boy.

"Perhaps. I was in a hurry for ice water. But that doesn't excuse your bursting in here without knocking."

"Well," said the boy, "you ought to read the bell card. It's one ring for the porter, two for me, and three for a gun; and when a guest rings for a gun in this hotel, the orders are to get it to him before the other fellow can beg his pardon."

539. "Is this the hotel clerk?" inquired the guest over the phone.

"Yes, this is the clerk. What's eating you now?"

"That's what I want to know."

540. *Judge:* "So they caught you with the silverware on you, did they? Tell me, whom did you plunder?"

Defendant: "Two fraternity houses."

Judge: "Mr. Bailiff, call up all the downtown hotels and distribute this stuff among them so that each gets its own property back."

541. *Salesman:* "What on earth do you put in your mattresses?"

Hotelkeeper: "The very finest straw, sir."

Salesman: "Now I know where the straw that broke the camel's back came from."

542. A man wrote to a country hotel to ask if his dog would be allowed to stay there. He received the following answer:

Dear sir: I have been in the hotel business for over thirty years.

Never yet have I had to call in the police to eject a disorderly dog in the small hours of the morning. No dog has ever attempted to pass off a bad check on me. Never has a dog set the bedclothes afire through smoking. I have never found a hotel towel in a dog's suitcase. Your dog is welcome.

P.S.: If he will vouch for you, you can come too.

Humor

543. When Samuel Rogers made a joke at which nobody laughed, he would say reflectively: "The curious part of that story is that stupid people never see the point of it." Whereupon, of course, everyone laughed uproariously.

544. Actor Sir Cedric Hardwicke listened while a man told a long story. But the man spoke so indistinctly and muffed his punch line so badly that the story wasn't funny. "Why did you laugh?" a friend asked Hardwicke afterward.

"I always do," the actor replied. "If you don't laugh, there's danger of their telling it over again."

Hunting

545. *Explorer* (just back from Africa): I brought back six tigers, two leopards and a potfer.
Friend: What's a potfer?
Explorer: To cook the meat in.

546. Two professors were members of a hunting party. One of the first things that they noticed was that the cabin stove was set on posts about four feet high. This excited their curiosity.

"Now," said one, "this man has discovered that heat emanating from a stove strikes the roof, and that the circulation is so quickened that the camp is warmed in much less time than would be required if the stove were in its regular place on the floor."

The other professor thought the stove had been raised above the window level so that pure, cool air could come in at night. Their host, more practical, thought the stove was elevated so that a supply of green wood could be put under it. They finally decided to call the guide to settle the dispute.

108

"Well, gents," he explained, "when I brought the stove up the river I lost most of the stove pipe overboard; we had to set the stove up that way so that what was left of the pipe would reach through the roof."

547. "Gus," called the new hunter, "are all the rest of the boys out of the woods yet?"

"Yep," said Gus.

"All six of them?"

"Yep."

"And they're all safe?"

"Yep," said Gus, "they're all safe."

"Then, by golly," said the hunter, "I've shot a deer."

Husband and wife

548. *Young Wife* (at post office window): "I wish to complain about the service."

Postmaster: "What is the trouble, Madam?"

Young Wife: "My husband is in Albany on business, and the card he sent me is postmarked Atlantic City."

549. After winning an argument with his wife, the wisest thing for a man to do is to apologize.

550. *Henpeck:* "Haven't I always given you my salary check the first of every month?"

Mrs. Henpeck: "Yes, but you never told me you got paid on the first and the fifteenth, you embezzler!"

551. The weary man had just settled down with his pipe and the evening paper.

"Sam," called his wife, "I've got a lot of things I want to talk to you about."

"Well, fine," said her husband. "Usually you want to talk about a lot of things you haven't got."

552. "For 20 years," mused the man at the bar, "my wife and I were ecstatically happy."

"Then what happened?" asked the bartender.

"We met."

553. *Wife:* "Every time you see a pretty girl, you forget you're married."

Husband: "You're wrong, my dear. Nothing brings home the fact with so much force."

554. "So your husband has got a job at last," said a neighbor of Mrs. Smith.

"Yes, he has," replied Mrs. Smith. "It is hard work and he says it is killing him. But thank goodness, it's permanent."

555. The luggage-laden husband stared miserably down the platform at the departing train. "If you hadn't taken so long getting ready," he sadly admonished his wife, "we would have caught that train!"

"Yes," she replied, "and if you had not hurried me so we wouldn't have so long to wait for the next one."

556. *Woman in a detective agency:* "I want my husband and the other woman followed night and day and a complete report on what she sees in him."

557. "My wife had a dream last night and thought she was married to a millionaire."

"You're lucky! My wife thinks that in the daytime."

558. *Wife to husband:* "Of course I spend more than you make, dear! I have great confidence in you."

559. The husband told the judge: "I came home and there was my wife in the arms of a strange man."

"What did she say when you surprised her?" asked the judge.

"Well, Judge, that was what hurt me the most," said the husband. "She turned around and saw me and then said, 'Well, look who's here. Old Blabbermouth! Now the whole neighborhood will know.'"

560. "They say your wife is outspoken."

"By whom?"

561. "I wish I knew where George was," remarked the young wife.

"I presume, my dear," said her mother-in-law, "that you mean you wish you knew where he is."

"Oh, no, I don't," was the firm retort. "I know where he is. He's in bed with a black eye and a headache. I want to know where he was."

562. The husband and wife were in the midst of a violent quarrel, and hubby was losing his temper.

"Be careful," he said to his wife, "you'll bring out the beast in me."

"So what!" replied the spouse. "Who's afraid of mice?"

563. A husband and wife were in sharp disagreement over what suit he should purchase. Finally the wife relented and said:

"Well, go ahead and please yourself. After all you're the one who will wear it."

Meekly the man replied: "Well, dear, I did figure I'd probably wear the coat and vest anyway."

564. *Husband to wife* (after going over the bills): "In case you're interested, dear, we're no longer keeping up with the Joneses—we've passed them."

565. An old man died and left his wife a few thousand dollars.

"How would you like to be his widow?" remarked a long-suffering husband.

"Ah, Pat," replied his wife, with emotion, "you know I would rather be yours."

566. The wife wanted to do something during the day, so at breakfast she asked her husband for ten dollars.

"Money, money, money!" he shouted. "Every day of the week you want more money. If you ask me I think you need brains more than you need money."

"Perhaps so," his wife agreed, "but I asked you for what I thought you had the most of."

567. If you want your wife to pay attention to what you say, address your remarks to another woman.

568. "My wife has an inferiority complex, Doctor."

"And you want me to cure it?"

"No, I want you to make sure she keeps it."

569. Father looked hard at his wife and then at his son. "That boy has taken money from my pocket!" he stormed.

"Henry," she protested. "How can you say that. Why, I might have done it."

Father shook his head. "No you didn't; there was some left."

570. In an army hospital, a wounded soldier was cooking up a letter to his wife. A kind-hearted nurse was writing it down for him.

"The nurses here," he dictated, "are a very plain lot."

"Oh, I say," the angel of mercy interrupted, "Don't you think that's a little unfair?"

The soldier grinned.

"Yes, I do," he declared, "but nurse, you can't imagine how happy my wife will be when she reads it."

571. The boys at the roundhouse observed that one of the crew was unusually glum, and asked what was bothering him.

"I think my wife is tired of me," he replied.

"What makes you think so?" inquired a marital-wise friend.

"Every day this week," he answered, "she has wrapped my lunch in a road map."

572. Husband and wife were having a polite difference of opinion. "It's obvious that I must be right and you wrong," contended the wife. "Since God created woman after man, it must follow that we're an improvement over the original model."

"Not at all," snapped the husband. "God had a very good reason for making woman after he had made man. He didn't want any advice."

573. "I can't figure you out," a housewife told her husband angrily. "Monday night you liked beans, Tuesday night you liked beans, Wednesday night you liked beans and now, all of a sudden, on Thursday night, you DON'T like beans!"

574. "Why did you shoot your husband?"

"Well, you see, we couldn't afford a divorce."

575. *Wife to husband:* "All right, I admit I like to spend money. But just name one other extravagance."

576. *Wife:* "I was a fool when I married you."

Husband: "I guess you were, but I was so infatuated at the time I didn't seem to notice it."

112

577. *Wife:* "You swore terribly in your sleep last night."
Husband: "What makes you think I was sleeping?"

578. Being a husband is like any other job—it makes it a lot easier if you learn to like your boss.

579. *Man:* "My wife has the worst memory I ever heard of."
Friend: "Forgets everything, eh?"
Man: "No, remembers everything."

580. The husband and wife were having breakfast, the former ensconced behind his morning newspaper.

"You had a very restless night, dear," said the wife, "and what's more you kept murmuring a woman's name in your sleep. Now, tell me, who is Daisy?"

"Oh-er," he stammered, "the fact is, my dear, Daisy is the name of a filly I backed yesterday. It won, 10-to-1, and here's your share."

Handing his wife a five-dollar bill, he hid himself once again behind his newspaper.

In the evening, at the dinner table, his wife once again returned to the attack.

"By the way," she said, "you know that horse you backed yesterday? Well, she telephoned this afternoon."

581. The farmer's wife lost her thumb when their light passenger car collided with a heavily-loaded freight truck.

A few hours later when she was discharged from the hospital, the claims adjuster for the trucking company called at her home.

She suggested a settlement figure which made the adjuster turn purple with rage.

"Madam," he exploded, "can't you see that your claim for $50,000 for a single digit is ridiculous?"

"You may think so," she countered, "but you don't seem to realize that that was no ordinary thumb. It was the one I've been keeping my husband under all these many years."

582. The young man, who had been calling frequently, at last spoke to Mabel's father about marrying the daughter.

"It's a mere formality, I know," he began, "but we thought it would be pleasing to you if it were observed in the usual way."

113

IDENTIFICATION

"And may I inquire," the father asked, "who suggested that asking my consent to Mabel's marriage was a mere formality?"

"Mabel's mother."

583. A sourish, aggressive-mannered woman boarded a subway train with her mild-mannered husband, and sought a seat. Finding none vacant, she let her disapproving gaze fall upon a tired-looking little man seated close by.

"Henry," she sternly remarked to her husband, "if I should ever catch you seated in a public conveyance while some woman was obliged to stand, I would never speak to you again as long as I should live."

The tired-looking little man regarded the husband with an expression of mingled awe and admiration.

"My friend," he remarked, "heaven has been kind to you. I only wish I could shut my wife as easily!"

584. *Husband:* "If a man steals, no matter what, he will live to regret it."

Wife (coyly): "You used to steal kisses from me before we were married."

Husband: "Well . . . ?"

585. The over-the-road driver rushed to the dispatcher's office immediately upon arrival. "What did my wife say when you told her I'd be late?" he inquired.

Dispatcher: "All she said was: 'Can I depend on that?' "

586. "I bet you think twice before you leave that wife of yours alone for an evening."

"Yes, I do. First I think up an excuse for going out. Then I think up a reason why she can't come along."

587. *Hank:* "My wife talks to herself."

Frank: "So does mine, but she doesn't realize it. She thinks I'm listening."

Identification

588. As a man threatened to jump from the window of a tall building in a southern city, a policeman stood just out of reach and tried to persuade him not to jump.

114

"Think of your mother and father," pleaded the cop. "Haven't any," came a surly reply.

"Well, think of your wife and family." "Haven't any," this time in a growl.

"Your girl friend, then." "I hate women!"

"All right, think of Robert E. Lee." "Who's Robert E. Lee?"

"Jump, you damyankee!"

589. "I tell you," said the housewife to the salesman, "I don't want a dictionary. I already have one. There it is, lying over there on the table."

"Lady, you can't fool me," retorted the salesman. "That's no dictionary; that's a Bible."

"How can you tell?" asked the woman, her eyes opened wide in amazement.

"That's easy," said the salesman. "By the dust on it."

590. A couple of policemen knocked on the door of the cabin of a hillbilly.

"Say Bill, Joe and I just found a dead man down by the creek and we came around here because we thought it might be you."

"How big was he?"

"Well, he was about your size—"

"Was he wearing a coonskin cap?"

"Yes, he was."

"A blue shirt?"

"Nope."

"Well, then it wasn't me."

591. "Here's a letter from your father. The letterhead identifies him as an undertaker."

"That's right, dear," he said. "What did you think he was?"

"Didn't you tell me some time ago that he was a doctor?"

"Oh, no. I never said that."

"But I'm positive you did."

"No, dear, you misunderstood. All I said was that he followed the medical profession."

592. The brash young man and his girl friend were returning to their seats in the theatre after the intermission.

115

IDENTIFICATION

"Did I step on your toes as I went out?" he asked the man at the end of the row.

"You certainly did," replied the other, rather expecting an apology.

"All right, Mary, this is our row," said the young man without so much as batting an eye.

593. A haughty dowager visited the hospital to see her chauffeur, who had been badly injured in an automobile accident. The head nurse hesitated, and then said: "He's a very sick man and should see no one but members of his family. Are you his wife?"

Highly indignant, the dowager blurted out: "I certainly am not; I'm his mistress."

594. *First salesgirl:* "How do you know the new window-dresser is married?"

Second salesgirl: "He always poses the models with their palms up."

595. The club bore was boasting of his ability to distinguish between different beverages. Finally, one of the listeners took a flask from his pocket and asked the connoisseur to taste it and tell him what it was. The man took a mouthful and promptly yelled, "Great Scott, that's gasoline!"

"I know," came the curt reply, "but what brand?"

596. A southern widow waited a short time after the death of her husband, and then married the husband's brother. She moderated somewhat her disregard for convention by hanging a picture of her late husband in a prominent place in the parlor. This mollified her friends to some extent until they heard her reply to a stranger who asked her who the distinguished man was. "Oh, that's my poor brother-in-law. He died recently."

597. *Detective:* "You're looking for your cashier? Is he tall or short?"

Banker: "Both."

598. When the great Charles Darwin was visiting the country house of a friend, the two boys of the family thought they would play a trick on the scientist. They caught a butterfly, a grasshopper, a beetle, and a centipede, and out of these evolved a strange com-

116

posite insect. They took the centipede's body, the butterfly's wings, the grasshopper's legs, and the beetle's head, glued them carefully together and presented it to Darwin for identification. Darwin looked at the bug and then at the boys.

"Did you notice whether it made a humming sound when you caught it, boys?" he asked.

"Yes," they answered.

"Then," said Darwin, with a twinkle in his eye, "it's a hum-bug."

Illness

599. When Rufus Choate, the great American lawyer, was on his last sick-bed, he was visited by one of his friends who said to him:

"Well, cheer up, Choate; I believe that your constitution will pull you through."

"Not at all," said Choate, "my constitution was gone long ago, and I am living on my by-laws now."

600. The hospital patient complained to a visiting friend that he hadn't been able to eat a morsel of food for all of four days.

"You haven't missed a thing," consoled the friend. "It tastes the same as it always did."

Illustration

601. "I shall now illustrate what I have on my mind," said the professor as he erased the board.

602. Once, when Toscanini was rehearsing Debussy's *La Mer*, he wanted to achieve a highly evanescent effect in one spot. At a loss for words to describe what he wanted, he took from his breast-pocket a large, white, silk handkerchief. He threw it high into the air, and every man in the orchestra was hypnotized as it floated softly, sensuously, to the floor. "There," the Maestro smiled happily, "play it like that."

Income tax

603. *First friend:* "Poor old Smitty. He was ruined by untold wealth."

Second friend: "Yep, he should have reported it on his income tax return."

604. An angry little man bounced into the postmaster's office. "For some time now," he shouted, "I've been pestered by threatening letters, and I want something done about it."

"I'm sure we can help," soothed the postmaster. "That's a federal offense. Have you any idea who is sending you these letters?"

"I certainly have," snapped the little fellow. "It's them pesky income tax people."

605. A mild little man walked into an income tax collector's office, sat down, and beamed on everyone.

"What can we do for you?" asked the clerk in charge.

"Nothing at all, thank you," replied the little man. "I just wanted to meet the people I'm working for."

606. On the suburban train, Jones had just read a long letter he had received that day from his old home town. Mellowed by the happy memories it brought back to him, he turned to the stranger seated beside him and happily remarked, "Did you ever get a letter that brought back visions of the past?"

Stark misery stared out of the other's eyes.

"Have I?" the man replied. "Only this morning I got one from the government, reminding me I still owed them some $2000 on my income tax of five years ago."

607. Next to being shot at and missed, nothing is quite as satisfying as an income tax refund.

608. On a crowded elevator, a friend asked Rep. Brooks Hays (D-Ark) how the last year had been for him. "Best year I ever had," said Hays. Then he spotted the Commissioner of Internal Revenue on the same elevator and quickly added, "I mean spiritually, not materially!"

609. One doesn't quarrel with the idea that George Washington never told a lie. However, it is well to bear in mind that in those days there were no income tax blanks.

610. "Dad, what is a savings account?"

"A savings account, son, is that part of a man's income which the government takes after permitting him to pay for the necessities of life."

611. A clergyman received a phone call from the local income-tax man inquiring about a $535 contribution listed as having been paid his church by a parishioner. "Did he make this donation?" the tax man asked.

The clergyman hesitated, then replied: "No—but he will, he will."

Inflation

612. A housewife found a ten cent piece inside a chicken she was cleaning, which prompted the crack that even the hens look upon a dime as nothing but "chicken feed" these days.

613. Buck-passing is not new—but they never passed faster than they do now.

614. *Son:* "Pop, what is creeping inflation?"

Father: "It's when your mother starts out asking for a new hat and winds up with a complete new outfit."

615. Billy walked into a drug store, laid a nickel on the counter, and asked for an ice cream cone.

"Cones are eight cents," the clerk behind the counter informed him.

"Then give me a package of chewing gum," said Billy.

"Sorry, gum is six cents."

With that Billy walked away leaving the nickel on the counter.

"You forgot your nickel," the clerk called out to him.

"You just keep it—it won't buy anything anyway," was little Billy's reply.

616. Six-year-old Willie was lecturing little George, aged three, on the value of various coins in his pocket.

"Now, this," he said, "is a dime. It will buy two candy bars. "This," he continued, "is a nickel. It will buy only one candy bar."

He fished around and brought out a third coin.

"And this," he said with a faintly contemptuous air, "is a penny. All it is good for is Sunday School."

INGENUITY

617. The high school lad had asked for more spending money.
"You don't know the value of a dollar, son," sighed the father.
"Yes, I do," replied the lad, "as of last week it was 61 cents, as compared with the 1939 standard."

618. *Bob:* "I'm getting stronger."
Helen: "How do you know?"
Bob: "Because a few years ago I couldn't carry ten dollars' worth of groceries and now it's easy."

Ingenuity. See also Resourcefulness

619. Returning after a lengthy absence to his family's spot on the beach, the youngster found them preparing to leave.
"Come along," said his mother. "We're going to a restaurant for a good dinner."
"I'm not hungry," was the reply. "I've eaten seven ice cream cones and three frankfurters."
"Where on earth did you get seven ice cream cones and three frankfurters?" asked his astounded mother. "You didn't have any money."
"I didn't need money. I just wandered all around the beach crying and making believe I was lost."

620. A Chinaman found his wife lying dead in a field one morning; a tiger had killed her.
The Chinaman went home, poured some arsenic, and returning to the field, sprinkled it over the corpse.
The next day the tiger's dead body lay beside the woman's. The Chinaman sold the tiger's skin to a mandarin, its body to a physician to make fear-cure powders, and with the proceeds he was able to buy a younger wife.

Installment purchase

621. The man wearing the rather frayed-looking suit entered a tailor's shop. "I hear that my son has owed you for a suit for three years," he commenced.
The tailor's face brightened. "That's right, sir," he replied. "And have you come to pay the bill?"

"Heck, no," replied the other. "I want one myself on the same terms."

622. The Pattersons' cook, whose countenance was nearly bright even at breakfast, looked very tired one morning. The man of the house asked what was wrong.

"I've been buying things on the lay-awake plan," she said.

"You mean lay-away plan, don't you?"

"No, I mean what I said. You buy things you can't afford, and then lay awake nights worrying how you're going to pay for them."

623. A California bank received the following brief note with a final payment on an auto contract:

"Dear Sirs: This should make us even. Sincerely, but no longer, yours."

624. All those who go through life gaily putting things on their accounts in shops or buying on the installment system should spare a thought from time to time for Peter the First of Portugal, who ascended his throne 600 years ago, and who, to protect his subjects from impoverishing themselves, forbade anybody either to buy or sell without immediate payment, and made the penalty for the second offense execution on the spot.

625. Jones was never an early bird at the office. One morning his boss exclaimed: "Late again. Have you ever done anything on time?"

"Yes, sir," was the meek but prompt reply. "I purchased a car."

626. An automobile salesman was pushing what he thought was a red hot prospect for a new car. The prospect, though, kept insisting he couldn't afford one.

"Listen," he said, "I'm still paying installments on the car I swapped for the car I traded in as part payment on the car I'm two payments behind on now."

627. *Maid:* "The installment man is here again, ma'am."

Lady of the house: "Tell him to take a chair."

Instructions

628. The American government, in studying the migratory habits of birds, bands them with a metal strip inscribed: "Notify Fish &

INSURANCE

Wild Life Service, Washington, D.C." The bands used to read, "Washington Biological Survey," abbreviated to "Wash. Biol. Surv." The inscription was changed to the present one shortly after a farmer shot a crow and disgustedly wrote the U. S. government: "Dear Sirs: I shot one of your pet crows the other day and followed the instructions attached to it and surved it. It was turrible. You should stop trying to fool the people with things like that."

629. A lady going from home for the day locked everything up well, and for the grocer's benefit wrote on a card: "All out. Don't leave anything." This she stuck on the door. On her return home, she found her house ransacked and all her choicest possessions gone. To the card on the door was added: "Thanks! We haven't left much."

Insurance

630. In the office of an insurance agent, an applicant for insurance handed in his completed form, and the agent looked it over.

"This seems to be in good order, Mr. Green," he said, "except for one little item. Where it asks the relationship of Mrs. Green to yourself, you should have put 'wife,' not 'strained.' "

631. An insurance agent, writing a policy for a cowpuncher, asked if he had ever had any accidents.

"No," said the cowboy, then added, trying to be helpful, "a bronc kicked in a couple of my ribs and a rattlesnake bit me a couple of years ago."

"Well!" said the agent. "Don't you call those accidents?"

"No," replied the knight of the branding iron, "they done it a-purpose."

632. A merchant took out a fire insurance policy and the very same day his store and its contents burned to the ground. The insurance company suspected fraud and arson, but couldn't prove anything. It had to content itself with writing the following letter:

"Dear Sir: You took out an insurance policy at 10 a.m., and your fire didn't break out until 3:30 p.m. Will you kindly explain the delay?"

633. A life insurance agent approached Mose, a very much-married Negro.

122

"Better let me write you a policy, Mose," he suggested.

"No, sir," said Mose most emphatically. "I ain't none too safe at home as things are now."

634. The owner of a movie house had just taken out a fire insurance policy. As he signed his name to the application blank, he turned to the insurance agent and asked, "Now, if my theatre was to burn down tomorrow, what would I get?"

"Oh, about two years I imagine," the agent replied.

635. "Why," said the insurance agent, "insurance is the greatest thing in the world. No man should be without it. I even carry a $50,000 policy, payable to my wife."

"It's too much," declared the harassed prospect. "What excuse can you give her for living?"

636. *Insurance agent:* "Don't you wish your office furnishings were insured against theft?"

Boss: "Yes, all except the clock. Everybody watches that."

Insurance, Life

637. "Well, Doc," asked the applicant for an insurance policy, "how do I stand?"

"I don't know," replied the Doc. "It's a miracle."

638. A farmer's barn burned down, and the agent for the insurance company, explaining the policy that covered the structure, told him that his firm would build another barn of similar size instead of paying the claim in cash. The farmer was furious. "If that's the way your company does business," he exploded, "you can just cancel the insurance policy on my wife."

639. An insurance salesman was having trouble getting through to his prospective customer.

"What is the maximum value of your husband's present policy?" he asked the housewife.

"If you should lose your husband, for example," he explained patiently, "what would you get?"

Thoughtfully, she looked around the rumpled, cigar-scented room. Then her face lit up and she brightly answered, "A parakeet!"

640. "So you don't believe Smith's widow is as sorry as she pretends?"

"Well, when I gave her the $50,000 insurance check, she stopped crying and said she'd cheerfully give $5,000 of it to have him back."

641. Life is cruel to men . . . When they are born, their mothers get the compliments and flowers. When they are married, their brides get the presents and the publicity. And when they die, their wives get the insurance and winters in Florida.

642. *Overheard on the beach:* "Mummy, may I go for a swim?"
"Certainly not, my dear, it's far too deep."
"But Daddy is swimming."
"Yes dear, but he's insured."

643. *Young bride:* "Now, dear, what will I get if I cook a dinner like that for you every day this year."
Young husband: "My life insurance."

Interference

644. "Everyone in town is talking about the Smiths' quarrel," remarked the wife. "Some are taking his part and some are taking hers . . ."

"And," interrupted her husband, "I suppose a few eccentric individuals are minding their own business."

645. "Your leisure hours must be quite a problem," a friend joshed the busy executive.

"The only problem I have there," snapped the executive, "is how to keep other people from wasting it."

646. The candidate was making a speech in the town square, and was being constantly interrupted by someone in the crowd shouting: "Liar!" The candidate finally stopped him by retorting: "If the fellow who keeps on interrupting will be good enough to tell his name instead of his calling, I'll be glad to meet him."

Joint effort

647. A famous organist put his hand on his chest, bowed, and announced: "I will now play the sonata, *Moonlight on the Pyramids.*

He came down on the keys. No sound. Presently the organ-blower peeped around the organ and said in a stage whisper: "Say, *we* will perform *Moonlight on the Pyramids.*"

648. A burglar who had entered a poor minister's house at midnight was disturbed by the awakening of the occupant of the room he was in. Drawing his knife, he said:

"If you stir, you are a dead man. I'm hunting for money."

"Let me get up and strike a light," said the minister, "and I'll hunt with you."

649. Competing in a race, the little boy kept dropping further and further behind, and his chances of winning seemed slim indeed; then suddenly his lips began to move with great regularity, his legs picked up speed, and he won the race.

Asked later what he was saying to himself, he said he had been talking to the Lord, saying over and over again, "Lord, you pick 'em up and I'll put 'em down. You pick 'em up and I'll put 'em down."

Journalism

650. A newspaper reporter was sent to cover a disastrous flood which had just wiped out a central Pennsylvania town.

After viewing the scene, the reporter went to the telegraph office and filed his story, which started out as follows:

"God is sitting on the hills of this little Pennsylvania town tonight . . ."

The hard-boiled telegraph editor read the first line and promptly sent back the following message:

"Rush interview with God."

651. "Remember," said the editor to the young lady reporter, "It was Joseph Pulitzer, the great newspaperman, who declared that accuracy is to a newspaper what virtue is to a woman."

"That, in itself, is not entirely accurate," said the young miss triumphantly. "A newspaper can always print a retraction."

652. A man rushed into the newspaper office and demanded to see the editor. "Sir," he cried, as he strode up and down the room, "your paper has libeled me. You have called me the lightweight champion."

"But that is true," returned the editor. "You are Mr. Fightwell, aren't you?"

"Yes, yes," cried the other, "but it's my brother who is the boxer. I'm a coal merchant."

653. "Dad," said the subscriber's little daughter, "I know why the editors call themselves 'we.' "

"Why?"

"So the fellow who doesn't like what's printed will think that there are too many for him to lick."

654. *Police sergeant:* "So you say you're an editor, eh?"

Prisoner: "Yes, sir."

Arresting officer: "That ain't so, Sarge! I searched his pockets and found money in them."

Justice

655. *Judge:* "My good man, under the American system of jurisprudence you are presumed to be innocent."

Defendant: "Then why all this effort to convict me?"

656. *Poet:* "This is a very unfair world."

Friend: "How so?"

Poet: "A banker can write a bad poem and people think nothing of it. But just let a poet try writing a bad check, and see what happens!"

657. "You told me that if I were sociable with the police magistrate, I would get off," complained the motorist to his friend.

"Well, were you?"

"Yes, I said 'Good morning, your Honor, and how are you today?' and he replied, 'Fine—$50.00.' "

658. It was the purpose of the trial to determine if the man at whom the finger of suspicion pointed really stole the complainant's overcoat. At last the judge got down to brass tacks.

"Did you steal this man's overcoat?" he demanded.

"No sir," declared the accused with a sickly grin. "I was just playing a joke on him."

"And where did you take this coat?" further demanded the irate judge.

"I took it off the coat rack in the restaurant and carried it home with me."

"Well," snapped the judge, "isn't that carrying a joke too far?"

659. "Judge, I don't know what to do."

"Why, how's that?"

"Well, I swore to tell the truth, but every time I try, some lawyer objects."

Justification

660. "My husband gets up in time for health exercises on the radio every morning."

"I didn't know he took 'em."

"He doesn't, but the girl in the apartment across the court does."

661. The landlord was charging his tenant with assault and battery.

"Tell me," demanded the judge, fixing his stern gaze upon the defendant, "do you think you had a right to kick your landlord down the stairs?"

The tenant-defendant reached into a bulging pocket and brought forth a long document marked "Lease." Firmly grasping the top edge of the instrument, he made a flinging motion so that the accordion pleats of the folded paper unfolded themselves, revealing a printed and signed agreement of extraordinary length.

"Look at this lease, judge," pleaded the defendant. "Don't you agree with me that anything they have forgotten to forbid, I've got a perfect right to do?"

Kiss—Kissing

662. As a married couple reminisced, the husband remarked, "By the way, I wonder whatever became of the old-fashioned girls who fainted when a man kissed them?"

His wife gave him a withering look. "What I'd like to know," she

127

retorted, "is what happened to the old-fashioned men who made them faint!"

663. *Shy young man:* "Do you shrink from kissing?"
Date: "If I did, I'd be nothing but skin and bones."

664. *Secretary:* "Your wife wants to kiss you over the telephone."
Employer: "Take the message and give it to me later."

665. The young artist kissed his model smack on the lips.
"I'll bet you do that to all your models," she said when she had regained her composure.
"No," he replied, "you are the first."
"How many have you had?" she inquired.
"Exactly four," he answered. "A rose, an onion, a banana, and you."

666. Bessie was just finishing her breakfast as her father stooped to kiss her before going downtown. The little one gravely took up her napkin and wiped her cheek. "What, Bessie?" said her father. "Wiping away Father's kiss?" "Oh, no!" said she, looking up with a smile. "I'se rubbing it in."

667. A pastor in Paris received a package from his nephew in America. It contained what appeared to be a very plain and ordinary necktie, suitable for one of his calling. He wore it one evening when he went calling on a very orthodox family. In the middle of a very profound philosophical discussion, the lights suddenly went out. It was pitch dark except for the pastor's "plain" tie, on which gleamed the request in bright phosphorescence, "Kiss me."

668. *Girl:* "Do you have any green lipstick?"
Druggist: "Green lipstick?"
Girl: "Yes, my date tonight is with a railroad man."

669. Gilbert Stuart, the celebrated portrait painter, once met a lady in the street in Boston, who saluted him with, "Ah, Mr. Stuart, I have just seen your miniature and kissed it, because it was so much like you."
"And did it kiss you in return?"
"Why, no."
"Then," said Stuart, "it was not like me."

128

670. "What would you do if you had five dates with the same man and he never tried to kiss you?" a coed asked.

The second coed replied promptly, "I'd lie about it."

Language

671. A beginner student at a Middle East college was constantly boasting about his mastery of the English language.

One day he told a fellow student: "I know the English well. I can even say to a person, 'Come here,' and he knows what I mean."

"Suppose you want a person to go there?" asked the other. "What do you do?"

The beginner thought a moment and answered: "I go over there and then say, 'Come here.' "

672. A young American girl traveling in Europe found herself in Germany, unable to speak a word of their language, and feeling rather lost and unhappy. As she crossed a street she sneezed and the policeman said, "Gesundheit!" The girl turned, threw her arms about his neck and cried happily. "Oh, you can speak English!"

673. A couple of gobs laying over for a day or two in Sweden decided to go to church. Knowing no Swedish, they figured to play safe by picking out a dignified looking old gentleman sitting in front of them and doing whatever he did.

During the service the pastor made a special announcement of some kind, and the man in front of them started to rise, at which the two sailors quickly got to their feet, to be met by roars of laughter from the whole congregation.

When the service was over and they were greeted by the pastor at the door, they discovered he spoke English, and naturally asked what the cause of the merriment had been.

"Oh," said the pastor. "I was announcing a baptism, and asked the father of the child to rise."

674. An African chieftain flew to the U.S. for a confab with the President and was met at the airport by a flock of newspaper reporters.

"Was your flight comfortable?" asked one of the reporters.

The chief exploded into a series of raucous noises: "screech, s-s-s-s, whistle, z-z-z-z, honk," and then in perfect English added, "Yes, it was most pleasant."

"How long are you planning on staying?"

Once again the chief preceded his remarks with the same noises before answering, "For about two weeks."

The reporter, not wishing to comment on the unusual noises, asked, "Tell me, Chief, where did you learn such perfect English?"

After the preliminary series of whistles and honks, the chief replied, "Short-wave radio."

675. "How is your wife?" the man asked the old friend he hadn't seen in years.

"She's in heaven," replied the friend.

"Oh, I'm sorry." Then he realized that was not the thing to say, so he added, "I mean, I'm glad." And that was even worse. He came out with "Well, I'm surprised."

676. The story is told of a number of spirits who demanded admission at the Celestial Gates. The keeper inquired who the first applicant might be.

"It's me," a voice replied. And St. Peter bade him enter.

Another knock. Another question. "Who's there?" Another answer, "It's me."

Finally there came a sharp rap. "Who's there?" demanded St. Peter.

"It is I," a voice replied.

"Another one of those school teachers!" grumbled St. Peter.

Lawyer-Client

677. *Thief:* (to the lawyer about to defend him): "How long do you think this business is going to last?"

Lawyer: "For me, two hours. For you, two years."

678. Apropos of counsel browbeating witnesses in murder trials, the case is recalled where the lawyer looked quizzically at the doctor who was testifying, and said:

"Doctors sometimes make mistakes, don't they?"

"Just as lawyers do, sometimes," was the reply.

"But doctors' mistakes are buried six feet under ground," said the lawyer.

"Yes," said the doctor, "and lawyers' mistakes sometimes swing six feet in the air."

679. *Client* (telephoning from prison): "They've shaved my head, cut a slit in my pants, and rolled up my sleeves. Now what will I do?"

Lawyer: "My advice to you is that no matter what you do, don't sit down."

680. Two friends, who hadn't seen each other for some time, met. One was on crutches.

"Hello," said the other man. "What's the matter with you?"

"Streetcar accident," said the man on crutches.

"When did it happen?"

"Oh, about six weeks ago."

"And you still have to use crutches?"

"Well, my doctor says I could get along without them, but my lawyer says I can't."

681. "Repeat the words the defendant used," said the lawyer.

"I'd rather not. They were not fit words to tell a gentleman."

"Then," said the attorney, "whisper them to the judge."

682. After a lengthy conference with the estranged husband, the lawyer reported to the man's wife, his client.

"Mrs. Cooley," he said, with a self-satisfied air, "I have succeeded in making a settlement with your husband that is eminently fair to both of you."

"Fair to both?" cried the disappointed client. "I could have done that myself! What do you think I hired a lawyer for?"

683. An adverse witness preceded each answer with: "I think." The distraught lawyer demanded for the third time the witness tell the court and jury "what you know and not what you think."

The witness quietly replied: "I'm not a lawyer; I can't talk without thinking."

684. A much married man was trying to chisel some free advice from a lawyer friend. "Isn't there some way a man can avoid paying alimony?" he inquired.

"Yes," replied the lawyer. "Two, in fact. He can either stay single or stay married."

Laziness

685. Abraham Lincoln once took a sack of grain to a mill whose proprietor was known to be the laziest man in the entire State of Illinois. After watching the miller at work for a while, the future President commented wearily, "I can eat that grain as fast as you're grinding it."

"Indeed," grunted the miller, "and how long do you think you could keep that up?"

"Until I starve to death," replied Lincoln.

686. "Why is it that you carry only one plank while everyone else carries two?"

"I guess," replied Slow Joe, "they're just too lazy to make two trips like I do."

687. The teacher had been reading to her class stories of the lives of famous inventors.

"Now then, Edgar, what would you like to invent?"

Little Edgar rose to his feet with a puzzled frown on his face.

"Well, teacher," said the lad, "I'd like to invent a machine that by simply pressing a button, all my lessons would be done."

The teacher shook her head.

"That's very lazy of you, Edgar," she reprimanded. "Now, let's hear from Tommy Thomas. Tommy, what would you like to invent?"

"Something to press the button," wily little Tommy replied.

688. An eastern go-getter spied a lazy Indian chief lolling indolently at the door of his tepee somewhere out west.

"Chief," remonstrated the go-getter, "why don't you get yourself a job?"

"Why?" grunted the chief.

"Well, you could earn a lot of money. Maybe fifty or sixty dollars a week."

"Why?" insisted the chief.

"Oh, if you worked hard and saved your money, you'd soon have a bank account. Wouldn't you like that?"

"Why?" again asked the chief.

"For gosh sakes!" shouted the exasperated go-getter. "With a big bank account you could retire, and then you wouldn't have to work any more—"

"I'm not working now," pointed out the Indian.

Leadership

689. "Now, Johnny," said the teacher, "if there were eleven sheep in a field and six jumped the fence, how many would there be left?"

"None," replied Johnny.

"Why, yes there would," said the teacher.

"No, ma'am, there wouldn't," persisted Johnny. "You may know arithmetic, but you don't know sheep."

690. The tenderfoot had spent the time since his arrival on the ranch asking innumerable questions. "Why is it," he asked Alkali Joe, "that you always slap your bronco on one side when you get in the saddle?"

"Wal," said the cowpuncher, "I figure that if I get one side goin' the other is pretty sure to follow."

Lesson

691. The king of an African tribe, after many years, faced the fact that his throne was wearing out. It was repaired a couple of times, but eventually collapsed and was replaced with a new one. The king, for sentimental reasons, hated to part with his old throne. So it was hoisted on ropes to the ceiling of his grass hut and stored there. Then one night, during a storm, the throne fell down and hit the king on the head.

The moral of the story is that people who live in grass houses shouldn't stow thrones.

692. "And in conclusion, my dear students, I shall give you a demonstration of the evils of the Demon Rum. I have here two glasses, one filled with water, the other with whiskey. I will now place a worm in each glass. Notice how the worm in the water squirms and vibrates with the very spark of life, while the worm in the whiskey

133

writhes in agony, curls up and dies. Now, young man, what is the moral of this story?"

Young man: "If you don't want worms, drink whiskey."

Livelihood

693. *Scientist:* "From our studies we find that other planets may not be able to support life."

Hard-working businessman: "It isn't exactly easy on this one either."

694. At a party, several young couples were discussing the difficulties of family budgets.

"I really don't want an awful lot of money," said one young matron. "I just wish we could afford to live the way we are living now."

Longwindedness

695. "Where have you been for the last two hours?" demanded the minister's wife.

"I met Mrs. Brown on the street and asked her how she was feeling," sighed the weary pastor.

Love

696. The newlyweds were honeymooning in Florida. As they walked arm in arm along the beach, he looked out toward the sea and said eloquently: "Roll on, thou deep and dark blue ocean, roll."

His bride gazed at the breakers for a moment, then in hushed and reverent tones, said, "Oh, Herman, you wonderful man. It's doing it!"

697. *Jessie:* "When did you first know that you loved me?"

Jimmie: "When I began to get mad at people who said you were brainless and homely."

698. The gang was having an old-fashioned sleigh ride and everybody was having a wonderful time. But one girl sighed deeply.

"What's the matter?" asked her boy friend.

"Nobody loves me," she whimpered, "and my hands are cold."

"Oh, that's all right," he whispered comfortingly, "your mother loves you, and you can sit on your hands."

699. *He:* "Why do you call it love at second sight?"
She: "I didn't know he was rich when I first saw him!"

700. "Ever been disappointed in love?" said a man to his friend.
"Twice," was the answer. "The first girl jilted me. The second one didn't."

Marriage

701. *Young man to phrenologist:* "I'm getting married, and would like to have my head examined!"

702. *Jim:* "When did you really begin to appreciate the value of a wife?"
Joe: "The first time I used her as an excuse for not attending a committee meeting in the evening."

703. *Father:* "There's plenty of time for Bessie to think of getting married. Let her wait till the right man comes along."
Mother: "I don't see why she should wait that long. I didn't when I was her age."

704. M. le Vicomte Sorigny, a distinguished member of the French Embassy, was present at the silver-wedding anniversary celebration of a bishop. Leaning over to his neighbor, the bishop's nephew, the vicomte asked, *sotto voce:* "Tell me, what is this silver wedding which we celebrate? I do not quite understand."
"Oh," replied the bishop's nephew, "don't you know? Why, my uncle and aunt have lived together for 25 years without ever having been separated."
"Ah," exclaimed the diplomat heartily, "and now he marry her? Br-ravo!"

705. Journalist Heywood Broun was standing next to a prim old lady at a wedding. "Can you imagine," she whispered as the couple met at the altar, "they've known each other scarcely two weeks, and here they are getting married!"
"Well," said Broun philosophically, "it's one way of getting acquainted."

706. *Ted:* "Too bad that Ed and his girl aren't good enough for each other."

Lee: "What makes you say that?"

Ted: "I've been talking to both families."

707. Herb Shriner reveals how his spinster aunt back in Indiana found herself a husband.

"She saw this fellow on a 'Wanted' poster," Herb explains, "and offered $100 more for him than the government did."

708. *Susie:* "You mustn't be discouraged. In this world there's a man for every girl and a girl for every man. You can't improve on an arrangement like that."

Millie: "I don't want to improve on it. I just want to get in on it."

709. Whether a man winds up with a nest egg or a goose egg depends a lot on the kind of chick he marries.

710. They say that people with opposite characteristics make the best marriages."

"That's why I'm looking for a girl with money."

711. An English soldier in a French village, seeing a wedding in process at a church, asked a Frenchman whose wedding it was.

"Je ne sais pas, M'sieu," answered the Frenchman.

A few hours later the same soldier saw a coffin going into the same church, and curiosity getting the better of him, he again asked the identity of the individual.

"Je ne sais pas," was the response.

"Blimey!" ejaculated the Tommy, "he didn't last long."

712. Marriage is like a railroad sign. You see a lovely girl and stop. Then you look. And after you're married you listen.

713. The girl who marries a man to mend his ways is apt to find out that he isn't worth a darn.

714. "Dearest," said the new husband to his bride, "do you really think I'll prove a satisfactory mate?"

"Oh, you'll do for a mate all right," answered the precious one. "Now, you look me over and tell me what you think of your captain."

715. An eight-year-old son of a lumberman asked a young girl of the same age if she would marry him when they grew up.

"I'm sorry," replied the young lady primly, "but it's quite impossible. In my family we always marry relatives. You see, my father married my mother; my grandfather married my grandmother, and even my uncle married my aunt."

716. *First father:* "My son doesn't want to get married."
Second father: "Wait until the wrong girl comes along . . ."

717. Marriage brings music into a man's life. He learns to play second fiddle!

718. *Young girl:* "The man I marry must shine in company, be musical, tell jokes, sing, dance, and stay home nights."
Married friend: "You don't want a husband, you want a TV set."

719. Two little girls were talking about getting married.
One said, "I am going to marry a doctor, for when I am sick, I can be well for nothing."
The other said, "I am going to marry a minister, for when I am bad, I can be good for nothing."

720. *Wife:* "Don't you think, dear, that a man has more sense after he is married?"
Husband: "Yes, but it's too late then."

721. A pretty girl is like a melody—after you marry her you have to face the music.

722. "So you and Henry are married. I thought all along it was just going to be another flirtation."
"So did Henry."

723. *Daughter:* "I can't marry him, Mother. He's an atheist and doesn't believe there is a hell."
Mother: "Marry him, dear, and between us we'll convince him he's wrong."

724. Two young women were chatting, when one noticed something odd, and said to the other, "You're wearing your wedding ring on the wrong finger."

"Yes, I know," said the second woman. "I married the wrong man."

725. Horrified father watching daughter select costly wedding gown said to his wife: "I don't mind giving her in marriage, but must she be gift wrapped?"

726. A minister advertised for a handyman and next morning a neat young man rang the doorbell. "Can you start the fire and have breakfast ready by 7:00?" asked the minister.

The young man thought he could.

"Can you polish all the silver, wash the dishes, and keep the house and grounds tidy and neat?" was the next question.

"Look, Reverend," protested the young man. "I came here to see about getting married, but if it's going to be anything like that, you can count me out right now."

727. "Dad," asked the small boy. "Why is a man not allowed to have more than one wife?"

"My son," replied the father, "when you are older you will realize that the law protects those who are incapable of protecting themselves."

728. The old-fashioned woman who saved her wedding dress for her daughter now has a daughter who saves her wedding dress for her next wedding.

729. *Son:* "Why do they rope off the aisles at weddings?"
Father: "So the bridegroom can't get away, son."

730. Two old schoolmates met after a lapse of several years. "It's nice to see you again," said the first. "Are you married?"

"Yes," said the second.

"I remember," laughed the first, "you always said you wouldn't marry the best man in the world."

"Well," confided her companion, "I didn't!"

731. A girl confided to a friend that she was going to marry an eccentric millionaire.

"But," the friend protested, "everyone thinks he's cracked."

"He may be cracked," the girl answered, "but he certainly isn't broke."

732. *Student:* "To whom was Minerva married?"
Professor: "My boy, when will you learn that Minerva was the Goddess of Wisdom? She wasn't married."

733. *She:* "You admit that marriage is a fine school?"
He: "Not for a man."
She: "Why not?"
He: "Because he loses a bachelor's degree without getting a master's."

734. *Lawyer:* "What's to be different about this will?"
Mr. Henpecked: "I'm leaving everything to my wife, provided she marries again. I want somebody to be sorry I died."

735. Marry an army man, girls—he can cook, make beds, sew, is in perfect health, and is already used to taking orders.

736. What is that spirit that keeps a woman thinking the man she is about to marry is better than the one she just divorced?

737. "I hope," said the girl's father impressively, "that you realize that when you marry my daughter you will be getting a very big-hearted and generous girl."

"Oh, I certainly do, sir," replied the fiance, "and I trust she has inherited those fine qualities from her father."

738. "You look positively happy all the time," said the young man to the elderly spinster. "I always thought unmarried women were grouchy."

"Well, I have a dog that growls, a fireplace that smokes, a parrot that swears, and a cat that stays out all night. What need do I have for a man around the house?"

739. When two important industrialists met at their club one day, one of them remarked to the other: "Well, I suppose now that your son is graduating from college, he will be going to work in your factory."

"No, I'm afraid not," rejoined the other. "He said he couldn't realize his life's ambition if he worked for me."

"And what is his life's ambition?" asked the first.

"To marry his wealthy employer's daughter," sighed the disillusioned father.

Marriage proposal

740. "Why don't you marry me?" he demanded. "There isn't anyone else, is there?"

"Oh, Oscar," she sighed, "there must be."

741. "So you desire to become my son-in-law?"

"No, sir, I don't, but if I marry your daughter, I don't see how I can get out of it."

Married life

742. Every married man should forget his mistakes. No use two people remembering the same thing.

743. A tired businessman's grueling day at the office was capped by his wife's announcement that the cook had walked out.

"Again?" moaned the husband. "What was the trouble this time?"

"You were!" charged the wife. "She said you used insulting language to her over the phone this morning."

"Good grief!" confessed the husband. "I thought all the time I was talking to *you.*"

744. In a New York restaurant, a woman was overheard to tell her henpecked husband: "Keep quiet. When I want your opinion I'll give it to you!"

745. The most popular labor-saving device for women is still a husband with money.

746. *Salesman:* "May I have tomorrow afternoon off to go shopping with my wife?"

Sales Manager: "Absolutely not!"

Salesman: "Thanks ever so much."

747. "Do you have the same trouble with your wife that I have with mine?"

"What trouble?"

"Why, there's no end to it. She constantly keeps nagging me for money, money, money, and then more money . . ."

"And what does she do with all the money you give her?"

"Who knows? I never give her any."

748. Brides soon learn that running a home is no different from running a car; the important thing to remember is to hold out the hand.

749. The girl of the house was beginning to fall for a young man rooming there. "Stay away from him," her mother advised. "I'm willing to bet he's a married man."

"But, Mother, he swears he's single."

"I don't care," said the mother, "he acts married. Every time he pays me he turns his back when he opens his wallet."

750. One way for a husband to learn about do-it-yourself is to criticize his wife's housekeeping.

751. "Dad, guess what? I've got my first part in a play," enthused the budding young actor. "I play the part of a man who's been married for 25 years."

"That's a good start, son," replied his dad. "Just keep at it and one of these days you'll get a speaking part."

752. "My husband and I never argue in front of the children," said a woman to one of her neighbors. "If any difference arises between us, we always send the children outdoors."

"Well, that explains everything," said the neighbor. "Just the other day I was remarking to my husband how well your children looked. I was right when I told him your children must spend a great deal of time outdoors."

753. "You look all in today, Bob, what's the trouble?"

"Well, I didn't get home until morning, and just as I was undressing, my wife woke up and said, 'Aren't you getting up pretty early, Bob?' So to avoid an argument, I put on my clothes and came to work."

754.   BEFORE

He walked, a spring in his step, a happy smile on his lips. He walked gaily, his hand on a little lavender note, which read: "Dearest: Yes, I love you and will marry you."

AFTER

He walked, his shoulders stooped, his mouth drooped. Glumly he walked, his hand on a little brown note, which said:
"1 lb. of potatoes
3 dozen eggs
½ lb. bacon—slice it thin."

755. A woman went to a medium and got into contact with her dead husband.
"James," she asked, "are you happy now?"
"I am very happy."
"Are you happier than you were with me on earth?"
"Yes, far happier," came the sepulchral voice.
"Tell me, James, what is it like in Heaven?"
"Heaven!" the voice said, "who's in Heaven?"

756. *She:* "I wonder why men lie so?"
He: "Because their wives are so inquisitive."

757. "I see," remarked young Mr. Brown, "that a man who speaks six languages has just married a woman who speaks three."
"That," replied the long-wedded Mr. Jones, "seems to be about the right handicap."

758. "I say a man should be master in his own house, or know the reason why."
"Most chaps know the reason."

759. *Mo:* "How are things going at home?"
Frank: "Well, the old woman ain't talking to me—and frankly, I'm in no mood to interrupt her."

760. *Traffic cop* (stopping motorist): "Mister, your wife fell out of the car three blocks back."
Motorist: "Thank goodness. I thought I'd gone stone deaf."

761. The bride was shy about asking her husband for money. "Jack, dear," she said at breakfast, "will you lend me $5 but only give me half of it?"
"Of course, darling," said her husband, puzzled, "but why only half of it?"

"Well, then you'll owe me $2.50 and I'll owe you $2.50, and we'll be square, won't we?"

762. "How long have you been married, Winifred?" asked an acquaintance.

"Twenty odd years," replied Winnie.

"Why do you call them odd?" queried the first with a look of puzzlement.

"Wait, just you wait," said Winnie. "Wait till you see my husband!"

763. A psychiatrist advised his timid little patient to assert himself. "Don't let your wife bully you. Go home and show her who's boss."

The patient went home, slammed the door loudly and roughly seized his wife. "From now on," he snarled, "you're taking orders from me, see? You're gonna make my supper this minute, and when it's on the table you're goin' upstairs and lay out my clothes, see? Tonight I'm goin' out on the town—alone, and do you know who's going to dress me in my tuxedo and black tie?"

"You bet I do," was the answer. "The undertaker!"

764. *Wife:* "Wake up, Egbert, there's a burglar going through your pockets."

Husband: "Now leave me out of this, Ethel. You two just fight it out between yourselves."

765. As she gazed through the family album, the wife reminisced about the early days of their marriage. Suddenly she turned to her husband.

"You know, Henry," she said, "when we were first married you used to catch me in your arms."

"Yeah," was Henry's blunt reply. "Now I catch you in my pockets."

766. "My wife is very irritable. The least little thing sets her off."

"You're lucky at that. Mine's a self-starter."

767. The wise husband meets a marital crisis with a firm hand—full of candy and flowers.

768. "You ought to brace up and show your wife who is running things at your house," a big, bossy man said to his henpecked friend.

"No need to," replied his friend, "she already knows."

769. "How's that married daughter of yours getting along in Chicago?" asked Mr. Smith.

"Oh, she's doing fine," replied Mrs. Brown. "She's got the prettiest little flat imaginable, lovely furniture, a nice car—and she's never had so many frocks. The only thing is, she can't stand her husband. But there's always something, isn't there?"

770. *Wife to her husband:* "I scratched the front fender a little, dear. If you want to look at it, it's in the back seat."

771. The anxious hostess was pressing her guests to provide entertainment.

"Is there any instrument you can play, Mr. Johnson?" she asked.

"Not away from home," he replied.

"What do you play at home?" she inquired.

"Second fiddle," Johnson murmured solemnly.

772. Jenkins and Smithers were discussing wives and their idiosyncrasies. "One annoying thing about wives," Jenkins observed, "is the way they always remember wedding anniversaries."

"Yes," Smithers agreed, "and husbands always forget them. How do you account for that?"

"Oh, that's easy," Jenkins replied. "Do you remember when you caught your biggest fish?"

"Do I!" Smithers exclaimed.

"But now, take the fish—" Jenkins murmured. "Do you think it remembers?"

773. *Jasper:* "My dear, I really don't believe you can ever teach that dog to obey you."

Mrs. Jones: "Nonsense, darling. Remember how obstinate you were when we were first married?"

774. A man who had been married for ten years consulted a marriage counselor. "When I first married," he said, "I was very happy. I'd come home from a hard day down at the shop. My little dog would race around barking, and my wife would bring me my slippers.

144

Now after all these years, everything's changed. When I come home, my dog brings me my slippers, and my wife barks at me!"

"I don't know what you're complaining about," said the marriage counselor. "You're still getting the same service."

775. "You seem to have plenty of money in your pockets these days. Nothing like the old days when you were always broke," said one office worker to another. "You must have found a lucky charm or something."

"Yes, I have," said the other, as he pulled out a rabbit's foot from his pocket.

"So that's what's bringing you your luck, eh?"

"In a way, yes. My wife touched it when she went through my pockets one night and hasn't been through them since. She must have thought it was a mouse."

776. "It's being rumored around town that you and your husband aren't getting along too well."

"Nonsense. We did have some words, and I shot him. But that's as far as it went."

777. "My wife explored my pockets last night."

"Did she find anything?"

"About the same as any other explorer. Enough material for a lecture."

778. It was the first time in all the three weeks that they had been married that she had seen him act that way.

"What's wrong, darling?" she asked. "You've been so secretive for the last few days I feel that something must be bothering you."

"Oh, it's nothing, sweetheart," he assured her. "Just forget all about it."

"But, dear," she persisted, "when we were married we agreed to share each other's trials and joys. Maybe I can help you if you are in trouble. Remember, if there are any worries, they belong to both of us."

"All right then, dear," he said, "a girl we used to know is suing us for breach of promise."

779. There's one advantage to being married—a man can't make a fool of himself without knowing it.

145

780. "Boss," said the young salesman, "I'm getting married next week and I'd like a raise."

"So you don't think two can live as cheaply as one, eh?" his employer rejoined. "You want some more money to meet your living expenses?"

"No, not exactly," explained the prospective bridegroom, "I'm already making enough money for us to live on."

"Then, why do you want a raise?"

"Well, it's this way," the young man explained. "In an unguarded moment, I told Mary how much I get, so I'd like to have a little additional for my own use that she doesn't know about."

781. Invited to tarry for a session at a tavern, a henpecked husband expressed his regret: "I can't; got to go home and explain to my wife."

"Explain what?" the bachelor asked.

"How do I know?" said the other wearily. "I'm not home yet."

782. "We've been married a year and never quarrel. If a difference of opinion arises and I'm right, my husband gives in."

"But what if he's right?"

"That has never occurred."

783. *Bachelor* (dreamily): "Sometimes I yearn for the peace and comfort of married life."

Married friend (wistfully): "I always do."

Military service

784. Two privates paused at the side of the road to puzzle over a dead animal they saw there. "It has two stripes," said one.

"That settles it," said the other. "It's either a skunk or a corporal."

785. An icy voice cut into an uninhibited telephone conversation: "Do you know whom you are addressing?"

"No," said the sergeant.

"Well, this is Colonel Humdinger."

"Colonel," said the sergeant, "do you know whom you are addressing?"

"No!" thundered the colonel.

"Thank God!" said the sergeant and quickly hung up.

146

786. *Young man to draft board:* "But you can't turn me down. I've proposed to three girls, told my boss what I think of him, and sold my car."

Millinery

787. *Wife:* "Oh, Henry, the lady next door has a hat just like my new one."
Hubby: "Now I suppose you want to buy another one."
Wife: "Well, it would be cheaper than moving."

788. *Jones:* "I think there should be only one head to a family."
Smith: "Brother, you said a mouthful! I just paid for hats for my four daughters."

789. Some men think women's hats are funny. Others have to pay for them.

790. "That was a beautiful hat your wife wore to church last Sunday. But it was so high I could hardly see the pulpit above it."
"If the good woman had worn the bill that came with it, you couldn't have seen the roof."

791. Frances Perkins, former Secretary of Labor, tells about turning to a gentleman seated behind her at a movie, and saying, "If my hat prevents your seeing this picture, I'd be happy to take it off."
"Please don't," said the man. "The hat's much funnier than the movie."

792. *Mrs. Brown:* "Whenever I'm down in the dumps, I get myself a new hat."
Mrs. Jones: "I've often wondered where you got them."

793. Women's hats are all different because no one likes to make the same mistake twice.

794. *Wife* (trying on hats): "Do you like this turned down, dear?"
Husband: "How much is it?"
Wife: "Twenty-five dollars."
Husband: "Yes, turn it down."

795. A customer, astonished at the high price tag on a new hat, was moved to comment:

147

"Why, there's nothing to this hat. Why should it cost so much?"

"Madam, nowadays you have to pay for the restraint," was the saleswoman's reply.

796. Emmy came home with a new hat, beaming with happiness. "What do you think of the latest model from Paris?" she asked her husband.

He took one look at the creation and replied, "That's not a model. That's a horrible example!"

797. Mrs. Hinkle had shown her husband a large lamp shade which she had just bought, saying, "Isn't it lovely, dear?"

Mr. Hinkle looked anything but pleased. "If you intend to wear that to church tomorrow," he said, "you'll go alone."

Mind, Presence of

798. Removing his shoes, he climbed the stairs, opened the door of the room, entered, and closed the door after him without being detected. Just as he was about to get into bed, his wife, aroused from slumber, turned and sleepily said, "Is that you, Fido?"

The salesman, relating the rest of the story, said: "For once in my life I had real presence of mind. I licked her hand."

799. A fisherman, returning home after a day of bad luck, met a friendly old man walking through the woods.

"Have any luck?" asked the old gentleman.

"Nope," replied the fisherman, "but yesterday before the season opened, I caught twenty bass of all sizes."

"Is that so?" replied the stranger. "Do you know who I am?"

"Can't say as I do," replied the fisherman.

"Well, young man, I'm the game warden."

"Now isn't that the strangest thing," said the fisherman. "Do you know who I am? I'm the biggest liar in the United States."

800. *Policeman:* "Why didn't you stop when I yelled back there?"

Motorist (with great presence of mind): "I thought you said 'Hello, Senator.' "

Policeman: "Well, you see, Senator, I was going to warn you about not driving too fast through the next town."

801. A man, returning home in the small hours of the night, found a burglar jimmying the lock on his front door. Thinking quickly, the man whispered to the prowler, "I'll open the door if you'll go in first."

802. A New York lawyer went to London to try to locate a young woman who had fallen heir to a large fortune. The police were called in to assist in the search. The case was placed in the hands of a young, clever, and personable detective. Several weeks passed by without any information being available, and the lawyer was beginning to feel concerned over the matter, when the young detective appeared on the scene and smilingly informed him he had located the heiress.

"Where is she?" asked the lawyer.

"At my place," replied the detective. "We were married yesterday."

803. Two girls boarded a crowded streetcar, and one of them whispered to the other: "Watch me embarrass a man into giving me his seat."

Pushing her way through the crowd, she turned all of her charms upon a gentleman who looked embarrassable. "My dear Mr. Brown," she gushed, "fancy meeting you on the streetcar. Am I glad to see you! Why, you're almost a stranger. My, but I'm tired."

The sedate gentleman looked up at the girl. He had never seen her before but he rose and said pleasantly, "Sit down, Bertha, my girl. It isn't often I see you on washday. No wonder you're tired. By the way, don't deliver the washing until Wednesday. My wife is going to the District Attorney's office to see whether she can get your husband out of jail."

Misinterpretation

804. A young businessman, a deacon in his local church, while in New York on business, was to purchase a new sign to be hung in front of the church. He copied the motto and the dimensions, but when he got to New York discovered he had left the paper behind.

He wired his wife: "Send motto and dimensions."

An hour later the reply came, and the new girl, who had just come

149

on duty, read it and fainted. The message read: "Unto Us a Child Is Born, 6 feet long and 2 feet wide."

805. The young matron listened attentively while the doctor prescribed a remedy for her nervous condition. "Madam," he said, "you require frequent baths, plenty of fresh air, and, above all, you should dress in warm clothes."

That evening she told her husband about it. "The doctor," she said, "told me I am in a highly nervous condition, dear, and that I must go to Miami Beach, then to a dude ranch out west, and, by all means, buy myself a full length sable coat."

806. "At your book sale last week," wrote the disappointed department store customer, "I made several purchases. One of the books was entitled 'One Hundred Ways to Please a Man!' Since you in no way indicated that this was a cook book, kindly call for same and credit my account."

Mistake

807. A worker was shorted two dollars in his pay envelope, and complained to the paymaster.

"You were overpaid two dollars last week and didn't object," reasoned the paymaster.

"I know," said the employee. "I don't mind overlooking one mistake, but when it happens the second time, I think it's time to complain."

808. A father had given his son a dollar for his birthday. All afternoon, the lad had trotted around his neighborhood, getting his bill changed to silver at the grocer's, back to a bill again at the baker's, and so on. Observing all this hustle and bustle, the father asked him the reason for his strange behavior.

"Well, you see, it's like this," replied the enterprising chap, "sooner or later somebody is going to make a mistake, and it's not going to be me."

809. "Have you ever made a serious mistake in compounding a prescription?" asked the customer of the pharmacist.

"Never but once," said the druggist. "That was the time I charged a man thirty cents instead of a dollar and a half."

810. A famous department store decided to honor its two-millionth customer. She was welcomed by the store president, interviewed on the radio, and loaded down with many packages of choice merchandise.

She then proceeded to her original destination—the complaint desk.

811. *Wife* (reading her husband's fortune on a weight card): "You are dynamic, a leader of men, and admired by women for your good looks and strength of character. It's got your weight wrong, too!"

812. *Child:* "Mother, have gooseberries got legs?"
Mother: "Why, of course not."
Child: "Then I think I swallowed a caterpillar."

813. "Look, madam," said the irate fellow who was strap-hanging on the bus, "you are standing on my foot."

"Oh, I am sorry," the lady standing next to him said. "I really thought it belonged to this man sitting down."

814. A young man called at the minister's office. "I just came to talk to you," he said, "and to ask you if it's right for any person to profit by the mistakes of another."

"Most certainly not," replied the minister.

Then the young man held out his hand and said, "Perhaps you'll return the $10 I gave you last June for marrying me."

815. *Judge:* "You admit that you stole eggs from this store. Have you any defense or excuse?"
Defendant: "Yes, I took them by mistake, your Honor."
Judge: "How is that?"
Defendant: "I thought they were fresh."

816. "There, now," said the sales manager as he and his newly-married chorine came within sight of Niagara Falls. "Didn't I tell you that if you'd be my wife you could look forward to the biggest cataract you'd ever seen?"

"Cataract?" she screamed. "I thought you said Cadillac!"

817. Jones took the ticket the agent gave him, picked up his change, and walked away.

151

A few moments later he was back again at the ticket window.

"I say," he said to the clerk, "you gave me the wrong change just a moment ago."

"I'm sorry, sir," said the agent with a shrug of his shoulders, "it cannot be rectified now. You should have called my attention to it at the time you bought your ticket."

"Well, that's all right with me, sir," said Jones, with a half-hidden smile, as he pocketed the five dollars too much he had been given and walked away.

818. When the sculptor Epstein was modeling the head of the great Einstein, his subject regaled him with stories about the Nazis, remarking that a hundred professors, in a book, had combined to deny the validity of his theory of relativity.

"If I had been wrong, really," commented Einstein, "one professor would have been enough."

819. A new member of a certain government bureau made life miserable for his associates by claiming to be absolutely infallible. What's more, he usually was. One day, however, he startled his co-workers by admitting that he had been wrong.

"No!" exclaimed one of his listeners.

"Yes," the man declared. "Once I thought I was wrong when I wasn't."

820. Mark Twain once opened an envelope addressed to his wife and then resealed it, marking across its face: "Opened by mistake to see what was inside. S. L. C."

Misunderstanding

821. Crossing the street one morning, I was nearly run down by an antiquated car, literally overflowing with about a dozen children. Since the red light had been against the woman driver, as she came to a halt I shouted: "Lady, don't you know when to stop?"

Glancing back at the moppets, she answered icily: "They aren't all mine."

822. *Purchasing Agent:* "How much do you take off for cash?"
Saleslady: "Sir!"

823. Married life seemed to have worn him down, so he went to his doctor for a check-up.

"There's nothing radically wrong with you," said the medico after a thorough examination, "all you need is a little sun and air."

"Yes, I suppose you're right," said the misunderstanding patient, "but my wife's dead set against having any children."

824. Joey Ray tells about a group of visitors being shown around a battleship. The guide paused before a bronze plaque on the deck and bowed his head. "This plaque," he said solemnly, "is where our gallant captain fell."

"Well, no wonder!" said one weary old lady. "I nearly tripped over the darned thing myself."

825. "Now," the lecturer asked, "is there a man in the audience who would let his wife be slandered and say nothing?"

A meek little man rose to his feet.

The lecturer glared at him. "Do you mean to say you would let your wife be slandered and say nothing?" she asked.

"Oh, excuse me, I'm sorry," the little man said apologetically. "I thought you said slaughtered."

826. *Customer:* "Give me a pound of those grapes. My husband is fond of them. Do you know if they have been sprayed with any kind of poison?"

Grocery Clerk: "No, ma'am; you'll have to get that at the drug store."

Money

827. There are more important things in life than money—but they won't go out with you if you're broke.

828. Money isn't everything, and don't let anybody tell you it is. There are other things, such as stocks, bonds, letters of credit, travelers' checks, and drafts.

829. A Westerner was visiting New York. Walking on a side street late one evening, he was held up by a bandit, who said: "Give me your money or I'll blow out your brains!"

"Blow away!" said the Westerner. "In New York you can live without brains, but not without money!"

Motherhood

830. Two nursemaids were wheeling their infant charges in the park, when one asked the other: "Are you going to the dance to-night?"

"I'd love to," the other replied, "but to tell the truth I'm afraid to leave the baby with its mother."

831. At a dinner party, several doting mothers were discussing their children's illnesses with the guest of honor, a noted pediatrician. One mother asked: "Doctor, what do you find to be the principal ailment of children?"

The doctor considered the question, then answered gravely, "Mothers, madam."

Mother-in-law

832. A young fellow who had recently been married had not yet learned all the ropes of matrimony. He consulted a married friend:

"I simply don't know what to call my mother-in-law. Since my own mother is living, it doesn't seem right to call my wife's mother 'Mother.' "

"That's simple," his friend said. "I had the same problem. The first year I addressed her as 'Say,' and after that I called her 'Granny.' "

833. A farmer's mule once kicked his mother-in-law to death. A tremendous crowd turned out for the funeral, all men, curiously enough. The minister, during the course of the obsequies, commented: "This old lady must certainly have been very popular, when one looks about and observes the large number of people who have left their work to come to her funeral."

"They're not here for the funeral," observed one of those who had come. "They're here to buy the mule."

834. Adam, they say, must have been a happy man; he had no mother-in-law.

835. An undertaker telegraphed a man that his mother-in-law had just died, and asked whether he should bury, embalm, or cremate her.

This was the reply: "All three. Take no chances."

836. A woman reported the disappearance of her husband to the police. "Is there any message you may wish to give your husband if we find him?" "Yes," she replied eagerly. "Tell him mother didn't come after all."

837. A wife in a small town said to her husband, "Last year for Christmas we sent mother a chair. What do you think we ought to do for her this year?"

The husband snorted loudly, "Electrify it."

838. A woman arrived late for the wedding. As she came rushing up to the door, an usher approached her for her invitation.

"I have none," she snapped.

"Are you a friend of the groom?" asked the usher.

"Certainly not!" the woman replied. "I'm the bride's mother."

839. "I'm surprised that your mother agreed to your marrying Jack when she dislikes him so."

"Well, she said she just wants to be his mother-in-law for a while."

840. *Solicitor:* "Could you please donate something to the Old Ladies' Home?"

Man: "Sure, help yourself to my mother-in-law."

841. *Judge:* "You say it was an accident that you shot your wife?"

Defendant: "Yes, your Honor. She got in front of my mother-in-law just as I pulled the trigger."

842. "You're charged with throwing your mother-in-law out of the window. Do you plead guilty or not guilty?"

"Guilty, your Honor. I did it without thinking."

"That's no excuse—you might have hit somebody on the head."

Motive

843. A reporter on holidays dropped in to see the editor of the local weekly.

"How on earth do you manage to sell a newspaper in a town where everyone must know what everyone else is doing?"

The editor smiled. "They don't buy my paper to find out who did what. They buy it to find out who's been caught at it."

844. The senior girl sniffed disdainfully as the pink-cheeked freshman boy cut in. "Why did you have to cut in when I was dancing?" she asked.

"Sorry," the freshman answered, hanging his head in humility. "I'm working my way through college, and your partner was waving a $5 bill at me."

Music

845. *Singer:* "How do you like my voice?"

Accompanist: "Madam, I've played the white keys and I've played the black keys. But never before have I seen anyone who could sing in the cracks."

846. A composer was once signed to do the complete score for a musical comedy in ten days.

"That will take a lot out of you," commented a well-wisher.

"Not out of me," countered the composer, "but out of Brahms, Bach, and Beethoven."

847. A henpecked-looking little man was escorting his wife to a concert. They arrived late. "What are they playing?" he whispered to his neighbor.

"The Fifth Symphony."

"Well, thank goodness," he said, "I've missed four of them, anyway."

Names

848. Tony, having his second son christened, was much concerned about getting the correct name on the birth certificate.

"Will you please name the baby just as I give it to you?"

"Surely," answered the minister, "why shouldn't I?"

"Well, you see, it's like this," replied Tony. "When I told you I wanted to name my first boy Tom, you wrote on his certificate 'Thomas.' This boy I want to name Jack."

849. A young girl, seeing names like "Surrender" and "My Sin" on the perfume counter, timidly asked the saleswoman: "Don't you have any for a beginner?"

850. Many years ago, the Brown Hotel in Louisville, Kentucky, adopted the custom of naming a room in the hotel for each winner of the Kentucky Derby. There was a Zev Room, a Gallant Fox Room, a Whirlaway Room, etc. But after the 1946 Derby, the management decided to abandon the practice. The winner that year was Assault.

851. It happened on one of those lake cruises. Most of the women were on deck—most of the men were below.

A stiff breeze started to kick up—it began to get cold top-side.

"Hey," one of the women shouted down to the men, "have you got a mackintosh down there to keep three women warm up here?"

There was a slight pause, then, "No mackintosh, but there's a MacMillan down here who's willing to try!"

852. A producer asked a star who had just read his new film script, "How would you like to play the role?"

Replied the star: "Under an assumed name."

853. "Why on earth," a man demanded of his friend, "did you name your boy Reginald Clarence?"

"Because," explained the new father, "I want him to be a good fighter—and in our neighborhood, any boy named Reginald Clarence has got to fight!"

Old age

854. An Irishman was held up by a bandit with the usual demand: "Your money or your life!"

"Take my life," said the Irishman. "I'll be after saving my money for my old age."

855. "Doctor," said the old gentleman as he entered the physician's office, "I've got to have a blood test. I'm going to get married."

The doctor eyed him admiringly. "Married?" he asked. "How old are you anyway?"

"I'm 78."

"And the bride—?"

"Oh, she's only 22."

"22?" cried the doctor. "Why, that kind of disparity could be fatal!"

"Well," shrugged the old man philosophically, "if she dies, she dies!"

856. A man was being interviewed by a reporter on his 100th birthday. He answered all the questions put to him quite promptly, until the reporter asked him to what he attributed the fact that he'd reached such a milestone.

There was a rather long pause, and then the old man drawled, "Well, I guess the main reason I got to be 100 years old was that I was born in 1857."

857. Who said old age doesn't have its advantages—who but grandpa can sing while brushing his teeth.

858. "If you had your life to live over," the prominent octogenarian was asked, "do you think you'd make the same mistakes again?"

"Certainly," said the old man, "but I'd start sooner."

859. "I'll be 96 tomorrow," boasted the old man, "and I haven't got an enemy in the world."

"That's a beautiful thought," said the minister.

"Yup," the old man said, "I've outlived every darned one of them."

Origin

860. The novelist Sam Adams was once asked by a youngster to help get him admitted to Groton. "You haven't a chance," Adams told him, "unless your father and grandfather too, were Groton boys in their day."

The youngster reflected briefly, then asked, "Say, how did they get the darned place started?"

861. The origin of the bagpipes was being discussed, the representatives of different nations eagerly disclaiming responsibility for the instrument.

Finally an Irishman said, "Well, I'll tell you the truth about it.

The Irish invented them and sold them to the Scots as a joke; and the Scots haven't seen the joke yet!"

Overweight

862. *Financial Wizard:* "Where in heaven's name does all that grocery money go that I give you?"

Wife: "Stand sidewise and look in the mirror!"

863. "I believe you are thinner than the last time I saw you, Mrs. Kane. Are you taking treatments or dieting to lose weight?"

"Oh, no, I'm losing weight because of all the trouble I'm having with my new maid."

"Why don't you fire her?"

"I'm going to, just as soon as she worries me down another ten pounds."

864. A fat lady stepped on the scales. They were out of order, and the indicator stopped at 75 pounds.

A slightly inebriated bystander watched her intently. "My gosh!" he marveled, "she's hollow!"

865. A very stout man was walking on the promenade of a seaside town when he noticed a weighing machine with this notice: "I speak your weight."

He put a penny in the slot and stood on the platform. A voice spoke up: "One at a time, please."

866. A tramp had heard it said that obese ladies were a soft touch. He was told that they were so good-hearted, and would give unstintingly and without hesitation. Acting upon this information he approached a certain fat lady and put on his act.

"Lady," he entreated, "please have mercy on me. I haven't eaten for four days."

"My," gasped the overweight one, "I certainly wish I had your will power."

867. When Jones met his old friend Smith, whom he hadn't seen in six months, he was shocked by his altered appearance. His face looked haggard and drawn, his eyes had a glassy stare, and the way his clothes draped his frame spoke eloquently of a considerable loss of weight.

"Good heavens, man!" exclaimed Jones. "Have you been ill?"

"No," replied Smith wearily, "but my wife is on a reducing diet."

868. Advice to the thin: "Don't eat fast."
Advice to the fat: "Don't eat, fast."

869. "What'll you do, little girl, when you're as big as your mother?"
"Diet!"

Parent-Child

870. *Little girl to her mother:* "It isn't fair. At night you tell me I'm too little to stay up, and in the morning you say I'm too big to stay in bed."

871. Isn't it surprising that Mrs. Brown can never see any faults in her children?" said Mrs. Smith.

"Mothers never can," laughed Mr. Smith.

"What a silly thing to say. Just like a man. I'm sure I could see faults in our children—if they had any."

872. "Mama," asked 7-year-old Joyce, "what does trans-atlantic mean?"

"Across the Atlantic, of course," replied her mother. "Trans always means 'across.' "

"Then I suppose," continued little Joyce, "transparent means a cross parent."

873. An indignant mother asked her young son: "Why didn't you tell me you wanted to go fishing?"

"Because I wanted to go fishing," answered the son.

874. *Little boy:* "Give me ten cents' worth of castor oil, please."
Druggist: "The tasteless kind?"
Little boy: "No—it's for my father."

875. Two modern youngsters were discussing the subject of piggy banks.

"I think it's childish to save money that way," little Mary opined.

"I do, too," replied Annie. "And I believe also that it encourages children to become misers."

"And that's not the worst of it," rejoined Mary. "It turns parents into bank robbers."

876. Just returned from summer camp, little Bobby was enthusiastically describing the many diverting projects in which he had participated.

His mother smiled indulgently. "I guess after all, dear, you were rather glad to get back home, weren't you?" she ventured.

"Well, not 'specially," replied the youngster. "But some of the other fellows were—those that had dogs."

877. A lady who was most proud of her little boy's scientific knowledge wanted to show him off in front of her bridge club.

"Bobby," she asked, "what does it mean when steam comes out of the spout of the kettle?"

"It means," said Bobby, "that you are going to open one of Daddy's letters."

878. A foreigner once commented, "You Americans are a strange people. You devote only one day out of the year to your fathers and an entire week to pickles."

879. "Now, Willie, you must not be selfish. You must let your brother have the sled half the time."

"But, Mother," replied the lad, "I do. I have it going down the hill and he has it coming up."

880. A boy broke a dish, and went to his mother and said, "Mother, I did it, and I'm sorry. And I hope this will be the end of the matter."

Partnership

881. Two brothers became owners of a country house through a joint inheritance. One, a go-getter and social climber, spent more than he could afford to fill his half of the house with the last word in decorations and mechanical devices. The other brother left his half exactly as he had found it, and simply enjoyed himself on it.

"This is unfair," grumbled the first one. "You owe it to me to do

161

something with your part of the house, just as I have done with mine."

"Very well," said the brother, "I will do something with my half. I'll set it on fire."

And the story goes, he did.

882. The high-pressure salesman was giving a pitch to a small manufacturer. "I'm the best man in the business," he boasted. "Put me to work for you and you'll really go places!"

"That may be so," said the tired, overworked owner, "but anybody I hire has to start at the bottom. First you gotta be my partner."

883. John wanted desperately to open his own electric appliance shop, but lacked the necessary capital to start.

"Look," said one of his friends, "why don't you get a partner? For instance, I hear Frank Hastings is in the same boat as you. Why not sound him out?"

"No," came back John's reply. "I know Frank pretty well. He was once engaged to my wife."

"So what has that got to do with it?" asked the puzzled friend.

"Heck, man," snapped back John, "you don't suppose I would take a smarter man than I for a partner, do you?"

Peace

884. "Me father and a man named Mulligan have been fightin' fer twinty years, but now they've stopped."

"Why? Did they bury the hatchet?"

"No, they buried Mulligan."

885. *She:* "Why can't we live peacefully like the cat and dog there together on the hearth. They never fight."

He: "No, they don't; but tie them together and then see what happens."

Photography

886. *Photographer:* "Look pleasant, please. As soon as I snap this picture, you can resume your natural expression."

887. A young scientist was the inventor of a rocket projectile. He took it to the testing grounds out in the desert. It was set up, touched off, and flew straight up for hundreds of miles. When it reached the peak of its flight, a camera photographed the entire earth.

A few days later someone asked how the picture had come out. "Not so good," was the sad reply. "Somebody moved."

Pleasure

888. A guy who goes for the cup that cheers somewhat too much was finally cornered by his wife in a bar where he was dreamily contemplating a slug of whiskey. Being in a genial mood, he offered her a sip, but when she took it she gagged and sputtered, finally coming out with: "How can you ever drink that horrible stuff?"

"See, I told you," said the husband, "and all the while you thought I was having a good time!"

889. *He:* "I'm keeping a record of all the good times we've had together."

She: "Oh, a diary?"

He: "No, stubs in a checkbook."

Point of view

890. Walter Richard Sickert, the painter, and James McNeill Whistler were once printing etchings together, when Sickert accidentally dropped a copper plate. "How like you!" said Whistler. A few minutes later Whistler dropped one. "How unlike me!" he said.

891. The baby sardine saw its first submarine, and went swimming in terror to its mother. "Don't be frightened, darling," she reassured him, "it's only a can of people."

892. Two Americans were cast away on a desert island in the middle of the Pacific for some three years. One day they stepped to the shores of the island and stood gazing out onto the horizon. Suddenly, one spotted a bottle being washed ashore. He raced out into the surf and pulled it in. It was one of those new king-sized Coca-Cola bottles. He looked at it; then suddenly, a frightening realization crossed his mind. "Joe," he shrieked, "we've shrunk!"

POINT OF VIEW

893. A lecturer on "Success" was giving his views on the way to get along in business.

"The best advice I can give any young man starting out in the business world today," he began, "is always to remember that one has to begin at the bottom in order to reach the top."

He was interrupted by a young fellow in the audience. "That's not the way I'm going to succeed in my line," said he.

"It's true in every line," said the speaker. "What business are you going into?"

"I'm going to dig oil wells," said the young man.

"Well, even in that line it holds good," replied the lecturer. "The oil starts from the bottom."

894. William Dean Howells, novelist and editor, was talking to a very conceited fellow author. "You know," said the latter, "I get richer and richer, but all the same I think my work is falling off. My new work is not as good as my old."

"Oh, nonsense!" said Mr. Howells. "You write as well as you ever did. Your taste is improving, that's all."

895. A reporter once interviewed William Jennings Bryan at an early stage of the latter's career.

"Put this in your paper, son," said Bryan. "A man simply *can't* make a million dollars honestly."

Years later, when Bryan, by reason of one legitimate activity or another had managed to accumulate a fairly substantial fortune, the reporter, now himself an editor and up in the world, chanced upon the golden-voiced orator and reminded him: "Do you recall what you once told me about rich men?" he chided him. "I certainly do," replied Bryan. "I said, 'A man simply can't make *two* million dollars honestly.' "

896. A visitor to West Point noticed that all the names engraved on a famous battle monument were those of men in the Union Army, killed in action during the Civil War. "Say," he called to a passing cadet, "what is this?"

"A tribute to the marksmanship of the Confederacy, suh!" drawled the cadet.

897. It was his small daughter's first plane trip, and her father was anxious to get her reaction. Shortly after the take-off, he asked her how she liked flying.

"Fine, Daddy," she replied excitedly. "But when do we start getting smaller?"

898. "Darling," cooed the beaming wife, "I haven't told you before, but I only paid five hundred dollars for this series of beauty treatments, and after only three weeks I've been taken for Marilyn Monroe."

"You," corrected her husband, "have been take for five hundred dollars!"

899. The woman lion tamer had her beasts under perfect control. At her summons, the fiercest lion came meekly to her and took a piece of sugar out of her mouth. The circus crowd marveled—all except one man.

"Anybody could do that," he yelled from the audience.

"Would you dare to do it?" the ringmaster yelled back scornfully.

"Certainly," replied the man in the spectators' stand. "I can do it just as well as the lion can."

900. *Son:* "Dad, what does pro and con mean?"

Dad: "Well, son, pro is your convincing unanswerable argument, and con is the other fellow's stupid drivel."

901. *Teacher:* "What is the half of eight, Frank?"

Frank: "Which way, Teacher?"

Teacher: "What do you mean?"

Frank: "On top or sidewise?"

Teacher: "What difference does it make?"

Frank: "Well, the top half of eight is zero, but the half of eight sidewise is three."

902. *Milkman* (inducted into the Army) wrote back home from camp as follows: "I sure like this Army life. It's nice to lie in bed every morning until 5:30."

903. A farmer was engaged in putting up a building.

"What are you building?" asked an observer.

"Well," answered the farmer. "If I can rent it, it's a rustic cottage nestled 'neath two tall pines. If I can't, it's a cow shed."

165

904. *Mother:* "Didn't I tell you not to let that man come over to your apartment last night? You know how things like that worry me."

Daughter: "But I didn't. I went over to his apartment. Now let his mother do the worrying."

905. In a college town a student called at a boarding house to ask about rooms.

"And what do you charge for your rooms?" he asked.

"Five dollars up," was the reply.

"Yes, but I'm a student," he said, thinking the price a little high.

"That being the case," replied the landlady, who had had experience to fall back on, "the price is five dollars down."

906. Two little flies were strolling along the ceiling of a New York penthouse apartment. "You know," remarked the first little fly, "human beings are so silly."

"People are silly?" replied the second little fly. "How do you figure that?"

The first little fly shrugged his wings. "Just take a good look," he chirped. "They spend good money building a nice high ceiling, and then what do they do but walk on the floor."

907. A little watch, dissatisfied with being in a pocket, envied Big Ben, the great tower clock. "I wish I could be up there," said the little watch. "I could then serve the multitude." And suddenly the little watch had its wish. It was drawn up to the tower. But from below it was invisible. Its elevation had become its annihilation.

908. Two men, members of a religious order, wanted to smoke while walking in the garden. They agreed that each would ask his superior for permission.

The first one returned to find the second one smoking and complained indignantly: "I was refused!"

"What did you ask?" inquired the second one.

"I asked if I could smoke while meditating."

"Oh," said the other, blowing his smoke reflectively, "I asked if I could meditate while smoking!"

909. Two retired farmers, lounging on a street corner in Norfolk, Virginia, one day, were suddenly aroused by a runaway team that

166

came dashing towards them at breakneck speed. The driver, scared nearly to death, had abandoned his reins, and was awkwardly climbing out of the wagon at the rear end.

One of the farmers shouted, "Brother Johnson, sure as you're born, that runaway horse is a powerful and monstrous sight to behold."

Johnson, the driver, shook his head doubtfully, and then replied in a philosophic tone: "That depends very much on whether you're standing on the corner observing him, or you're on the other side of the tail-board of the wagon."

910. "I love to hear the alarm clock ring in the morning," said the man eating breakfast in a diner. "I can't understand people who curse it because it wakes them up. To me it is the symbol of being itself, the sign that the city is functioning again and that soon the streets and buildings will be filled with active participants."

"What eloquence!" said the guy sitting next to him. "Are you a poet?"

"No," said the man, "I'm a night watchman."

Police

911. Two men were traveling on a motorcycle on a windy, winter day. When it became too breezy for one, he stopped and put his overcoat on backwards to keep the wind from ballooning it away from him. A few miles further on, the motorcycle hit a tree, killing the driver and stunning the fellow with the reversed coat. Later, when the coroner visited the scene, he asked a rookie policeman standing nearby: "What happened?" "Well," the officer replied, "one of them was dead when I got here, and by the time I got the head of the other one straightened around, he was dead, too."

912. The candidate for the police force was being verbally examined.

"If you were by yourself in a police car, and were pursued by a desperate gang of criminals in another car doing forty miles an hour on a lonely road, what would you do?"

"Fifty," promptly replied the candidate.

POLITENESS

913. *Teacher:* "What's the greatest copper-producing country in the world?"

Student: "Ireland."

914. *News item in the Muscatine, Iowa, Journal and News-Tribune:* "Local police are puzzled over the finding of a car parked outside the Methodist Church containing a full case of Scotch whiskey. So far they have found no trace of the owner, but Captain Casey is diligently working on the case."

Politeness

915. Humorist Oliver Herford was on a crowded trolley one afternoon, holding his young nephew on his knees. A pretty young blonde boarded the car, stepped in front of them and reached for the strap.

Herford eyed her appreciatively. Then, nudging his nephew, he said, "My boy, why don't you get up and give the lady your seat?"

916. When a fussy German nobleman pushed his way into the British Embassy demanding to see the Ambassador, he was met with the polite request: "Please take a chair." "Young man!" stormed the German, "do you know who I am?" And he proceeded to pour out a string of imposing titles. The Ambassador's secretary looked up in well-simulated awe, and said, "In that case, sir, please take two chairs."

917. "I am glad to see you home, Johnny," said the father to his small son who had been away at school, but who was now home for his Christmas vacation. "How are you getting on at school?"

"Fine," said Johnny. "I have learned to say 'Thank you' and 'If you please' in French."

"Good," said the father. "That's more than you ever learned to say in English."

918. The old man neglected to assist his wife onto the streetcar.

"John," she said, "you are not so gallant as when you were a boy."

"No," was the answer, "and you are not so buoyant as when you were a gal."

Politics

919. A public office holder died and at his funeral an office seeker approached the Governor of the state and asked if he could have the dead man's place.

"I have no objection," said the Governor, "if the undertaker is willing."

920. "There are hundreds of ways to make money," said a politician, "but only one honest way."

"What's that?" asked his opponent in debate.

"Aha," retorted the first, "I thought you wouldn't know."

921. Politics makes strange postmasters.

922. Churchill was once asked the qualifications for a politician. Without hesitation, he answered:

"It is the ability to foretell what will happen tomorrow, next month, next year—and to explain afterward why it did not happen."

923. A political office in a small New Hampshire town was vacant. The office paid $250 a year and there was keen competition for it. One of the candidates, Ezekiel Hicks, was a shrewd old fellow, and a neat campaign fund was turned over to him. To the astonishment of all, however, he was defeated.

"I can't account for it," said one of the leaders of Hicks' party, gloomily.

"With all that money we should have won. How did you lay it out, Ezekiel?"

"Well," said Ezekiel, slowly milking his chin whiskers, "ye see thet office only pays $250 a year salary, an' I didn't see no sense in paying $900 out to get the office, so I bought a little truck farm instead."

924. Two political officeholders were dourly discussing the behavior of one of the faithful who had been put on the county pay roll.

"I thought," said one politico, "when we rewarded him with that soft job down at the county jail, he would be satisfied. Why, about all that bird has to do is tear a page off the office calendar each month!"

The other sighed. "I know," he rejoined, "but now he's starting to complain that February is such a short month!"

925. During a political campaign in a New England state, a man who had been elected Senator several times, and who thought that therefore he had a lifelong right to the office, was addressing a meeting:

"Fellow citizens," he began, "I stand before you on my record. If you had a hired man who had worked for you for a long time, would you not think it right for you to go right on employing him?"

At this point, a voice from the rear of the hall broke in with:

"Not if he got to thinking that he owned the whole darned farm."

926. The farmer had gone and had himself elected to the legislature. After he'd served in the law-making body for thirty days, he came home for a week end.

"Martha," he said to his wife, "I've discovered one thing—it's the first insane asylum I've ever seen or heard of that's run by the inmates."

927. A real philosopher was the candidate who was defeated in the election and said he was glad he was defeated because he wouldn't have to keep all the promises he had made during his campaign.

928. It was during the Parliamentary election of 1857, and the author Thackeray was contesting for the Oxford seat against a Mr. Cardwell. A few days before the election, the contestants met in the street and stopped for a chat. In taking leave, Thackeray said to his opponent: "Well, good day to you, and may the best man win!"

"I hope not," said Cardwell, with witty politeness.

929. Two Negroes attended a political meeting where a candidate was making a speech.

In a few minutes one said to the other, "Who's that man?"

"I don't know," was the reply, "but he sure does recommend himself."

930. A local politician decided to give the Negro who showed the best reason for being a Republican the generous reward of a fine, fat turkey.

One said he was a Republican because that party had set the slaves free. The second said he was a Republican because of its tariff policy, but the turkey went to the third who said:

"I'm a Republican because I want that turkey."

931. A politician was being interviewed by the press. One reporter asked, "Do you feel that you have influenced public opinion, sir?"

"No," he answered. "Public opinion is something like a mule I once owned. In order to keep up the appearance of being the driver, I had to watch the way he was going and follow closely."

932. Three men were arguing over whose profession was first established on earth. Said the surgeon, "The Bible says that Eve was made by carving a rib out of Adam. I guess that makes mine the oldest profession."

Said the engineer, "Not at all. An engineering job came before that. In six days the Earth was created out of chaos—and that was an engineer's job."

Said the politician, "Yes, but who created the chaos?"

933. A man ran for sheriff in a small western town, but he received a sound beating at the polls, getting only a mere 125 votes out of a total of 32,000.

The next day he walked down the main street with two guns hanging from his belt.

Confronted by a group of puzzled and indignant citizens, he was asked, "See here, you have no right to carry those guns. After all you aren't the one who was elected sheriff."

"Listen here, my friends," he said, "a man with no more friends than I've got in this community needs to carry a gun."

934. The politician's name had been bandied about quite frequently in the press, and he was complaining to a friend about it.

"But I don't see anything wrong in that," declared the friend. "You're getting a lot of publicity out of it."

The politician couldn't see it that way at all. "But half those lies they tell about me aren't true," he protested.

935. "Dad, are political plums raised from seed?"

"No, my boy—by expert grafting."

171

PRACTICABILITY

936. It was during the Democratic convention in Baltimore, and there had been an enthusiastic banquet at one of the hotels. The next morning a prominent Republican met one of the Democratic delegates and said:

"I understand there were some Republicans at the dinner last night."

"Oh, yes," replied the Democrat, kindly, "one waited on me."

937. "I am out of politics for good," announced the political leader.

"Whose?" questioned the cub reporter.

938. A candidate for sheriff called upon a minister to ask his support at the up-coming election.

"Before I give you my decision," said the minister, "let me ask a question. Do you partake of intoxicating beverages?"

"Before I reply," said the candidate, cautiously, "is this an inquiry or an invitation?"

939. *Teacher:* "Johnny, what are the three great American parties?"
Johnny: "Democratic, Republican and cocktail."

940. "I just got out of prison this morning," a traveler told his seat companion as they were riding along on a train. "It's going to be tough facing old friends."

"I can sympathize with you," said the other, "I'm just getting home from Congress."

941. *Voter:* "Why, I wouldn't vote for you if you were St. Peter himself."

Candidate: "If I were St. Peter, you couldn't vote for me. You wouldn't be in my district."

Practicability

942. The Reverend Frederick Brown Harris, chaplain of the U.S. Senate, was on a return flight from a religious convocation in Honolulu when one of the plane's engines conked out. The pretty hostess bustled about, reassuring the passengers, but Chaplain Harris felt she needed a little reassurance herself.

"Nothing can happen to this plane," he told her. "There are eight bishops aboard."

The hostess forced a smile and said she would relay the comforting news to the captain. In a few minutes she was back, looking uncertain.

"I told the captain," she said. "He said he would rather have four engines."

943. G. K. Chesterton and several other literary figures were asked one evening what book they would prefer to have with them if stranded on a desert isle.

"The complete works of Shakespeare," said one writer without hesitation.

"I'd choose the Bible," interrupted another.

"How about you?" someone asked Chesterton.

"I would choose," replied the portly author, *"Thomas's Guide to Practical Shipbuilding."*

Prayer

944. A woman churchgoer stopped outside to chat with a friend after services. Suddenly, she remembered she had left her purse on the seat. When she returned, it was gone. She sought out the minister and found that he had picked it up.

"I felt that I had better hold it," he explained. "You know, there are some in the congregation of such simple faith as to believe it might be an answer to a prayer."

945. The five-year-old daughter in the minister's family had been, as she thought, unjustly disciplined. When at last it came bedtime she knelt as usual for prayer at her mother's knee. Earnestly she prayed:

"O, Lord, please make all the bad people good; and, Lord, if it's possible, please make all the good people nice."

946. "I'm not saying she's a bad cook," said the boy friend, "but I know now why her family prays before every meal."

947. "Do you say your prayers every night, Judy?" asked the minister.

"Oh, no; Mummy says them for me," was Judy's reply.

"Indeed; and what does she say?" queried the gentleman of the cloth.

"She says, 'Thank God you're in bed.' "

948. A little boy was saying his bedtime prayers in a low voice. "I can't hear you, dear," whispered his mother.

"I wasn't talking to you," was the firm and prompt reply.

949. Little Gerald, climbing a tree, began falling toward the ground. "Oh, Lord, save me, save me," he whispered. Then a pause. Finally, "Never mind, Lord, my pants just caught on a branch."

950. A sailor's wife approached the pastor of her church just as he was stepping into the pulpit, and handed him a note. The note said: "Harold Peat, having gone to sea, his wife requests the congregation to pray for his safety."

The minister hastily unfolded the note, and with his mind on the sermon he was about to make, he announced: "Harold Peat, having gone to see his wife, requests the congregation to pray for his safety."

951. A British soldier one night was caught creeping back to his quarters from the nearby woods. Taken before his commanding officer, he was charged with holding communications with the enemy. The man pleaded he had gone into the woods to pray by himself. That was his only defense.

"Down on your knees and pray now!" roared the officer. "You never needed it so much!"

Expecting immediate death, the soldier knelt and poured out his soul in eloquent prayer.

"You may go," said the officer simply, when he had finished. "I believe your story. If you hadn't drilled often, you could not do so well at review."

952. "Do you say prayers before eating?" the minister asked the little boy. "No, sir, I don't need to," replied the child. "My mother's a good cook."

953. Junior fully expected a long wait for his food when his father asked the minister to say grace at the table. To his surprise, the prayer was brief.

Looking up at the guest with a grin, Junior said approvingly, "You don't pray so long when you're hungry, do you!"

174

Preaching

954. The new minister's car broke down just after the morning service, so on Monday he drove it to the local garage for repairs. "I hope you'll go a little easy on the price," he told the mechanic. "After all I'm just a poor preacher."

"I know it," came the answer. "I heard you preach."

955. A clergyman, called suddenly away and unable to officiate at the Christmas services in his own church, intrusted his new curate with the duty. On his return home, he asked his wife what she thought of the curate's sermon.

"The poorest I ever heard," she confided. "Nothing in it at all."

Later in the day, the clergyman, meeting his curate, asked him how he had got along.

"Excellently, excellently, sir," he replied. "I didn't have time to prepare anything myself, so I preached one of your sermons."

956. The clergyman was preparing his sermon as his small daughter watched.

"Daddy," she asked, "does God tell you what to say?"

"Of course, honey," he answered, "why do you ask?"

"Oh," was her reply. "Then why do you scratch some of it out?"

957. A sexton, cleaning up the pulpit after Sunday service, took a peek at the preacher's manuscript. Along the left margin were instructions such as: "Pause here," "Wipe brow here," "Use angry fist gesture," "Look upward."

Near the end was a long paragraph of texts, opposite which the preacher had marked in large capital letters: "ARGUMENT WEAK HERE. YELL LIKE HELL!"

958. A preacher, being considered for a call to Minneapolis, was asked to preach a trial sermon to the new congregation. He unfortunately chose a text from St. Paul—and that was it. The whole thing was called off.

959. Church services were over, and three prominent members walked home together, discussing the sermon.

"I tell you," said one enthusiastically, "our minister can dive deeper into the truth than any other preacher I ever heard."

"Yes," said the second man, "and he stays under longer."

"Yes," said the third, "and comes up drier."

960. A wealthy farmer decided to go to church on Christmas. After the services, he approached the minister with great enthusiasm. "Reverend," he said, "that was a damned good sermon you gave. Damned good!"

"I am satisfied," replied the minister, "that you were pleased with it, but it would be nice if you didn't use those terms in expressing yourself."

"I can't help it," responded the farmer. "I still think it was a damned good sermon, and I was so impressed that I put a one hundred dollar bill in the collection basket.

"The hell you did," gulped the over-excited minister.

961. "Brothers," said the colored preacher, "the subject of my sermon today is 'Liars.' How many in this congregation have read the 69th chapter of Matthew?" Nearly every hand went up.

"You are the very people I want to preach to," the reverend said. "There is no such chapter."

962. The pastor of a little church in Vermont was famous for the fact that every one of his sermons lasted exactly twenty-two minutes. Then, one unfortunate Sunday, the sermon lasted three-quarters of an hour.

At dinner his mortified wife asked him what had gone wrong.

"It was just one of those things," the pastor answered moodily. "My secret device was to slide a cough drop under my tongue just before beginning the sermon. It always melted in exactly twenty-two minutes. That way I knew when it was time to stop. This morning I was talking over forty minutes before I realized my cough drop was a suspender button."

963. A young clergyman, after preaching a funeral sermon, wished to invite the mourners to view the remains, but became confused and exclaimed:

"We will now pass around the bier."

964. A preacher once asked Joseph Jefferson, the actor, "Why is it you always have a great audience, while I always have only a small one?"

Jefferson answered, "I act as if I believe in what I say, while you preach as if you did not believe what you preached."

965. A minister and a doctor joked with each other about their respective professions. When the minister inquired about the health of an elderly member of his congregation, whom he knew the doctor was attending, the physician put on a very serious mien.

"Poor Thompson," he sighed. "To tell you the truth, he needs your help more than mine."

"Is it that bad?" inquired the minister with concern.

"Yes," replied the doctor, shaking his head. "I've been trying to get him to take a nap every day and he just won't do it."

Precaution

966. The new commander, inspecting the camp's water supply, asked what was being done about contamination.

"Well, sir," said the non-com, "we boil it first."

"Fine," nodded the general.

"Then we filter it," said the sergeant.

The general nodded approvingly.

"And then," continued the sergeant, "just to play safe, we drink beer."

967. *His Honor* (sternly): "Well, what's your alibi for speeding sixty miles an hour through the residential section?"

Meek Defendant: "I had just heard, your Honor, that the ladies of my wife's church were holding a rummage sale, and I was hurrying home to save my other pair of pants."

968. A couple of coeds were talking about their future plans. One remarked that she intended to get an airline hostess job. "That way," she said, "I'll meet lots of men."

"Might be an idea," agreed her companion, "but wouldn't you meet as many men doing something else?"

The first gal shrugged, "Could be," she admitted, "but not strapped down."

969. "I see by the papers that your creditors are pressing you for payment," said a friend to the Senator.

"Yes," replied the veteran legislator, "I arranged that. In this era of investigations I want it made perfectly clear that I haven't more than enough money than to cover my current expenses."

970. He had had at least one too many when he walked up to the sergeant's desk.

"Offisher, you'd better lock me up," he pleaded. "Jush hit my wife on the head with a bottle."

"Did you kill her?" demanded the officer.

"Don't think so. Thash why I want to be locked up."

971. "Well, my dear," said a businessman who had married his secretary, "I must get someone to replace you at the office."

"I've been thinking of that," replied the bride. "My cousin is just leaving school."

"What's her name?"

"George Burns," said the bride.

Prejudice

972. A fashionable woman thought she would like to share some hospitality with a few soldiers at a camp nearby. So in a letter to the Commanding Officer, she invited two men to dine at her house the following evening. But, she specified, on no account must they be Jews.

The next night two colored soldiers were shown into the drawing room at the appointed time. Somewhat embarrassed, the hostess asked, "Are you certain there hasn't been some mistake?"

"No, ma'am," replied one of the soldiers. "Colonel Cohen never makes a mistake!"

973. A year or two before his death, Booker T. Washington made an address in a small town in Georgia. When he had finished, an old Confederate soldier, white-haired and white-moustached, pushed forward to the platform, his face aglow with enthusiasm.

"Doctor Washington," he declared, "I want to do now what I never thought I'd be doing—I want to clasp your hand and pledge you my support for the great work you are doing. And furthermore, I want to tell you this: that was the best speech I ever heard in my life and you are the greatest man in this country today!"

"I am afraid you do me too much honor," said Washington. "Wouldn't you regard Col. Roosevelt as the greatest man we have?"

"Huh!" exploded the Southerner. "I've had no use for him since he invited you to eat a meal with him at the White House."

Preparedness

974. Two little girls were discussing their families. "Why does your grandmother read the Bible so much?" asked one.

Replied the other: "I think she's cramming for her finals."

975. A business executive stopped his car each morning as he passed a state institution for the mentally ill. In the yard one of the inmates was continually going through the motions of winding up and pitching an imaginary baseball.

Finally one of his friends asked, "Why do you stop each morning and watch that unfortunate fellow go through his act?"

"Well," he answered, "if things keep going the way they are, I'll be in there catching for that guy, and I want to get on to his curves."

976. The car screeched to a stop in front of the hospital emergency entrance. An excited young man jumped out, took the steps three at a time, and went spinning through the revolving door.

"What seems to be the trouble, sir?" asked the anxious nurse.

"My wife's going to have a baby."

"Well, bring her in."

"Oh, the baby isn't due for another month. I'm just timing myself to see how fast I can get here!"

Prescription

977. In a midwestern medical school, a student was having a hard time with a number of questions which proved too difficult for him.

One of the questions was: "How would you go about inducing copious perspiration?"

This was his answer: "I would have the patient take the medical examination in this college."

978. A professor at medical school asked one of the students how much of a certain drug should be administered to a patient, and received the following reply: "Five grains."

A few minutes later, the same student raised his hand. "Professor," he said, "I'd like to change my answer to that previous question."

The professor looked at his watch and replied, "I'm sorry, young man, but it's too late. Your patient has been dead for forty seconds."

Professional fees

979. Newell Dwight Hillis, the famous preacher, once made use of the services of a young physician who was not an ardent church goer. But the doctor never sent a bill.

"Look here, Doctor," Hillis said finally, "I have to know how much I owe you."

After thinking it over, the doctor said, "I'll tell you Hillis, I hear you're a pretty fair preacher, and you seem to think I'm a pretty good doctor. I'll make a bargain with you. I'll do all I can to keep you out of heaven, if you'll do all you can to keep me out of hell, and it won't cost either of us a cent."

980. A famous surgeon was in the habit of charging his patients in accordance with their means. So he sent a bill for $2000 to one of his patients, who happened to be a very wealthy manufacturer, for a delicate operation which he had performed. The businessman was indignant at what he thought was an outrageous fee.

"It was up to you," said the surgeon. "You could have gone to another surgeon who would have operated for half the amount—and that would have been cheaper for your heirs, too."

981. Though she'd never had much truck with doctors, Aunt Maisie got through the examination and treatment pretty well. As she was leaving, the physician said, "I'd like to see you again in two weeks." She kept the appointment, but was indignant at the end of the month to find the doctor had charged her for both visits.

"The second one was your idea," she told him over the phone. *"You* wanted to see *me."*

982. A rich but ignorant Englishman once went to the famous painter Turner and ordered a painting. When it was finished he refused to pay the price that the painter demanded.

"What!" he said, "all that money for a square yard of canvas and a little paint!"

"Oh," replied Turner, "if it's just paint and canvas that you want, here's a half-used tube, and over in the corner you will find some canvas. I won't charge you for them."

983. *Wife* (to husband returning from doctor): "Well, did the doctor find out what you had?"

Husband: "Almost. I had $22, and he charged me $20."

984. The minister had just married a Negro couple, and the bridegroom asked what the fee was. "Oh, pay me whatever you think she is worth to you," said the minister. The young man looked long and lovingly at his bride, then, rolling his eyes, he said: "Lawd, suh, you has done ruined me fo' life; yo' sho' has."

985. "That was a close one," admitted the doctor. "If you hadn't such a strong constitution, I doubt very much if I would have been able to pull you through."

"Then just remember that, won't you, Doctor, when the time comes for you to make out your bill."

986. Bringing babies safely into the world was a prominent physician's specialty. He always scaled his fees to the client's capacity to pay. After delivering a son and heir for a socially prominent and rich lady he was rather amazed to hear the woman say:

"I realize, of course, that your services have been the sort that cannot be fully paid for. However, I hope you will accept as a token of appreciation from me this purse which I myself have embroidered."

The physician wasn't in the mood to let her off that easy.

"Fees of the physician," he said rather coldly, "are usually paid in money, not merely in gratitude. A doctor must eat, too, you know."

"What is your fee?" she asked.

"Three hundred dollars," he replied.

Whereupon the lady opened the purse she had brought as a token of her appreciation, took out five one hundred dollar bills, kept two, and gave three to the physician.

987. A lawyer went to a judge to complain that the client for whom he had just won a case had refused to pay his fee.

"Did you present your request in writing?" asked the judge.

"Yes, I did, sir," replied the lawyer.

"And what did he have to say?" continued the judge.

"He told me to go to the devil," answered the lawyer.

"Then what did you do?"

"Well, then I came straight to you, sir."

988. Doctors are wonderful. Mine certainly put me on my feet. The bill was so large I had to sell the car.

989. *Filling station attendant:* "Boss, your doctor's in here with a flat tire."

Proprietor: "Swell! Diagnose the trouble as a puncture wound resulting in a prolapsus of the perimetric membrane and prescribe plastic surgery to be followed by the administration of violent flatulents, and charge him accordingly. That's what he has been doing to me for years."

990. A certain clergyman used to tell of a young couple who came to his house late one evening to be married. When the minister had performed the ceremony, the groom took him aside, and whispered:

"I am sorry, sir, I have no money to pay your fee, but if you will take me down into your cellar, I will show you how to fix your electric light meter so that it won't register."

991. "I wish the boys wouldn't call me Big Bill."

"Well, why not?"

"Well, you know, those college nicknames stick, and I'm studying to be a doctor."

992. Igor Stravinsky was offered $4000 to compose the music for a Hollywood film. "It is not enough," he said.

"It's what we paid your predecessor," replied the producer.

"My predecessor had talent," responded Stravinsky. "I have not. So for me the work is more difficult."

993. *Young doctor:* "Why do you always ask your patients what they have for dinner?"

Old doctor: "It's a most important question, for according to their menus I make out my bills."

994. *Patient:* "How can I ever repay you for your kindness to me?"

Doctor: "By check, money order, or cash."

Proof

995. An American who put his name down for a seat in the first rocket ship to Mars wanted to insure himself with a British company. His proposal was accepted, the premium being that for normal flying plus fifty per cent. A special clause was inserted in the policy, stating: "Non-return is no proof of death."

996. John Erskine, the author, was once invited to give a lecture at the University of Chattanooga. President Alexander Guerry of the University went down to the station to meet him. Said Dr. Guerry to Dr. Erskine: "I asked one gentleman if he was Dr. Erskine and he said emphatically, 'I should say not.' I asked a second man and he said, 'I wish I were.' That shows that at least one man has read your books."

"That it does," said Dr. Erskine. "But which one?"

997. "I just got an order for forty thousand dollars," boasted one salesman to another.

"You're kidding," countered the other.

"I sure am not!" insisted the first. "I can prove it to you. Here's the cancellation."

998. In a village election in rock-ribbed Republican Vermont, one Democratic vote was discovered before the tabulation had been completed. Election officials stopped to ponder this marvel, then decided to complete the count. Another Democratic vote turned up.

"That settles it," said one official. "That dad-burned fool voted twice."

Psychiatry

999. A sad-looking character was shown into the office of a prominent psychiatrist. "I've lost all desire to go on, Doctor. Life has become too hectic, too confused."

"Yes," said the doctor, clucking sympathetically. "I understand. We all have our problems. You'll need a year or two of treatments at $50 a week."

There was a pause. "Well, that solves your problem, Doc. Now about mine?"

1000. "Now, tell me about the dream you had," the psychiatrist said to the young lady on the couch.

"Well, I dreamed I was walking down the street with nothing on but a hat."

"And you were embarrassed?" suggested the doctor.

"Indeed I was!" agreed the lady. "It was last year's hat."

1001. A farmer brought his brother to see the psychiatrist. "My brother," he explained, "thinks he's a hen."

"Really," said the psychiatrist, "and how long has he been thinking on those lines?"

"For about four months," replied the farmer.

"And you did nothing about it?"

"No, doctor."

"That's too bad. Why in the name of all that's reasonable didn't you bring him to see me sooner?"

"Well, to tell you the truth, doctor, we needed the eggs."

1002. Because of his refusal to eat, the frantic mother had taken her little son to the great psychiatrist, who coaxed the boy with every conceivable goody in vain. Finally he said, "What would you like to eat?"

"Worms," was the calm reply.

Not to be outdone, the medico sent his nurse out for a plate full of the wrigglers. "Here," he barked to the boy.

"I want them fried," came the answer.

The nurse did and returned with the plate.

"I only want one," said the food hater.

The doctor got rid of all but one. "Now," he exploded, "eat!"

The boy protested, "You eat half."

The doc did, then he dangled the remaining half in the little fellow's face. The boy burst into loud tears.

"What's the matter now?" yelled the infuriated medic.

"You ate my half," the little boy wailed.

1003. The attractive woman psychiatrist was attending a convention. At one of the lectures the man sitting next to her began to pinch her. Annoyed, she was about to give him an angry retort, when she changed her mind.

"Why should I get angry?" she decided. "After all—it's his problem."

1004. A man was consulting a psychiatrist. Among other questions, the doctor asked: "Are you troubled by improper thoughts?"

"Why, no," answered the patient. "To tell the truth, doctor, I rather enjoy them!"

1005. A young psychoanalyst was telling an older colleague about his troubles in getting intelligent responses from his patients. "Suppose you ask me some of your questions," the older analyst suggested.

"Well, my first question is, what is it that wears a skirt and from whose lips comes pleasure?"

"A Scot blowing a bagpipe," the veteran answered.

"Right," said the younger one. "Now, what is it that has smooth curves and at unexpected moments becomes uncontrollable?"

"Bob Feller's pitching."

"Right! What do you think of when two arms slip around your shoulder?"

"Why, a football tackle," replied the veteran.

"Right," said the young doctor. "All your answers were amazingly correct. But you'd be surprised at the silly answers I keep getting!"

1006. The psychiatrist married a very ugly woman. "I know," he told friends, "she's ugly, she has a bad figure, she's cross-eyed, and not very bright—but, boy, what nightmares she has!"

1007. One night, an eminent alienist found himself standing at the wrong end of a large pistol. He was shocked when he recognized the thug who was holding him up.

"Look here," he protested. "Don't you know me? I'm your benefactor. Don't you remember I once saved you from the electric chair by proving you were crazy?"

The stick-up man laughed a hearty laugh. "Sure I remember you! And ain't holding up your benefactor a crazy thing to do?"

1008. One thing a woman likes about visiting a psychiatrist: she can lie when asked her age.

1009. *Herb Shriner:* "One of the questions those Army psychiatrists always asked us was, did we like girls? We always said yes, but they never gave us any."

1010. The school authorities were very concerned about little Albert. He drew pictures of black cows, black houses, black dogs—and one day he drew a black landscape with black waves breaking on a dark beach.

They investigated his home life—and found nothing there to depress him. They called in a psychiatrist—and the most careful tests failed to show any manic-depressive tendencies. Finally they discovered the reason. He'd lost all his crayons except the black one.

1011. *Secretary to psychiatrist:* "There's a man outside who says he has a dual personality."

Psychiatrist: "Tell him to go chase himself."

Public speaking

1012. Some people don't have much to say, but you have to listen so long to find it out.

1013. Two handsomely minked ladies accosted Lewis Browne, famous lecturer and author, in a New York theatre lobby one matinee afternoon and asked: "Do you lecture?"

"Yes," replied Mr. Browne.

"Oh, did you lecture yesterday morning at Town Hall?"

"Yes."

"Oh, we thought we recognized you. We were there. Oh, you were just won-der-ful won-der-ful! What's your name?"

1014. Mark Twain was once called upon to respond to the toast, "Literature."

"Ladies and gentlemen," he began, in his unforgettable drawl, "I am sorry to say that Literature is in a pretty bad way. Shakespeare is dead and gone. Milton has been gathered unto his fathers. Tennyson is no longer with us, and, ladies and gentlemen, I am not feeling very well myself!"

With that, he sat down.

186

1015. The speaker was being interrupted continually by a voice from the gallery calling: "Speak up, sir! Speak up, sir!"

"I am speaking up," retorted the lecturer, at last, "and I utterly decline to speak down to the level of the ill-mannered person in the gallery."

1016. Once, when called upon to speak at a public gathering, the late King George VI, then Duke of York, told his audience that he had read somewhere that the Royal Family were "obvious" persons. He wasn't quite sure what the expression meant, so he looked it up in the dictionary and found one of the definitions to be "goes without saying." He further stated that on the occasion in question he would like to be "obvious" and "go without saying," and with that he sat down.

1017. Called on for an impromptu speech at a dinner one night a Yale graduate bethought himself of his alma mater and lauded her by proclaiming that the "Y" stood for youth, when all might enjoy the benefits of college; the "A" for the appreciation for all the finer things which college makes possible; the "L" for that loyalty from which all sincere endeavor stems. After about an hour of all this he ended with "E" which he said stood for the efficiency of the graduates of Old Eli.

Out in the audience, one drowsing listener murmured to his neighbor, "Thank God he didn't attend the Massachusetts Institute of Technology."

1018. Booth Tarkington, the author, was once asked to act as master of ceremonies at the burial service of a fellow author.

"Where is he going to be buried?" he inquired.

"He is going to be cremated," was the answer.

"Well, if that's it, you don't want a master of ceremonies," declared Tarkington. "What you want is a toastmaster."

1019. It is said that a man once shot an after-dinner speaker who talked too much and too long.

Immediately after the deed, the man took himself to the sheriff's office, and said:

"I just killed an after-dinner orator."

The sheriff replied:

"You are in the wrong place. You want to go to the game warden's office. You collect the bounty there."

1020. William Allen White, the famous Kansas editor, was once subjected to one of those toastmasters who insist upon demonstrating their own eloquence before giving the speaker of the evening a chance. The toastmaster delivered himself of a long drawn out address and then continued on with an elaborate introduction.

At last White had his opportunity. "Sometimes," he began, "I like to lapse into the field of statistical analysis. At the moment, I am wondering about the disposition of toastmasters, and it occurs to me that if all the toastmasters in the world were laid end to end—it would be a wonderfully good idea."

1021. General Dwight D. Eisenhower, speaking at the National Press Club, told his audience that he regretted he was not more of an orator.

"It reminds me of my boyhood days on a Kansas farm," Ike related. "An old farmer had a cow that we wanted to buy. We went over to visit him and asked about the cow's pedigree. The old farmer didn't know what pedigree meant, so we asked him about the cow's butterfat production. He told us that he hadn't any idea what it was. Finally we asked him if he knew how many pounds of milk the cow produced each year.

"The farmer shook his head and said: 'I don't know. But she's an honest old cow and she'll give you all the milk she has!' "

1022. On his return home from a meeting, the fond wife asked her husband, "How was your talk tonight?"

"Which one," he retorted, "the one I was going to give, the one I did give, or the one I delivered so brilliantly to myself on the way home in the car?"

1023. The chairman of the dinner, who tipped the scales at 220, mopped his brow and sank into his chair. The guest of honor jumped to his feet. "Gentlemen," he cried, "they tell a lovely fable in my country that when a baby is born, its guardian angel bestows upon it a kiss. If the kiss is on the brow, the child is destined to be an intellectual; on the eyes, it will be a great beauty; if it is on the fingers, he will be a great artist. Now I am not in a position to tell you where

188

the angel kissed our presiding officer, but you'll have to admit he makes a wonderful chairman."

1024. *At a banquet:* "Well, did they like your speech after the dinner?"

"Rather! When I sat down everybody said it was the best thing I'd ever done."

1025. The important man was about ready for his speech, when a news photographer was observed jockeying for a vantage point for an action shot. The chairman, fearing that the speaker would be annoyed, called the photographer and said: "Don't take his picture while he is speaking. Shoot him before he starts."

1026. A reporter stopped a hurrying diplomat and asked him what he thought about a then current international problem.

"Please don't bother me," snapped back the diplomat impatiently. "I'm on my way to make a speech and this is no time to ask me to think."

1027. I am like the man who was boiling a pot of coffee and frizzling some bacon over a little fire that he made on the prairie. The fire caught the grass of the prairie, and the man had to run along behind to keep the skillet over the blazing grass, and by the time he had his bacon done he was two miles away from the pot of coffee.

1028. The long-winded lecturer had been holding forth for over an hour, except for brief pauses from time to time to gulp a hasty drink of water. Finally, during one such intermission, an old man in the audience leaned toward his neighbor and announced in an audible whisper: "First time I ever saw a windmill run by water!"

1029. *Toastmaster:* "What is the hardest part of your work as a lecturer?"

Lecturer: "As a rule the hardest part of my work is waking up the audience after the man that introduces me has concluded his remarks."

1030. "You have a marvelous gift for oratory," said a reporter to George Bernard Shaw. "How did you develop it?" Replied Shaw:

PUNCTUALITY

"I learned to speak as men learn to skate or cycle, by doggedly making a fool of myself until I got used to it."

Punctuality

1031. "What are you doing on Sunday?" the boss asked his secretary one Friday evening.

"Oh, nothing," replied the girl, expecting an invitation.

"In that case," said the boss, "I hope you will be here *punctually* on Monday morning."

1032. *Husband* (shouting upstairs to wife): "For the last time, Mary, are you coming?"

Wife: "Haven't I been telling you for the last hour that I'll be down in a minute."

1033. It was so tough for Joe to get up mornings that he went to his doctor, who prescribed a pill. Joe took the pill, slept well, and was awake before he heard the alarm clock. He dressed and ate breakfast leisurely. Later he strolled into the office and up to the boss, saying:

"I didn't have a bit of trouble getting up this morning."

"That's good," replied the boss, "but where were you yesterday?"

1034. *Office Manager* (to new employe): "You should have been here at nine o'clock."

New employe: "Why, what happened?"

Punishment

1035. Little Bobby ran to his mother sobbing as though his heart would break.

"What's the matter, Bobby?" she asked.

"Daddy was hanging up a picture and dropped it on his toe."

"Why, that's nothing to cry about; you should laugh at that."

"I did," sobbed Bobby.

1036. An irate visitor darted angrily up to the beekeeper and complained:

"One of your bees just stung me, and I want you to do something about it."

The beekeeper answered soothingly: "Certainly, madam, just show me which bee it was and I'll have it punished."

1037. *Judge:* The prisoner is sentenced to a fine of one hundred dollars and seven days' imprisonment.

Prisoner: Judge, I wish you could reverse your sentence.

Judge: Very good then: seven dollars fine and a hundred years' imprisonment.

Recommendation

1038. "I hope you've enjoyed your stay here," said the proprietor of a country resort to a departing guest, "and that you will recommend our place to others."

"Well," said the departing guest, "I wouldn't send my enemies here, because it isn't bad enough; and on the other hand, I wouldn't send my friends here, because it isn't good enough."

1039. A certain workingman had been employed for some time as gardener on a large estate. He had finally been dismissed because of his dishonesty. Feeling sorry for the man's wife and family, his employer gave him a letter of recommendation, worded as follows:

"I hereby certify that the bearer has been my gardener for over two years, and during that time he has gotten more out of my garden than any man I ever employed."

Religion

1040. Two ministers of different faiths were the best of friends, although they often disagreed on religious questions. One day they had been arguing, a little more heatedly than usual, on some theological point, when one of them said, "That's all right. We'll just agree to disagree. The thing that counts is that we're both doing the Lord's work, you in your way and I in His."

1041. A Roman Catholic priest was showing Charles W. Gilkey, formerly dean of the chapel, University of Chicago, through the new Church of St. Thomas. Finally, they came to the place where the priests lived. Dean Gilkey looked on it with envious eyes. "It's better than our parsonage," he said.

With a twinkle, Father Shannon replied: "You Protestants have better halves; you surely would not begrudge us better quarters."

1042. Al Smith, when governor of the State of New York, was one of a party of twenty convivials at a mid-winter week end party at the home of a friend in the mountains of New Hampshire. While a tremendous place in the summertime, in the winter it was a pretty lonely spot. The place was opened by the host especially for this occasion. On Sunday, Al Smith and two other Catholics in the party got up at four-thirty in the morning to drive a full twenty miles to attend six o'clock Mass. The Governor bundled himself into about four sweaters and a fur-lined heavy top coat, since it was about thirty degrees below zero. He took a last look at his non-Catholic friends sleeping peacefully, and murmured as he stepped out into the cold, "Wouldn't it be awful if it turned out that they were right and we were wrong?"

1043. Spurgeon, the noted English pastor and writer, once noted a weather vane on the roof of a barn. That was nothing out of the ordinary in his country. What was unusual was the inscription written under it: "God is Love."

"Just what do you mean by putting that text there?" Spurgeon asked the farmer. "Do you think God's love is changeable like that?"

"You don't get it," the farmer replied. "What I mean is, no matter which way the wind blows, God is still Love."

Resourcefulness

1044. "I don't like that woman," said Jones to his wife, when the door bell rang and a caller was announced. "Do you mind if I go upstairs and remain there until she leaves?"

"All right, my dear," said the wife, going to the door to greet the visitor.

The husband waited upstairs for a long time, until he thought the caller must surely have left. Then he called down to his wife:

"Dear," he said, "has that terrible old bore gone yet?"

The caller was still there but the quick-witted wife was equal to the occasion. She called back:

"Yes, my dear," she said, "she left more than an hour ago. Mrs. Robinson is here now."

192

1045. They were a large family—husband, wife, and five children—and they were having difficulty finding an apartment in the big city. Everywhere they went they met with the same obstacle—landlords universally objected to large families. They were just about at their wits' end when father suddenly was struck with a brilliant idea.

"Dear," he said to his wife, "tomorrow I want you to take the three youngest ones to the cemetery to visit your mother's grave, while I take the other two and we continue with our apartment-hunting."

After searching all day, he finally found a place that suited him, but not before he was confronted with the usual question: "How many children have you?"

Before answering he heaved a deep sigh. Then pointing to the two youngsters, he said: "Five. But three are with their dear mother in the cemetery."

The truth it was—and he got the apartment!

1046. A woman who ran a boardinghouse would get her knives sharpened from four to five times a week. When the knife sharpener asked why she had her knives sharpened so often, the woman whispered, "Well, it's cheaper than buying tender meat."

1047. It was in Los Angeles that a drunk who wanted to go to El Paso climbed onto a bus that was about to leave. Immediately, he started to make a nuisance of himself. After remonstrating with the man for several minutes, the driver lost his patience.

"Okay, mister," he said. "You either quiet down or this bus ain't leavin' for San Francisco tonight."

"San Francisco?" mumbled the drunk. "Lemme out o' here. I don't want a San Francisco bus."

He scrambled out of the door. The driver turned and winked at his passengers—and the bus left for El Paso.

1048. Charles Coghlan, the actor, was a man of great wit and resource. He also liked the ladies. His wife had barely left on an out-of-town trip one morning when he got in contact with one charming young lady. But Mrs. Coghlan had forgotten something, and was returning home when she saw her husband helping the young lady from a cab. She confronted the pair. Coghlan thought quickly.

"My dear," he said to his wife, "allow me to present Miss Blank. Mrs. Coghlan, Miss Blank."

The two ladies bowed coldly while Coghlan added: "I know you two ladies have ever so many things you want to say to each other, so I will ask to be excused."

With that he tipped his hat, hopped into the cab and rode away.

1049. Women drivers posed a problem even during the reign of Louis XVI. It was fashionable in those days for a woman to drive her own carriage. In the narrow, crowded streets of 18th century Paris, this custom created perennial traffic jams. The King directed d'Argenson, one of his ministers, to have it stopped. But d'Argenson hesitated. He stood to lose his post by issuing such an order, as many of the ladies had great power in court. The task required delicate handling. With a master stroke of genius, he solved his dilemma by proclaiming the following ordinance:

"Ladies under 30 years of age are forbidden to drive carriages."

1050. "How did you make your neighbor keep his hens in his own yard?"

"One night I hid half a dozen eggs under a bush in my garden, and next day I let him see me gather them."

1051. A psychiatrist was examining a selectee.

Psychiatrist: "What's your occupation?"

Selectee: "I'm a gag writer for radio."

Psychiatrist: "Let's see you invent a gag."

Selectee (rising slowly, goes to the door and looks down at the long line of other selectees): "O.K., you guys can go home now, the job's taken."

1052. Somebody told us about a little boy and an old man who had lost ten dollars. After listening to the oldster's story, the kid, who had found the money, decided it must be his, and handed it over.

"Hey," says the old gent, "you're an honest boy, but what I lost was a $10 bill, and you've given me ten ones."

"That's right," says the boy. "Last time I found one, the man didn't have any change."

1053. Jones, a good family man, had been enticed into a game of poker, and as the hands of the clock moved relentlessly toward the morning's wee hours, he grew more and more apprehensive.

Finally, at 3 a.m., he had a sudden inspiration. He called his home, and when the little woman answered the telephone, he shouted in frenzied haste: "Don't pay the ransom, I'm back."

1054. "I've decided on a name for the baby," said the expectant mother. "I shall call her Minerva."

The young husband didn't care very much for her selection but, being a tactful fellow, was far too wise to object verbally.

"Fine," he agreed. "That's a beautiful name. The first girl I ever loved was called Minerva, and the mention of the name revives for me happy memories."

There was a brief moment of silence, then: "We'll call her Lucy; I think that's better," said the young wife.

1055. When an ex-army officers' association decided to hold a ball recently, a few committee men thought the word "formal" on the tickets might discourage some husbands.

But they got around this by sending the tickets anyway and following them later with a note to all the wives. It read: "Last week your husband was sent tickets for the Army Officers' Ball. Has he told you about it yet?"

The turnout was a record.

1056. As the crowded elevator descended, greying Mrs. Jones became increasingly furious with her husband, who was delighted to be pressed against a gorgeous blonde.

As the elevator stopped at the main floor, the blonde suddenly whirled, slapped Mr. Jones and said: "That will teach you to pinch."

Bewildered, Mr. Jones was halfway to the parking lot with his wife when he choked—"I—I—didn't pinch that girl."

"Of course, you didn't," said his wife, consolingly. "I did."

1057. *Warden:* "I've been in charge of this prison for 20 years and that calls for a celebration. What kind of a party would you boys suggest?"

Prisoners: "Open house!"

1058. *Uncle:* "But how could you possibly play truant from a correspondence school?"

Nephew: "I send them an empty envelope."

195

RESOURCEFULNESS

1059. Science solves everything. When they found they couldn't open the railroad car windows, they air-conditioned the whole train.

1060. When Charles Lamb worked for the India Company, he detested his job, coming in late in the mornings and departing earlier in the afternoon than any of the other clerks. Still, he got all his work out on time, winning high praise from his employers. At last his literary efforts began to bear fruit, and he left his menial job for good.

"How is it, Charles," a fellow-clerk asked him at the door, "that you always came in late for your work and left early, yet you always turned out more work in less time than the rest of us?"

Lamb smiled slyly: "Not at all. I never did one-fourth of it myself," he confessed. "You see, I always marked most of it 'Refer to Mr. Smith.' I figured that in an organization as large as the India Company there must be several Smiths handy around somewhere. And, do you know, there were—for none of my papers was ever returned to me!"

1061. Dwight L. Moody, calling on a ministerial brother in an eastern city, was invited to spend the following day, Sunday, with his host. The resident minister said that he would like to have Mr. Moody preach, but was ashamed to ask him to do so.

"Why?" inquired Mr. Moody.

"Well," was the reply, "our people have acquired the bad habit of going out before the close of the meeting, and it would be an imposition to ask you to conduct the service."

"I will stop and preach," said the evangelist.

On Sunday morning, Mr. Moody opened the meeting, and then said: "My friends, I am going to speak to two kinds of people today, the sinners first and then the saints."

After earnestly addressing the supposed sinners, he informed them that they could now take their hats and go. But the whole congregation stayed and heard him to the end.

1062. A man received from the income-tax office a "Second Notice" that his instalment was overdue, and dire things would happen to him if it were not immediately forthcoming.

Hastening to the collector's office, the man paid up and said: "I would have paid this before, but I didn't get your First Notice."

Replied the clerk: "Oh, we ran out of First Notices. Besides, we find that the Second Notices pull in the dough a lot faster."

1063. When Lincoln was captain of the "Bucktail" Rangers in 1832, he was as ignorant of military matters as his company was of drill and tactics. On one occasion, his troop, marching in platoon formation, was confronted by a gate. Captain Lincoln had no idea of the proper order; but his quick wit did not desert him.

"Company dismissed for two minutes!" he commanded. "At the end of that time, 'fall in' on the other side of the fence."

1064. "Young man," said the angry father from the head of the stairs, "didn't I hear the clock strike four when you brought my daughter home?"

"You did," admitted the boy. "It was going to strike eleven, but I grabbed it and held the gong so it wouldn't disturb you."

The father muttered: "Dawgone! Why didn't I think of that in my day!"

Restaurant

1065. For more than a year, a man had eaten in a small restaurant whose sign read, "Mary's Home Cooking," but never once had he seen Mary. Finally his curiosity got the better of him and he said to the waitress, "I've been having lunch in here for a long time, and Mary is never around. Where is she?"

"She's just where the sign says she is," the waitress answered, "Home cooking."

1066. The boy looked at the prices of the menu at the drive-in, then turned to his date and said, "What will you have, my plump little doll?"

1067. "Are you the girl who took my order?"

"Yes, sir," replied the waitress, politely.

"Well, I'll be darned!" remarked the patron. "You don't look a day older."

1068. *Customer:* "Hey, waiter, this steak is burnt black."

Waiter: "Yes, sir; it's a mark of respect. Our head waiter died this morning."

197

REVENGE

Revenge

1069. Two Hollywood writers rented a house for a year, and got a promise from the landlord to redecorate the place. When it became obvious that he wouldn't keep his promise, the writers had their attorney draw up a paper giving them permission to decorate the house at their own expense. The landlord was happy to sign.

Two days before they moved out, they had the whole place painted black.

1070. A certain minister was in his study when a servant announced that a young man wanted to see him on an urgent errand.

When the young man had entered, he said to the clergyman:

"Say, I want to join your church."

Persistent questioning developed the fact that the young man belonged to an altogether different faith. In view of this, the minister advised him that he would have to undergo an intensive course of instruction before he could be admitted to the minister's church, but the young man was persistent and determined to join.

"What is your hurry?" asked the preacher.

"Well, my family has done me 'dirt' and I want to disgrace them," said the young man.

1071. A youngster taken to see Santa Claus kicked him in the shins, saying: "That's for last year."

1072. A prominent Episcopal clergyman had his name left out of the telephone directory because he had been receiving so many calls. A merchant of the same name in the neighborhood began to be pestered with calls asking him to officiate at weddings, funerals, etc. He went to the rector and asked him to have his name put back in the book. The minister, however, refused.

The merchant determined to complain to the telephone company, and was in the act of writing a letter one Saturday night when his phone rang and the timid voice of a young man asked if he would marry him at once. A happy thought came to the merchant.

"No," he said, "I'm too damned busy preparing my sermon for tomorrow."

Reward

1073. Johnny was proud of a book he had brought home from school as a prize in natural history. Questioned by his mother, the boy said that the teacher had asked how many legs on an ostrich, and that he had answered three.

"But an ostrich has only two legs," observed the curious mother.

"Yes, I know," replied the victorious lad, "but the rest of the class all said four."

1074. At a dance, a wallet was lost containing $600. The owner, hoping to retrieve it, got up on a chair and made the following announcement:

"Ladies and gentlemen, may I have your attention, please. I just lost my pocketbook with $600 in it, and to the man who finds it I shall give $50."

From the rear of the hall came a voice: "I'll give $75."

Romance

1075. *Jim:* "Why did you break your engagement?"
John: "She wanted to get married."

1076. Just let a man become bent on matrimony and, presto, an accommodating woman will show up to straighten him out.

1077. A sultan kept his harem three miles from where he lived. Every day he sent his man servant to bring a wife to the palace. The sultan lived to be 83, but the servant died when he was only 30. The moral of this story is: It's not the women that will kill you, but the running after them.

1078. When Clark Gable played his very first love scene, the story goes that he was scared to death. The director soothingly told him to put on an expression of longing. Gable did his best. He tried to think of a big, juicy tender steak; this did the trick so well that he continued to use the idea for romantic scenes ever after.

1079. "You mean to say that you're engaged to five different boys at once?"

"Yeah, I can hardly wait until after Christmas to straighten things out."

1080. *Bored girl:* "You remind me of the ocean."
Boy-with-a-line: "On account of my being so wild, magnificent, and romantic?"
Gal: "No, because you make me sick."

1081. The Smiths were on the balcony and could hear the young couple in the garden below. Mrs. Smith nudged her husband and whispered, "I think he wants to propose. We ought not to listen. Whistle at him."
"Why should I?" her husband asked. "Nobody whistled at me."

1082. *Girl:* "I maintain that love-making is just the same as it always was."
Boy: "How do you know?"
Girl: "I just read about a Greek maiden who sat and listened to a lyre all evening."

1083. *He:* "Please, darling, whisper those three little words that will make me walk on air."
She: "Go hang yourself."

1084. "So you were engaged to Agnes for five years and then she gave you back your ring? That's what I call a cruel blow."
"Oh, it wasn't too bad. In fact, it worked out rather nicely. In the years that Agnes and I were engaged, the ring doubled in value and when she gave it back I was able to get a better girl with it."

1085. Said one girl to another, speaking of her two beaus: "If I could only combine their respective qualities, I'd be the happiest girl in the world. Clarence is gay, debonair, and rich. He's also handsome and witty. But it's Reggie who wants to marry me."

1086. "I really don't ask much in life," said the pretty young blonde. "All I want is a nice man to love and understand me. Is that too much to expect of a millionaire?"

1087. *Boy:* "Dad, how do they catch lunatics?"
Father: "With face powder, fancy dresses, and pretty smiles, my son."

1088. *Portia:* "How did you make the acquaintance of your second husband?"

Dorothy: "It was quite romantic. You see, I was crossing the street with my first husband, when my second husband came along in a car and ran him down. That was the beginning of our friendship."

1089. *Hank:* "You used to say there was something about me you couldn't help loving."

Claire: "But it's all spent now."

1090. *Uncle:* "You boys of today want too much money. Do you know what I was getting when I married your aunt?"

Nephew: "No, and I'll bet you didn't either."

1091. *He* (making the time-worn excuse): "I'm afraid we'll have to stop here; the engine's getting pretty warm."

She: "You men are such hypocrites; you always say the engine."

1092. "Dad," inquired the high school junior, "what can I do when a pretty girl keeps talking to me day after day in class?"

"Well," replied papa. "You can have your seat changed, of course, but if she's like your mother, she'll get you in the long run, regardless."

1093. After lavishing untold wealth in money, furs, cars, and jewelry on a beautiful blonde show girl, a certain old New York playboy finally made her his wife.

"That old relic," an acquaintance hooted. "Do you suppose that could be a love match?"

"Heck, no," rejoined the other. "The old coot married her for his money."

1094. *Gloria:* "I hear you have accepted him. Did he happen to mention that he had proposed to me first?"

Gwendolyn: "Not specifically. He did say, however, that he had done a lot of foolish things before he met me."

1095. "Should I marry a man who lies to me?"

"Lady, do you want to be an old maid?"

1096. The little girl asked, "What makes a man always give a woman a diamond engagement ring, Daddy?"

Replied Daddy, "The woman."

SALARY

1097. A blushing young woman handed the clerk a telegram form containing only a name, address, and the word *Yes*.

"You know," said the clerk, "you can send ten words for the same price."

"I know," she said, "but wouldn't I look eager if I said it ten times?"

1098. The more perfect a man is the more girls try to altar him.

1099. Friends of a young farmer who was known for his inability to think of anything to say to women were amazed when, the morning after the shy one met a girl at a dance, it was announced that he had become engaged. One asked how it happened.

"Well," said the bashful man, "I danced with her three times and I couldn't think of anything else to say."

1100. A famous quarterback took back his fraternity pin from the campus beauty. He found she was faithful to the end.

Salary

1101. A well-known lawyer was always lecturing his office boy— whether he needed it or not. One day he chanced to overhear the following conversation between his boy and the one employed next door.

"How much does he pay you?" asked the latter.

"I get $3000 a year," replied the office boy—$25 a week in cash and the rest in legal advice."

1102. *Employe:* "Boss, I came to see if you could raise my salary."

Boss: "Go back to work and don't worry. I've managed to raise it each pay day so far, haven't I?"

1103. A kindly disposed man was walking down the street one Saturday, when he saw a man and woman in violent dispute.

"Here, here, this won't do," he exclaimed.

"What business is it of yours?" demanded the belligerent one, angrily.

"Not any," said the kindly disposed man, mildly, "except that I would like very much to help settle this dispute."

"There ain't no dispute," returned the other. "She *thinks* she's not going to get my week's wages and I *know* darned well she isn't. That's no dispute."

1104. "And about the salary?" said the movie star.

"Well," said the producer after a moment's thought, "suppose we call it $5,000 a week?"

"All right."

"Of course, you understand that the $5,000 is merely what we will call it—you will get $500."

1105. An employer was talking to a friend about what to do with a young salesman, who had embezzled a large amount of money and lost it all on the market.

"Keep him on the job and take it out of his pay," the friend advised.

"But he couldn't ever pay me back that way," said the employer, "the amount is too large and his wages too small."

The advisor thought a moment.

"Well, then," he said, "why don't you raise his salary?"

Salesmanship

1106. A wholesale shoe salesman had been calling on a certain dealer for more than a year, without a chance of getting an order. The dealer was friendly, almost too friendly, constantly promising to "give your house some of my business." But he never seemed to get around to doing so.

The dealer, it seems, was quite a practical joker. The salesman, on the other hand, knew that if he could ever once get the better of his prospect, all would be well. Finally, on one occasion when the dealer had repeated his usual formula, he added, "Next time you come in I'll surely have an order for you." The salesman walked away, apparently satisfied. In half an hour he returned, set his portfolio on the counter, took out his order book and stood with pencil poised. "Well, here I am for that order you promised me the next time I came in. This is the 'next time,' so let's go!" And by golly, it worked!

1107. The sales manager was giving advice to the salesmen. "Soft soap," he said, "in some form pleases all, and generally speaking, the more lye you put in, the better."

SALESMANSHIP

1108. Two clothing merchants were bragging to each other about their salesmen. "One of my men," said one of them, "is the smartest salesman in the city. Why, the other day a man came in for a pair of shoelaces, and before he left my man had sold him a suit of clothing and an overcoat."

"Humph, that's nothing," replied the other. "Last week we had a woman come in to buy a suit of black clothing in which to bury her husband. And before she left, my salesman had sold her a suit with an extra pair of trousers."

1109. A Protestant boy wanted to marry a Catholic girl. Her parents felt that it would be advisable for the lad to adopt the family religion. Accordingly he began to read Catholic literature, and attend classes taught by a priest.

All went well until one day the mother came home to find her daughter lying on the sofa, sobbing her heart out.

"It's . . . it's Paul," the girl wailed. "There isn't going to be any wedding!"

"Whatever is the matter, darling? Doesn't he love you any more?"

"It isn't that," daughter explained. "We . . . we oversold him! He's going to be a priest!"

1110. A salesman is a man with a shine on his shoes, a smile on his face, and a lousy territory.

1111. A home-freezer salesman had demonstrated his appliance for a farmer and his wife. They held a whispered conference, but finally rejected the machine. As the salesman was about to depart, the farmer asked: "What would you give me if I sold one of them freezers for you?"

"I'll give you $25 for every one you sell," the salesman replied.

"Well, I bet I can sell my wife one," declared the farmer. He did, too—and pocketed the commission!

"The trouble with you fellows," he confided, as he helped the salesman unload the freezer, "is that you don't know nothin' about selling!"

1112. A salesman who had a long run of bad luck suddenly rushed into his home and began to turn the room upside down.

"What have you lost, dear?" asked his wife.

"I've taken an order today," he revealed, "and I've misplaced the address of my firm."

1113. A salesman was explaining to his buddy the reason for his sudden affluence.

"I sell ladies' stockings. Sometimes if the woman of the house is really interested, I put them on for her," he said.

"You must sell plenty that way," the friend commented.

"No," said the salesman, "my legs look lousy in women's stockings."

1114. A pawnbroker loaded his show window with unredeemed saxophones, banjos, tubas—and shotguns. "Very interesting display," commented a friend, "but does it sell merchandise?"

"Does it!" enthused the pawnbroker. "One day a fellow buys a sax or a tuba. Two days later his neighbors buy the shotguns."

1115. The young, newly-hired salesperson was looking extremely depressed.

"Come, come!" said the store owner. "Don't look so down-in-the-mouth. It's difficult at first, but you'll soon get onto it. With a little experience you'll get along all right."

"It isn't that," said the man. "When I got home last night I practiced my sales talk on my wife, and now I've got to buy her a vacuum cleaner."

1116. The automobile salesman was making his pitch to a prospective customer: "Just look at those beautiful lines and that attractive upholstery. Its purchase would be a most timely one."

"Timely?" asked the prospect. "In what way?"

"Because if I don't make this sale, my boss will fire me!"

1117. An insurance man walked into a lunch-room and, taking his place on one of the vacant stools, ordered bread and milk. The fellow sitting on the next stool asked:

"On a diet?"

"No. Commission."

1118. An ex-serviceman, carrying a chair, approached the proprietor of a secondhand store and asked how much it was worth.

"Three dollars," answered the storekeeper.

The young man looked surprised. "Isn't it worth more than that?"

"Three dollars is the limit, son," the older man repeated, shaking his head. "See that?" He pointed to a crack in the chair leg. "And look here where the paint is peeling."

"All right then," said the veteran, tugging at his wallet. "I saw this chair in front of your store marked $10, but I thought there was some mistake. For $3 I'll take it."

1119. The big businessman had died and gone to—well, not to heaven. He had hardly become settled when a hearty hand slapped him on the back, and into his ear boomed the voice of a salesman who had pestered him so much on earth.

"Well, Mr. Brown," chortled the salesman, "I'm here for the appointment."

"What appointment?"

"Don't you remember? Every time I entered your office on earth you told me you would see me here."

1120. St. Patrick was perhaps as shrewd as any man who ever trod the sod of Erin. He was not, of course, an Irishman, but a Scot who emigrated to the island as a missionary. Pagan Ireland then worshipped at the shrine of the Druids, and Patrick was smart enough not to try to make over the country at one fell swoop. Rather, he eased his religion upon the folk in gentle, homeopathic doses.

When the populace set about celebrating a pagan feast day, Patrick would promptly "discover" that the birth of some Christian saint, by chance, fell upon that exact date. He would tactfully suggest a simultaneous celebration. Thus, gradually the saints usurped all of the red letter days on the Irish calendar! Patrick had made his "sale," but the prospects all believed they had "bought." Which is as it should be.

1121. Two salesmen were talking. "You know," said one, "I made some very valuable contacts today."

The second replied, "I didn't make any sales, either."

1122. *Reporter* (to city editor): "Here's the perfect news story."
City Editor: "Man bites dog?"
Reporter: "No . . . the bull threw the salesman."

206

1123. "I want some invisible hair nets for my wife," said a customer.

"Here you are, sir. That will be twenty-five cents."

"Are you sure they're invisible?"

"Invisible!" exclaimed the salesman. "Why, I've been selling them all morning and we've been out of stock for nearly two weeks."

1124. *Customer:* "Now, Mr. Grocer, are you sure those eggs are fresh?"

Grocer: "Boy, feel those eggs and see if they're cool enough to sell yet."

1125. *Employer:* "Son, I'm surprised at you. Do you know what they do with boys who tell lies?"

Office Boy: "Yes, sir. When they get old enough, the firm sends them out as salesmen."

1126. When a man wrote to the B. F. Goodrich Company asking for some information, he added, "I don't want any advertising material—and no salesman." It was difficult to put the information into a letter; so the company ignored the warning and sent a salesman.

The fellow didn't wait for an explanation. "I told them," he said to the salesman, 'no salesman'!" The caller—a youngster just out of the company's training school—sighed and replied, "Mister, I'm as close to a no-salesman as they've got."

1127. The cub salesman asked his boss if he could refund the money to an irate customer who discovered that the lot he had bought was under water.

"What kind of a salesman are you?" demanded the boss. "Go out there and sell him a motor boat."

1128. An enterprising salesman decided to bypass the merchandising manager and go directly to the store president. When asked, "What are you trying to sell?" the salesman replied, "I'm not here to sell you. My boss asked for a survey of the city to find out whether there was a store good enough to handle his product."

Sarcasm

1129. "Oh, but she's good to her inferiors," once said a kind lady to Dorothy Parker, to which Miss Parker replied, with a puzzled frown: "But where does she find them?"

1130. *Wife* (coming home late for dinner): "I've been to the beauty parlor."
Husband: "Oh, you didn't get waited on, did you?"

1131. Mark Twain's hostess at the opera had chattered so much that no one in her box had been able to enjoy the singing. At the end of the performance she said, "Mr. Clemens, I want you to be my guest next Friday night, too. They are going to give *Tosca,* then."
"Charmed," said Twain, "I've never heard you in that."

1132. *Rev. Jones:* "Sheriff, there's a dead mule in front of my house."
Sheriff: "I thought you ministers took care of the dead."
Rev. Jones: "We do. But first we get in touch with their relatives."

1133. The butcher was busy waiting on a customer when a woman rushed in and said, "Give me a pound of cat food, quick!"
Turning to the other customer, who had been waiting for some time, she said: "I hope you don't mind my getting waited on before you."
"Not if you're *that* hungry," replied the other woman.

1134. The sour-faced, oddly-dressed lady was poking among the brooms in the hardware store when a clerk asked if he could help her.
"Nothing here is worth buying," she snapped. "Flimsy, cheap straw, poor handle, shoddy material!" Seizing the broom she shook it under the nose of the bewildered clerk and said angrily: "Not like the brooms they used to make! Give the floor one good sweep and it would fall apart! What's it good for?"
"Well," said the clerk, "you might find that it flies wonderfully."

1135. "I never said I didn't like her," remarked a woman in sort of self defense. "I merely remarked that all the polish she had was on her fingernails."

1136. The customer had picked out six apples at the grocery store.
"That will be $1.35, please," said the clerk.

The customer handed the clerk $1.50 and started to walk out of the store.

"Just a minute, sir," called the clerk after him, "you forgot your change."

"That's all right, you keep it," retorted the customer. "That makes us even; I stepped on a grape on the way in."

1137. *Artist:* "I'd like to devote my last picture to a charitable purpose."

Critic: "Why not give it to an institution for the blind?"

Secret

1138. "She told me," a woman complained to a friend, "that you told her the secret I told you not to tell her."

"Well," replied her friend in a hurt tone, "I told her not to tell you I told her."

"Oh, dear," sighed the first woman. "Well, don't tell her I told you that she told me."

1139. The tiny boy had been taken for an automobile ride by a friend of the family. On his return his mother asked him, "Did you thank Mr. Swank for taking you for a ride?"

There was no reply. The mother repeated her question, but still there was no answer.

"Jimmie," she said, "did you hear me? Did you remember to thank Mr. Swank for the ride?"

"Yes," whispered Jimmie, "but he told me not to mention it."

Self-appraisal

1140. A three-piece orchestra, piano, bass, and drums, was playing in a night club. The piano player, who was the band leader, told his colleagues to "keep on playing, while I go out front and see how we sound."

1141. A business manager, in search of talent within his own organization, passed out a list of questions to his younger workers. One question asked, "What is your chief reason for believing that you possess executive ability?"

209

Many of the answers were duplications, but one stood out as unique. It read, "I think I would make a very successful executive because I seldom get lonesome, and would not mind working in a private office."

1142. A district attorney was having trouble with one of the witnesses, a rather pugnacious old man.

"Are you acquainted with any of the jurors?" asked the D.A.

"More than half," grunted the witness.

"Are you willing to swear that you know more than half of them?"

The old man flicked a glance over the jury box. "If it comes to that," he drawled, "I'm willing to swear I know more than all of them put together."

1143. A prominent businessman fell in love with an actress and decided to marry her, but for the sake of prudence he employed a detective agency to report on her life.

The report read: "The lady has an excellent reputation: her past is without a blemish; and she has a circle of impeccable friends. The only breath of scandal is that lately she's been seen a great deal in the company of a businessman of doubtful reputation."

1144. A successful manufacturer who was responsible for the operation of a considerable factory said to his associate: "I wish you would look about the shop for an hour or so each day and tell me what you see that is wrong there. Don't trouble to speak of the things which are going well. It's the mistakes I wish to learn." The suggestion was accepted. There was hardly a day from that time forth for many years in which something was not found that needed adjustment or correction. It is of the very essence of success that a manufacturer should be his own sternest critic.

1145. Volunteering as a blood donor at a Texas hospital, a young woman was asked by the nurse, "Do you know your type?"

"Oh, yes," came the reply. "I'm the *sultry* type."

Self-confidence

1146. It is told of Col. Abraham Gruber that when he was very young and looking for employment, he passed a lawyer's office, where he saw a sign reading, "Boy Wanted." He removed the sign and rushed up to the lawyer with it, placing it on his deck.

"Why did you bring up that sign?" asked the lawyer.

"Why keep it out any longer? I am going to take the place," said young Gruber.

1147. *Jimmy:* "Aw, you're afraid to fight."

Johnny: "Naw, I'm not, but if I fight my mom'll find out and spank me."

Jimmy: "How'll she find out?"

Johnny: "She'll see the doctor going into your place."

1148. "Dupont," said Admiral Farragut to his officer who failed in an important enterprise, "do you know why you did not get into Charleston harbor with your ironclads?"

"It was because the channel was crooked, sir," replied the officer.

"No, Dupont, it was not that," said Farragut.

"Well, the rebel fire was perfectly horrible."

"Yes, but it wasn't that."

"What was it then?"

"It was because you didn't believe you could get in."

1149. Self-confidence has often proved the one great secret of a successful career.

When the little Corsican, Napoleon Bonaparte, a feeble youth at the beginning of his wonderful career, was presented to the Convention of France as the man who could rescue the country from its peril, the president fixed his eyes on him dubiously and said: "Are you willing to undertake our defense?" "Yes," was the calm and confident reply. "But are you aware of the magnitude of the undertaking?" asked the president again. "Fully," said Napoleon, fixing his piercing eye upon the questioner, adding, "and I am in the habit of accomplishing that which I undertake."

Spelling

1150. To his son who was attending college, the deacon of a church wrote as follows:

"Dear Son: I suggest that you add penmanship to the other courses you are taking, so that you may learn that the small 'e' and the 'l' are not the same height. Until your mother deciphered your last letter for me, I was sure that you and the other young man sharing your room both had coeds—not colds."

1151. Mrs. Jones was reading a letter at breakfast. Suddenly she looked up suspiciously at her husband.

"Henry," she said, "I've just received a letter from mother saying she isn't accepting our invitation to come and stay, as we do not appear to want her. What does she mean by that?" I told you to write and say that she was to come at her own convenience. You did write, didn't you?"

"Er—yes, I did," said the husband. "But I—I couldn't spell 'convenience,' so I made it 'risk.' "

1152. According to a news dispatch from New York City, an executive there has given up trying to get clean, correctly-spelled letters from his secretary. Instead, according to the report, he rubber stamps an explanation on each messy missive: "She can't type—but she's beautiful!"

1153. A Boston lady was expressing her indignation at the indecent words being painted on the walls and sidewalks of the city.

"What will outsiders think of us?" she cried. "Why, some of the words aren't even spelled right!"

1154. The teacher had been trying to regularise the spelling— brilliant in its originality—of the Tough Boy of the class. He made the suggestion that the Tough One might remember the spellings better if he learned the meanings of the words.

"Spell 'straight,' " said the teacher.

"S-t-r-a-i-g-h-t," spelled the Tough One.

"Right," said the teacher. "And now what does it mean?"

"Without soda water," replied the Tough One.

Sports

1155. "Bullfighting," according to Pedro, "is the most popular sport in South America."

"Isn't it revolting?" asked his fair companion from Detroit.

"No," said Pedro, "that's the second most popular sport."

1156. It seems that the devils challenged the angels to a baseball game.

"That's silly," said the angels. "You know all the good ball players are up here."

"Yes," answered the devils, "but where are all the umpires?"

1157. *Smith:* "If two old maids, ages 39 and 41, took a bottle of 12-year-old Scotch to a baseball game and sat in row five, section Q, what inning is it?"

Jones: "I give up."

Smith: "It's the last of the 5th and the bags are loaded."

1158. A midwestern university held entrance exams for a group of ex-GIs. One of the questions was, "Name two ancient sports."

An ex-sergeant racked his brain, finally came up with an answer that passed him. He wrote, "Antony and Cleopatra."

1159. *Freshman:* "I'm a little stiff from bowling."

Coach: "I don't care where you're from. Get out there and get going."

1160. *Neighbor:* "They tell me your son is on the college football team. Do you know what position he plays?"

Proud Mother: "I'm not sure, but I think he is one of the drawbacks."

1161. They arrived at the ball game during the fifth inning.

"What's the score, Jim?" he asked of a fan.

"Nothing to nothing," was the reply.

"Oh, good!" she exclaimed. "Then we haven't missed a thing."

Stinginess

1162. The group had met to discuss the abolition of the practice of tipping. McPherson was not showing much enthusiasm.

"Surely, McPherson, you are planning to join our group. The membership fee is only one dollar a year."

"In that case," replied McPherson, "I might as well keep on tipping."

STUPIDITY

1163. Two Englishmen were discussing the Scots. "One thing you can say for them," commented one, "is that they have a fine sense of humor. I wonder where they get it."

The second considered for a moment, then replied, "It must be a gift."

1164. The stingy salesman, while on an out-of-town sales trip, sent his wife a check for a million kisses as an anniversary present.

The wife was quite annoyed and sent back a postcard: "Dear Chuck, Thanks for the anniversary check. The milkman cashed it for me just this morning."

Stupidity

1165. A husband decided that on his wife's birthday he'd surprise her with a new Cadillac convertible. He drove the car home and parked it in front of the house. He then went in and asked the little woman to come to the front door.

When she appeared, the husband pointed proudly to the parked Cadillac and asked, "How do you like it, honey?"

Whereupon the wife turned to him and said, "What's the matter, stupid, couldn't you answer the $64,000 question?"

1166. *Policeman:* "Excuse me, sir, but your lights are out."
Motorist: "Thanks, but it really doesn't matter."
Policeman: "How are your brakes?"
Motorist: "Rotten."
Policeman: "By the way, do you have your license?"
Motorist: "No, never had one."
Policeman: "That's three violations. I'll have to arrest you."
Motorist's wife: "Oh, don't pay any attention to what he says, officer. He always talks that way when he's drunk."

1167. A Hollywood starlet, who was more beautiful than brainy, visited friends one day and asked to be shown through their new greenhouse. Pausing a moment before one plant, she asked its name.

"It belongs to the Begonia family," was the host's answer.

"Oh," gushed the beauty, "how nice of you to look after it while they're away."

214

Success

1168. The occasion was a testimonial dinner for the town's leading citizen.

"Friends," the leading citizen said, "when I first came to your city 50 years ago, I had only one suit on my back, one pair of shoes, and all my earthly possessions were wrapped in a red handkerchief over my shoulder. This city has been good to me—and I worked hard. Now, I am president of the bank; I own ten buildings and five companies. Yes, friends, your town has been good to me."

After the banquet, an awed youngster approached the great man and asked timidly, "Please, sir . . . what did you have in that red handkerchief when you first came to town?"

"Well, son, if I recall rightly, I had about $300,000 in cash and $850,000 in securities!"

1169. "What is your formula for success?" asked the young man of the successful financier.

"Patience, my lad," said the old man. "Anything in the world can be accomplished if one only has patience."

"I'll wager I can name one thing that cannot be done, even with the utmost patience," said the young man.

"And, what's that?"

"Carrying water in a sieve," answered the youth.

"Is that so? Well, even that can be achieved," was the reply, "if one will only have the patience to wait until it freezes."

1170. Asked by an ambitious young man for the secret of success, the wealthy merchant had this to say:

"There is no easy secret. You must jump at your opportunity."

"But how can I tell when my opportunity comes?" asked the youth.

"You can't," agreed the businessman. "You've just got to keep jumping."

1171. A minister and his wife were talking about two of his congregation members. "Yes," said the minister, "I knew both of them as boys. One was a clever, handsome fellow; the other a steady, hard worker. The clever lad was left behind in the race, but the hard worker, well, he died and left $200,000 to his widow. It's a great moral."

"Yes," smiled his wife, "it certainly is. I heard today that the clever one is going to marry the widow."

Superstition

1172. A visitor once commented to Niels Bohr, the famous atom scientist and Nobel prize winner: "I'm surprised to see that you have a horseshoe hanging over your door. Do you, a man dedicated to science, believe in that superstition?"

"Of course not," smiled Bohr, "but I've been told that it's supposed to be lucky whether you believe in it or not."

1173. "My good man," said the visitor to the prisoner in the penitentiary, "how did you happen to come to this sad place?"

"Well, sir," replied the convicted man, "you see in me the unhappy victim of the unlucky number 13."

"Indeed!" said the visitor. "How was that?"

"Twelve jurymen and one judge, sir."

1174. The smiling, confident young man entered a New York bank. He stepped up to the manager's desk and began, "Good day, sir. Has your bank any need for a highly-intelligent, college-trained man?"

The manager handed him an application form and offered to assist him in filling it out.

"Your name?"

"Theophile Babinger."

"Experience?"

"Just out of college."

"I see," said the manager. "And what kind of position are you seeking?"

"Well," mused the young man, "I want something in the executive line, such as a vice-presidency, for example."

The manager put down his pencil. "I'm really very sorry," he said sarcastically, "but we already have twelve vice-presidents."

The young man waved a hand, then stated with a happy confidence, "Oh, that's all right; I'm not superstitious."

1175. The vacuum cleaner salesman was demonstrating in a Chicago skyscraper apartment building. The door-bell rang.

"It's probably my husband," gasped the housewife. "He's insanely jealous. Jump out of the window."

"But this is the thirteenth floor," protested the salesman.

"Go on," she said, "jump—this is no time to be superstitious."

1176. *Hostess:* "Now, when you set the table for dinner tonight, be sure you put the forks on the left side of the plate."

Servant: "Yes, mum."

Hostess: "And be careful to put the plates so that the designs are straight and even."

Servant: "Yes, mum."

Hostess: "And above all, make sure that the napkins are folded neatly."

Servant: "Yes, mum, but why are you so superstitious?"

Surprise

1177. The businessman was phoning his home. "Hello, honey." he said, "would it be all right if I brought a couple of fellows home for dinner tonight?"

"Why, certainly, dear. I'd *love* to have them."

"I'm sorry," apologized the businessman after a brief pause. "I must have the wrong number."

1178. Many a wife surprises her husband on their wedding anniversary simply by mentioning the date.

Suspicion

1179. The professor in one particular class had just concluded an experiment concerning atoms. He commented: "Please note that at the beginning of the experiment there were twenty-seven atoms; now there are only twenty-six. Students," he demanded pointedly, "what happened to that other atom?"

There were several moments of tense silence. Then a low voice from the rear of the room said slowly, "Don't anybody leave this room."

1180. A man and his wife were sitting together in the living room one evening. The phone rang and the man answered. "How on earth should I know?" he said, as he put the receiver to his ear. "Why don't you call the Coast Guard?" Then he hung up and returned to his newspaper.

"Who was that, dear?" inquired his wife.

"I haven't the faintest idea," replied the unsuspecting spouse. "Some stupid fellow wanted to know if the coast was clear."

1181. The country doctor came home all worn out and prepared for a good night's sleep, but no sooner had he retired than the phone beside his bed rang loudly. He nudged his wife: "Listen dear, see who it is; say you expect me soon, or anything you think of."

The wife answered the phone. "Doctor is not at home," she reported.

"Well, this is Mrs. McTavish," rattled a voice in the receiver. "I've got a pain in the chest and I want to see him as soon as he comes in."

The doctor whispered some instructions to his wife, which she repeated to the prospective patient. "Do that and I'm sure you'll soon feel all right."

"Thanks very much," said the lady on the phone, "but tell me, is that gentleman who seems to be with you qualified to advise me?"

Taciturnity

1182. When Coolidge was Vice-President, he was obliged to attend many dinners. His hostesses invariably despaired of him, because they could never get him to talk. One such lady had the bright idea of putting him next to Alice Roosevelt Longworth, thinking surely that that brilliant conversationalist could get him started.

Mrs. Longworth did her best on numerous topics, but the Vice-President ate his way through soup, fish, and entree, replying only in monosyllables. Nettled, she determined to get a rise out of him somehow.

"It must be very boring for you to have to go to so many dinners," she said testily.

"Well," replied the unruffled Coolidge, "a man has to eat somewhere."

Tact

1183. A glamorous Hollywood star had her picture taken. She fumed at the result.

"I can't understand it," she screamed. "The last time I posed for you, the photographs were heavenly."

"Ah, yes," the cameraman replied. "But you must remember I was eight years younger then."

1184. "I must say these are fine biscuits!" exclaimed the young husband.

"How could you say those are fine biscuits?" inquired the young wife's mother, in a private interview.

"I didn't say they were fine. I merely said I must say so."

Talent

1185. Smith took his wife to the circus, and the man on the flying trapeze, high above the crowd, hung precariously by his toes as he swung through the air.

Mrs. Smith watched incredulously as the trapeze artist, still hanging by his toes and swinging, arched his back and forced his head through his legs. Mrs. Smith rose to her feet with mouth agape as the performer reached behind his back with one hand and drew forth a violin, and reached behind his back with the other hand and drew forth a bow.

As the flying trapeze man swung 100 feet above the audience, hanging on by his toes, he began playing a tune on his fiddle behind his back.

"Oh, John!" exclaimed Mrs. Smith. "Isn't he wonderful?"

Smith shrugged and grunted: "He ain't no Heifetz."

1186. "I understand your wife is a finished soprano."

"No, not yet; but the neighbors almost got her last night."

1187. For weeks, the destitute concert violinist shivering in his tenement had enviously watched the daily arrival of a bad neighborhood violinist who played in the courtyard below.

When the bad violinist sawed out his wretched tunes, windows in the tenement opened and tenants threw out wads of money.

One day the concert violinist decided to try the same thing. He played brilliantly but his take was only a meagre eighty-five cents.

Completely bewildered, he put the question to the neighborhood violinist that afternoon.

TARDINESS

"That's simple," said the second-rate novice. "The answer is that you also have to be a bookmaker in addition."

1188. Pianist Rachmaninoff told this story about his boyhood:

"When I was a very little fellow," he said, "I played at a reception at a Russian count's, and, for an urchin of seven, I flatter myself that I swung through Beethoven's *Kreutzer Sonata* pretty successfully.

"The *Kreutzer*, you know, has in it several long and impressive rests. Well, in one of these rests the count's wife, a motherly old lady, leaned forward, patted me on the shoulder and said:

" 'Play us something you know, dear.' "

Tardiness

1189. A fellow who had "just two drinks" was driving the wrong way, against traffic, on a one-way street. He'd gone only a few blocks when a cop stopped him, asking: "Where do you think you're going?"

"I don't know for sure," answered the driver, "but wherever it is, I must be late. Everybody's comin' back already!"

1190. In the middle of his lunch a man noticed the clock behind the counter and made a dive for his hat and coat.

"Two o'clock," he cried. "I've got to get over to the bank. My wife is supposed to meet me there at one o'clock sharp, and I don't want to be late."

1191. "Late again, I see, my man. How do you account for this chronic tardiness?"

"It's inherited, sir; you see my father was the late Patrick O'Brien."

1192. The boss was berating his porter for coming to work later each day. "Don't you want to amount to something?" he asked. "Don't you know that you will never get anywhere unless you get up early in the morning?"

"Well, Ah don't know," replied the porter. "Ah've noticed that them that gets up early goes to them that gets up late to get paid."

1193. A bachelor was breakfasting in a restaurant when he saw an inscription on an egg: "Should this meet the eye of some young man who desires to marry a farmer's daughter, age 18, write . . ."

The bachelor wrote and in a few days received the following note: "Your letter came too late. I am now married and have three children."

1194. "I'm really not late, boss," said the tardy secretary, hanging up her hat. "I just took my coffee break before coming in."

1195. The Bank of England requires its employees to sign a daily register and record their reasons if they are late.

London weather being what it is, the first tardy gentleman generally writes "fog" opposite his name and those who follow, "ditto."

One morning, the first latecomer wrote in the book, "wife had twins." Under the twice-blessed gentleman's name mechanically followed twenty others, each with "ditto" dutifully noted.

Taxes

1196. A lady with a young boy drove into a service station and asked that her tires be checked. Before the attendant could get to his chore, her son leaped out of the auto and said he would check the tires. "You get back in the car and let the man do it," the woman told him. "What do you think we pay gasoline taxes for?"

1197. Everyone has wondered who hit Joe Louis hardest during his ring career. When asked, Joe simply shrugged his shoulders. "That's easy, Uncle Sam!"

1198. Everybody should pay his taxes with a smile. I tried it, but they wanted cash.

1199. A stranger, dashing into a house in answer to a woman's screams, found a frightened mother who explained that her young son had swallowed a quarter. The stranger grabbed the child by the feet and shook him vigorously until the coin fell from the boy's mouth. "Doctor," the woman gasped with relief, "it certainly was lucky you happened by. You knew just how to get it out of him."

"I'm not a doctor, madam," the stranger explained. "I'm a Deputy Collector of Internal Revenue."

1200. Taxes are just like golf—you drive your heart out for the green, and then end up in the hole.

TAXES

1201. A Topeka, Kansas, assessor recently ran across the best answer yet to the question on the tax assessment blank: "Nature of taxpayer." The answer: "Very mean."

1202. "I don't understand the difference between direct and indirect taxes," a puzzled wife told her husband.

"It's about the same thing," he explained briefly, "as you asking me for money and going through my pockets at night when I'm asleep."

1203. When an old South African native was told he had to be taxed because the government, like a father, protected him from enemies, cared for him when he was sick, fed him when he was hungry, gave him an education, and for these purposes needed money, the old native said:

"Yes, I understand. It is like this: I have a dog and the dog is hungry. He comes to me and begs food.

"I say to him: 'My dear faithful dog, I see you are very hungry. I am sorry for you. I shall give you meat.'

"I then take a knife, cut off the dog's tail, give it to him, and say, 'Here, my faithful dog, be nourished by this nice piece of meat.'"

1204. The man who dived from a pier to rescue an income tax collector prefers to remain anonymous. So does the man who pushed the tax collector in.

1205. One thing in favor of death over taxes—death doesn't get worse every time Congress meets.

1206. The taxpayer is beginning to feel like the sick man about whom the doctor inquired, "Nurse, did the patient take the medicine religiously, as I ordered?"

"No, sir," replied the nurse. "He cursed every time he took it."

1207. "And now, gentlemen," continued the Congressman, "I wish to tax your memory a bit."

"For heaven's sake," muttered a colleague, "why hadn't we thought of that before."

1208. *Disgruntled taxpayer:* "We don't get as much government as we pay for."

Irked businessman: "That's one of the few things we can be thankful for."

1209. *Wife to husband:* "Dear, there's a man from the Eternal Revenue Department here to see you!"

Teacher-Pupil

1210. Little Jimmy was one of the gladsome youngsters in a Louisiana school. His teacher told the class of the Roman who swam across the Tiber three times before breakfast.

"Three times!" involuntarily said the wondering Jimmy. "Did you say three times, Miss Jones?"

"Why, yes, Jimmy," responded the teacher. "You don't doubt that a trained swimmer could do it?"

"No, ma'am," was the smiling reply of little Jimmy. "I just wondered why he didn't make it four, and get back to the side where he left his clothes."

1211. *Teacher,* patiently: "If one and one makes two, and two and two makes four, how much does four and four make?"

Old-enough-to-vote hillbilly pupil: "That ain't fair, teacher. You answer the easy ones and leave the hard one for me."

1212. *College Miss:* "Professor, I want you to suggest a course in life for me. I have thought of journalism—"

Professor: "What are your own inclinations?"

College Miss: "Oh, my soul yearns, throbs, and pulsates with an ambition to give the world a life-work that shall be marvelous in its scope and weirdly entrancing in the vastness of its structural beauty!"

Professor: "Woman, you're born to be a milliner."

1213. One of the Sunday school teachers in a large and fashionable church was explaining to his class the significance of the color white.

"White," he explained, "stands for joy. That is why a bride wears white when she's married. Her wedding day is the most joyous occasion of a woman's life."

"Then, why," queried the little boy, "do the men all wear black?"

1214. *Student:* "Do the Canadians have a Fourth of July?"
Teacher: "Of course not!"
Student: "What do they do? Go from the third to the fifth?"

1215. Little Johnny's mother had just presented the family with twins, and the household was in a state of excitement. Father beamed with pride as he took Johnny to one side.

"If you'll tell your teacher about it, I'm sure she'll give you a day's holiday," he said.

That afternoon Johnny came home from school radiant. "I don't have to go to school tomorrow," he proudly announced.

"Did you tell your teacher about the twins?" asked the father.

"No, I just told her I had a baby sister. I'm saving the other for next week."

1216. The teacher was trying to get over the intricacies of subtraction. "You have ten fingers," she said. "Suppose you had three less, then what would you have?"

"No music lessons," Johnny promptly replied.

1217. *Teacher:* "What do we call a person who keeps on talking when people are no longer interested?"
Pupil: "A teacher."

1218. *Sunday School Teacher:* ". . . and that is the story of Jonah and the whale. Now, Willie, what does this story teach us?"
Willie: "Only this: that you can't keep a good man down."

1219. *Auntie:* "And how did Jimmy do in his history examination?"
Mother: "Oh, not at all well, but then, it wasn't his fault. Why, they asked him things that happened before the poor boy was born."

1220. *Teacher:* "If your mother gave you a large apple and a small apple and told you to divide with your brother, which would you give him?"
Tommy: "Do you mean my little brother or my big brother?"

1221. "My little boy is so sensitive," said the mother, bringing her son to school for the first time. "Never punish him. If he's naughty, just slap the boy next to him; that will frighten him, and accomplish your purpose."

1222. "If you had six apples and I asked you for three, how many would you have left?" asked the instructor in arithmetic.

"Six," promptly replied Willie.

1223. *Teacher:* "This makes five times I have punished you this week. Now, Willie, what have you got to say?"

Willie: "I'm glad it's Friday."

1224. Alan, arriving home from school, beamed with such happiness that he almost forgot he was hungry.

"I didn't know my second grade teacher liked me so well, Mommy," he confided. "I heard her talking to some of the other teachers, and she must be awfully fond of me! Do you know what she said?"

"What did she say, Alan?" queried his mother.

"She said that the happiest day of her life was the day little Alan Williams was promoted into the third grade."

1225. The children had all been photographed, and the teacher was trying to persuade them each to buy a copy of the group picture.

"Just think how nice it will be to look at it when you are all grown up and say, 'There's Rose; she's married,' or 'That's Harold; he's a sailor.'"

A small voice at the back of the room piped up with, "And there's teacher; she's dead."

1226. The teacher was conducting an oral examination among her grade school pupils.

"Willie, tell me what you know about George Washington," she asked. "Was he a soldier or a sailor?"

"I think he was a soldier," replied little Willie.

"Why do you think he was a soldier?"

"Because I saw a picture of him crossing the Delaware, and anybody who would stand up in a rowboat sure ain't no sailor," was Willie's prompt comeback.

Technique

1227. "With a single stroke of the brush," said the school teacher taking his class through the art gallery, "Joshua Reynolds could change a smiling face into a frowning one."

"So can my mother," said a small boy.

TECHNIQUE

1228. The most successful elephant hunter in all history was on his deathbed. There he decided to reveal the secret which enabled him to capture more elephants than any other hunter.

"I use a spyglass, a pair of tweezers, and a mason jar," he said. "First I climb a tree and use the spyglass to locate an elephant. It's easy to find elephants, you know, although capturing them is hard. Then I turn the spyglass around. This makes the elephant very small. So I pick him up with the tweezers and drop him into the mason jar."

1229. A widow, viewing her husband laid out in a funeral parlor, expressed regret that she had ordered a brown, rather than a blue, suit for the occasion.

"We can fix that," said the obliging mortician. "Just drop back again about 6 o'clock."

Sure enough, when the widow called at 6, the change had been made. "It was easy," the mortician told her. "The woman whose husband is in the next room decided she preferred her husband in a *brown* suit . . ."

"So you traded suits?"

"Oh, no, we just switched heads!"

1230. Two men were looking for a lost horse. They asked a half-witted boy if he had seen it. The boy went off, and after a while came back leading the horse.

"How did you find him so quickly?" they inquired.

"I went over there and sat on the fence, and thought where I would go if I was a horse. And I did and he had!"

1231. He didn't want to marry her for her money, but he didn't know how else to get it.

1232. A preacher whose congregation usually spurned seats in the front of the church was surprised to see one man, a stranger, in the first row. After the sermon, the pastor asked the man why he sat down in front. The man replied that, being a bus driver, he wanted to find out how the preacher got people to move to the rear.

1233. "Your little boy is really very bright," the note accompanying the report card read. "But he spends entirely too much time playing with the girls. However, I am working on a plan to break him of the habit."

So Mama signed the card and sent it back with this reply: "Let me know if it works, and I'll try it out on his father."

Thrift

1234. *Wife modeling a new hat before husband:* "It didn't cost a thing. It was marked down from $20 to $10, so I bought it with the $10 I saved!"

1235. *Man* (to wife in swank decorator shop): "Instead of doing the room completely, dear, why don't we just paper it with dollar bills and bank the difference."

1236. "My boy," said the successful man lecturing his son on the importance of thrift, "when I was your age I carried water for a gang of bricklayers."

"I'm proud of you, father," answered the boy. "If it hadn't been for your pluck and perseverance, I might have had to do the same sort of thing myself."

1237. "Living in the past has a good point—it's cheaper!"

1238. When it comes to saving money, you've got to hand it to the women.

Tipping

1239. "What's the average tip on this train?" asked the traveler of the porter who brushed his coat.

"Two dollars," said the porter without batting an eye.

The traveler gave him two dollars and said, "You must make quite a lot of money on this job."

"Not as much as you might think," said the porter. "You're the first average I've had in six months."

1240. *Tourist* (having looked over historic castle): "I've made a stupid mistake."

Butler: "What was it?"

Tourist: "I tipped his lordship instead of you."

Butler: "That's awkward. I'll never get it now."

227

1241. The bill for his lunch in the dining car was $1.45, and the diner pulled out two one-dollar bills. The waiter brought, in change, a fifty-cent piece and a nickel. The guest looked up at the waiter, who gazed solemnly at the change tray. With a grunt of annoyance, he pocketed the half dollar and, to his astonishment, the waiter grinned widely.

"That's all right, sir," he chuckled. "I just gambled and lost. Just gambled and lost, that's all."

1242. A generous tipper at a hotel found a new waiter serving him breakfast one morning. "Where is my regular waiter?" he asked. "You know, that boy named Mose."

New Waiter: "Sir, Mose isn't serving you any more. I won you in a crap game last night."

1243. As a friend stuffed his soiled clothes in his laundry bag, he put a coin in the pocket of the trousers. Asked why, he said:

"I told the woman who does the washing that any money she found in my clothes she could keep," he told me. "She's old and lame, and it makes me feel good to give her this tip without hurting her pride."

Tit for tat

1244. "When an American has nothing else to do, he can always spend a few years trying to discover who his grandfather was," remarked Paul Bourget to Mark Twain.

"Right, Monsieur," answered Twain, "and when all other interests fail for a Frenchman, he can always try to find out who his father was, I reckon."

1245. Every morning for years, at about 11:30, the telephone operator in a small Sierra-Nevada town received a call from a man asking the exact time.

One day the operator summed up nerve enough to ask him why the regularity.

"I'm foreman of the local sawmill," he explained. "Every day I have to blow the whistle at noon so I call you to get the exact time."

The operator giggled. "That's really funny," she said. "All this time we've been setting our clock by your whistle."

1246. *Johnny* (offering some candy): "Here, darling, sweets to the sweet."

Mary: "Oh, thank you, and won't you have some of these nuts?"

1247. "Dear Clara," wrote the young man, "pardon me, but I'm getting so forgetful. I proposed to you last night, but really forgot whether you said yes or no."

"Dear Will," she replied by note, "so glad to hear from you. I knew that I had said no to somebody last night, but had forgotten who it was."

1248. "I'd like to have you look these shoes over and tell me whether they're worth mending," asked the physician of a repairer of shoes.

"I wouldn't spend any money on them," said the cobbler. "They're not worth it."

"All right, thank you," said the doctor as he turned to go.

"Fifty cents, please," said the shoe mender.

"Fifty cents! For what?" asked the medico. "You haven't done a thing."

"Neither did you the other day," said the shoe man, "when you examined me and charged me five dollars after telling me you found nothing wrong with me."

1249. "How much is the hotel bill?"

"Seventy-five dollars."

"Seventy-five dollars?"

"Yes—forty for room, thirty-five for meals."

"Thirty-five dollars for meals? But we didn't eat a meal here."

"The meals were here. If you didn't eat them, that's your fault."

"Then I will charge you thirty-five dollars for kissing my wife."

"But I didn't kiss your wife."

"That's okay. She was here. If you didn't kiss her, that's your fault."

"Your bill will be forty dollars."

1250. *Father:* "Son, when Lincoln was your age, he was earning his own living."

Son: "Yes, Father, and when he was your age he was President of the United States."

1251. Just prior to the Civil War, Susan B. Anthony was endeavoring to enlist the support of Horace Greeley, editor of the New York *Tribune,* in the cause of woman's rights. The great editor was opposed to woman's suffrage, among other reasons declaring that women were useless in wartime.

"What would you do," he demanded, "in the event of civil war?"

"Just what you would do, Mr. Greeley," promptly replied Miss Anthony. "I should sit in my office and write articles urging other people to go and fight."

1252. The following advertisement appeared in a small town newspaper:

"The man who picked up my wallet on Main Street was recognized. He is requested to return it."

The next day this reply was published:

"The recognized man who picked up your wallet requests the loser to call for it."

1253. Beatrice Lillie once attended a garden party wearing the famous Peel pearls. She was approached by a lady of great pretensions, who remarked: "What lovely pearls; I suppose they are genuine?" Beatrice indicated that they were. "Of course," said the lady, "you can always tell by biting them. Let me try." "Certainly," said Lady Peel, sarcastically, "but of course you know that you can't tell real pearls with false teeth."

1254. A man who had been waiting fifteen minutes on a Chicago street finally hailed a cab. Just as it drew up to the curb, a befurred dowager waddled up to the cab and climbed in triumphantly.

The gentleman, maintaining a cold calm, addressed the driver: "Did you come to the curb on my signal?"

"I certainly did."

"Then take this money," said the gentleman, "and drive around the block as long as it lasts."

The cab rolled away. After circling the block three times it stopped where the gentleman stood waiting. The dowager bounced out in a rage; the gentleman gallantly doffed his hat, entered the cab, and drove off.

1255. Wong, a Chinese servant, asked his master for permission to attend the funeral of another Chinese.

"All right," said his master, "and I suppose you'll put some food on the grave as the Chinese usually do."

"Yes, sir," Wong answered.

"Look here, Wong, when do you think your friend will eat that food?"

"As soon, sir, as the friend you buried last week will smell the flowers you put on his grave," was the crushing answer.

1256. *Angry father* (at 3 A.M.): "Well, young lady, where have you been until this hour?"

Daughter: "I've been sitting up with the son of the sick man you tell Mother you were sitting up with."

1257. A stranded English actor went into a sordid eating house in New York for a cheap meal. He was horrified to recognize his waiter as a colleague who had played with him in London.

"Great Scott!" he gasped. "You—a waiter—in this place!"

"Yes," replied the other in dignified scorn, "but I don't eat here."

1258. A frowning woman walked up to a little boy she caught smoking.

"Does your mother know you smoke?" she demanded.

"Lady," he countered, "does your husband know you stop and talk to strange men on the street?"

1259. Three girls had grown up together. Two of them married, and thereafter continually annoyed their spinster friend with tactless remarks about her unhappy condition.

She laughed off their comments good-naturedly until one day they went a bit too far.

"Now, tell us truthfully," they twitted her, "have you ever really had a chance to marry?"

With a withering glance, she retorted: "Suppose you ask your husbands."

1260. "I'm sorry the manager isn't in," said the clerk to the pompous individual who had strutted in. "Is there anything I can do for you?"

"No," snapped the visitor. "I never deal with underlings. I'll wait until the manager returns."

About an hour later the pompous one became impatient. "How much longer do you think the manager will be?" he demanded.

"About two weeks," was the reply. "He just left on his vacation."

1261. It was lunch hour at the plant, and Pat's two buddies decided to play a little joke on him during his absence. They drew the features of a donkey on the back of his coat. In due time, Pat returned and presently hove in sight bearing the decorated coat.

"What's the trouble, Pat?" asked one casually.

"Nothing much," replied Pat, equally indifferent, "only I'd like to know which of you wiped his face on my coat?"

1262. "Some of you pedestrians walk as if you owned the streets."

"Yes, and some of you motorists drive around just as if you owned your own cars."

1263. The District Attorney was questioning a Kentucky Colonel in court. Unable to shake his testimony, he turned to sarcasm.

"They call you colonel, do they not?" he sneered. "In just what regiment are you a colonel?"

"Well," drawled the witness, "it's like this. The 'Colonel' in front of my name is like the 'Honorable' in front of yours. It doesn't mean a thing."

1264. Two Irish friends greeted each other while waiting their turn at the bank window.

"This reminds me of Finnegan," remarked one.

"What about Finnegan?" inquired the other.

" 'Tis a story that Finnegan died, and when he greeted St. Peter, he said: 'It's a fine job you've had here for a long time.' 'Well, Finnegan,' said St. Peter, 'here we count a million years as a minute and a million dollars as a cent.' 'Ah!' said Finnegan, 'I'm needing cash. Lend me a cent.' 'Sure,' said St. Peter, 'just wait a minute.' "

1265. A romance of long standing had gone on the rocks, and a friend was questioning the would-be bridegroom.

"Why, after all these years," he inquired, "did you break your engagement to Mary?"

"Well," replied the other sadly. "I only did to the engagement what she did to me."

1266. The new elevator man went to his boss and asked to have the day off to help his wife with housecleaning.

"Jim, I am always glad to grant any reasonable request," said the employer, "but your wife has 'phoned saying she would not need you."

"Mr. Jones," replied Jim. "There are two persons in this building who handle the truth loosely and I am one of them. I am not married."

1267. A motorist and his wife hadn't spoken for miles. They'd gotten into a quarrel and neither would budge. Suddenly the man pointed at a mule in a pasture they were passing.

"A relative of yours?" he asked.

"Yes," the wife replied, "by marriage."

1268. *He:* "Why do you weep and snuffle at a picture show over the imaginary woes of people you never met?"

She: "For the same reason that you scream and yell when a man you don't know slides into second base."

1269. A minister, rather noted for his close calculations, also operated a small farm in Vermont.

One day he observed his hired man sitting idly by the plow, as his horses took a needed rest. This rather shocked the good man's sense of economy. After all he was paying the man $1.00 an hour. So he said, gently but reproachfully, "John, wouldn't it be a good plan for you to have a pair of shears and be trimming the bushes while the horses rest?"

"That it would," replied John agreeably. "And I suggest, your Reverence, that you take a peck of potatoes into the pulpit and peel them during the anthem."

1270. *Judge:* "Did you see that shot that was fired?"

Witness: "I only heard it."

Judge: "That is pure hearsay and inadmissible as evidence."

As the witness left the stand and as his back was turned to the judge, he laughed out loud. At once the judge called him back and was about to hold him in contempt of court.

Witness: "Did you see me laugh?"

Judge: "No, but I heard you."

Witness: "Isn't that the same kind of inadmissible evidence, Judge?"

1271. *Alice:* "Gracious, it's been five years since I've seen you. You look so much older, too."

Beatrice: "Really, my dear. I doubt if I would have recognized you, but for your coat."

1272. A sailor stationed on a far-flung U. S. outpost was noted for his loyalty to his fiancée. Then one day he received a callous letter telling him that she was going to marry a 4-F, and would he please return her picture.

He was so upset by this treachery that his buddies rallied to avenge their pal. A collection of photographs, snapshots, and pin-up girls was made from every fellow on the base. They were packed into a huge crate and shipped to the fickle wench.

Upon opening the crate, she found a note reading: "Please pick out your picture and return the rest to me. This is a little embarrassing but I don't remember which one is yours."

1273. A conceited bachelor was invited to dinner by a lady of consequence, but didn't accept. Meeting her on the street a few days later, he said in his best manner, "I believe you asked me to dine with you last week."

"Yes, I believe I did," responded the lady, adding, "and did you come?"

1274. The speaker stood up to speak, but was spellbound. The big and jubilant audience dazed him, and as he stammered and stuttered to get started, someone in the audience shouted: "Tell 'em all you know, Bill. It won't take long."

"I'll tell 'em all we both know," he shot back. "It won't take any longer."

Traffic, Automobile

1275. Hopelessly snarled in a traffic jam, the wife asked, "What shall I do?"

"I don't know," the husband answered, "but I'm sure if you climb into the back seat, you can figure it out."

1276. *Two men following a woman driver:*
"She's got her hand out the window," remarked one of the men. "What does that mean?"

"Only one thing for sure," replied the other. "The window is open."

1277. A young lady stalled her car at a traffic light. She stamped on the starter and tried again, while behind her an impatient citizen honked his horn steadily. Finally, she got out and walked back. "I'm awfully sorry, but I can't start my car," she told the driver of the other car. "If you'll go there and start it for me, I'll stay here and lean on your horn."

1278. *Sign on back of truck:* "Please don't hug me. I'm going steady."

1279. Two motorists met on a bridge too narrow for two cars to pass.

"I never back up for an idiot," shouted one driver.

"That's all right," replied the other quietly, as he shifted into reverse, "I always do."

1280. A woman trying to maneuver her sedan out of a parking space banged into the car ahead, then into the car behind, and finally, pulling into the street, struck a passing delivery truck. A policeman who had been watching approached her. "Let's see your license," he demanded.

"Don't be silly, officer," she said. "Who'd give *me* a license?"

1281. *Smart aleck tourist:* "What's your speed limit?"

Native son: "Ain't got none! You fellers can't go through here too fast to suit us."

1282. The world gets out of the way for a man who knows where he is going—so they say.

At a lecture, the speaker stated fervently: "He drove straight to his goal. He looked neither to the right nor to the left, but pressed forward, moved by a definite purpose. Neither friend nor foe could delay him nor turn him from his course. All who crossed his path did so at their own peril. What would you call such a man?"

"A truck driver!" shouted a voice.

TRAFFIC, AUTOMOBILE

1283. "The woman driver wouldn't have trouble squeezing into a parking space if she'd imagine it was a girdle or a pair of shoes."

1284. The reason there were fewer wrecks in the horse-and-buggy days was because the driver didn't depend entirely on his own intelligence.

1285. *Lady driver to mechanic:* "Fix my horn, my brakes don't work."

1286. *Young lady driver* (presenting parking ticket at police station): "Did one of your men lose this? I found it on my windshield!"

1287. Natives who beat drums to beat off evil spirits are objects of scorn to smart American motorists who blow horns to break up traffic jams.

1288. The biggest problems for traffic planners: Urban, suburban, and bourbon drivers.

1289. "How did you happen to hit the man?" asked the judge.
"I didn't," said the driver. "I came to a stop sign and stopped. I motioned for him to go across, and he fainted."

1290. In a contest in Surrey, England, for slogans for highway safety posters, one youngster came up with this suggestion:
He looked; she didn't.
He is; she isn't.

1291. To insist on drinking before driving, is to put the quart before the hearse.

1292. *Tom:* "What part of an automobile kills the most people?"
Harry: "The nut behind the wheel."

1293. The Sunday-school teacher was describing how Lot's wife looked back and turned into a pillar of salt, when little Jimmy interrupted. "My mother looked back once while she was driving," he announced triumphantly, "and *she* turned into a telephone pole!"

1294. "It's not just the work I enjoy," confided the cab driver, "it's the people I run into."

1295. Two drunks went tearing down the street in a high-powered Chrysler at better than sixty miles an hour.

"Whew! This is awful," cried the one seated alongside the driver. "I just can't take it."

"Okay, then," replied the driver. "Jush close your eyes like I'm doing."

1296. "I've had my eye on you for some time, miss," said the motorcycle cop.

"Fancy that," was the airy reply. "And I thought you were arresting me for speeding."

1297. *Officer:* "Why did you keep on going after I whistled?"

Lady driver: "Sorry, officer, I'm pretty deaf."

Officer: "Well, don't worry, lady, you'll get your hearing in the morning."

1298. A lot of friction on the highways is caused by half the drivers trying to go fast enough to thrill their girl friends, and the other half trying to go slow enough to placate their wives.

1299. While they were waiting for the police to arrive, another chap ran over to the scene of the accident.

"Are you a doctor?" pleaded the driver.

"Yes, but I'm afraid I can't help you. I'm a veterinary doctor."

"You'll do all right," said the motorist. "I'm just a jackass to think I could do eighty-seven miles an hour and beat the train to the crossing."

1300. Statistics prove that locomotives are not afraid of automobiles.

1301. The new traffic cop had been told by the inspector to overtake and stop a speeding car. Ten minutes later he called in to report: "Car was being driven by an actress. I stops her, pulls out my notebook. She snatches it, writes her autograph, and leaves me standing."

1302. His car and her car met head-on. Both drivers got out and, with the fine courtesy characteristic of motorists nowadays, both began to apologize profusely. "I'm so sorry," said the woman. "It was all my fault."

"Not at all," the man gallantly responded. "It is I who am to blame."

"But," interrupted the woman, "I insist it was my fault."

"In a sense, that may be true, but, my dear madam, the fact is that I am responsible for the collision. You see, I saw you coming blocks away, and I had ample opportunity to turn off on some side street."

1303. *Judge:* "I am revoking your driver's license, and you will not be allowed to drive a car for two years. You're a danger to pedestrians."

Motorist: "But, your honor, my living depends on it."

Judge: "Yes, and so does theirs."

1304. A motorist had been haled into court, and when his name was called the judge asked what the charges were against the defendant.

"Suspicious actions, your Honor," answered the arresting officer.

"Suspicious actions?" queried His Honor. "What was he doing that seemed suspicious?"

"Well," replied the officer, "he was running within the speed limit, sounding his horn properly, and trying to keep on the right side of the street, so I arrested him."

1305. *Judge:* "Could the motorist have possibly avoided you?"

Injured pedestrian: "He could have, your Honor. He had the choice of hitting me or the missus, and he picked me."

1306. The trailer truck driver hauling a load of new cars was having headlight trouble. Unable to correct the trouble, he finally climbed up and turned on the lights of the front car. Pulling his rig back on the highway, the trucker saw an approaching car suddenly swerve, smash through a guardrail, and skid into a cornfield. He halted the truck, ran back to the overturned car, and pulled out two stunned but uninjured occupants.

"What happened?" demanded the trucker.

"Well, as I was telling Sam," explained the dazed motorist, "if that thing is as wide as it is high, we'd better get off the road."

1307. If all the cars in the nation were placed end to end, some fool would pull out and try to pass 'em.

Travel

1308. It was Mrs. Shiplett's first ocean voyage, and she was deathly ill. Wanting to comfort her as much as he could, the steward told her: "Don't be so downhearted, lady, I have never heard of anyone dying of seasickness."

"Oh, don't tell me that," was her reply, "it's only hope of dying that has kept me alive so far."

1309. Two women were preparing to board the airliner. One of them turned to the pilot and said, "Now please don't travel faster than sound. We want to talk."

1310. *Traveler* (on an English train): "Shall I have time to get a drink?"

Guard: "Yes, sir."

Traveler: "Can you give me a guarantee that the train won't start?"

Guard: "Yes, I'll take one with you."

1311. She had insisted on taking along every garment she owned, and they arrived at the station loaded with baggage.

"I wish," said the husband thoughtfully, "that we had brought your piano."

"Now, don't be sarcastic," came his wife's frigid reply.

"I'm not being sarcastic," he said wistfully. "I left the tickets on it."

1312. The conductor was perplexed. "Who on earth," he sputtered, "would want to steal a Pullman ladder?"

Just then the curtain parted and the little old lady poked her head through cautiously.

"Conductor," she whispered, "you may use mine if you like. I won't need it until morning."

1313. A man touring Europe sent back to his son a picture postcard which bore the following message: "Dear Son: On the other side you will see a picture of the rock from which the Spartans threw their defective children. Wish you were here! Dad."

1314. A certain Mr. Jones, who had recently come into a great fortune after having been a member of the lowest income group, decided that he and his wife should take a very grand holiday.

TRAVEL

After much deliberation they settled for a round-the-world cruise on a liner of extreme luxury.

They loaded themselves with luggage, and reserved the largest and most expensive suite on the ship.

When the Captain scanned his passenger list to find the most likely influential people to dine at his table, he came across Mr. Jones's name, and, on inquiring who he was, was told that he had booked the No. 1 suite and had filled half the luggage space with his trunks and baggage.

Here seemed the right man. The Captain sent the chief steward to the Jones's cabin with an invitation to join him for dinner.

The steward was extremely surprised to receive the following reply: "What? I spend a fortune to get the finest and best suite on this beautiful ship, and now I'm expected to eat with the crew!"

1315. A rich man lying on his death bed called his chauffeur, who had been in his service for years, and said:

"Ah, Sykes, I am going on a long and rugged journey, worse than ever you drove me."

"Well, sir," consoled the chauffeur, "there's one comfort—it's all down-hill and you won't be needing any gasoline."

1316. An old lady was taking her first train ride, and at night the porter came through the coach with pillows.

"How much are they?" she asked.

"Twenty-five cents," the porter replied.

"I'll take six," she said. "I could never get them that cheap in a department store."

1317. He was making his first ocean voyage and was in his cabin, groaning with seasickness.

"Shall I send you some dinner, sir?" asked the steward.

"No," was the reply. "Just throw it overboard and save me the trouble."

1318. A farmer went to the large city to see the sights, and took a room at a hotel. Before retiring, he asked the clerk about the hours for meals.

"We have breakfast from 7 to 11, dinner from 12 to 3, and supper from 6 to 8," explained the clerk.

"Say," inquired the surprised farmer, "when will I ever get to see the town?"

1319. A customs officer asked the feminine traveler:
"Have you anything special to declare, madam?"
"No," she replied, "not a thing."
"Then, am I to understand, my lady," the officer replied, "that the fur tail hanging down from under your coat is your own?"

1320. A young lady was going on a sight-seeing tour of Detroit. Going out Jefferson Avenue, the driver of the bus called out all the places of interest.
"On the right," he announced, "we see the Dodge home."
"John Dodge?" the lady asked.
"No, madam, Horace Dodge."
Continuing on further, he called out: "On the far left corner we have the Ford home."
"Henry?" she suggested.
"No, lady, Edsel."
Still farther out on Jefferson: "On the near-left crossing you will see Christ Church."
"Jesus, or am I wrong again?" the lady sheepishly asked.

1321. An American woman visiting in Paris before World War II went to a bureau which provided men as escorts. When informed that she could engage either a Northerner or a Southerner, she asked the difference, and was told the Southerners were gallant and debonair, while the Northerners were smooth talkers and romantic.
"Well, then," she said, "I'll take a Southerner from as far north as possible."

1322. "We are now passing Guinness's, Ireland's largest brewery," said the conductor-guide.
"We are not!" said the tourist—and he hopped off the coach.

Twins

1323. George had just become engaged, and his friend Harry went over to congratulate him.
"Well, old boy," said George, as he grasped his friend's hand,

"my congratulations to you! Is it true that you are engaged to one of the Enright twins?"

"Yes," replied George enthusiastically, "I'm happy to say it is so."

"But," inquired George, "how do you ever tell them apart?"

"I don't try to."

1324. A mother brought her four-year-old twins to a store for a final fitting of identical coats. Wouldn't the twins like to see themselves in the mirror, the store owner asked.

"Oh, that won't be necessary," the mother replied. "They never do—they just look at each other."

Usefulness

1325. *Salesman:* "Ladies and gentlemen, I have here the famous flexible comb that will stand any kind of treatment. You can bend it double—you can hit it with a hammer—you can twist it—you can—"

Interested listener: "Say, mister, can you comb your hair with it?"

1326. "You don't make very good music with that instrument," said a bystander to the man with the big bass drum, as the band ceased to play.

"No," admitted the tympanist, "I know I don't; but I drown a heap of bad music."

1327. *John:* "You remind me of an airplane."

Jim: "How come?"

John: "You're no good on earth."

Vacation

1328. *Al:* "How do you afford such long holidays?"

Gene: "Easily. One month on the sands and eleven months on the rocks."

1329. A vacation is an experience that is simultaneously broadening and flattening.

1330. *Phil:* "Where are you going on your vacation?"

Will: "Haven't decided yet. I want to take a trip around the world, but my wife wants to go some place else."

1331. *Uncle:* "Well, Frankie, what are you going to do this vacation?"

Frankie: "Last year I had chicken pox and mumps. This year I don't know what I'm going to do."

1332. "You didn't take a vacation this year, did you?"
"No, I thought I needed a rest."

1333. One summer evening when Thomas A. Edison returned home from his work, his wife said, "You've worked too long without a rest. You must take a vacation."

"But where will I go?" he asked.

"Decide where you'd rather be than anywhere else on earth and go there," was the answer.

"Very well," promised Mr. Edison, "I will go tomorrow."

The next morning he returned to his laboratory.

Veracity

1334. A Hollywood producer got in early one morning to find his wife awake and raging. "Where have you been?" she demanded. "Well," the producer explained, "we previewed my new picture, and then I got to talking to the leading lady—a very lovely person. We went to Romanoff's, had a few drinks, and then she said she'd like me to see her to her apartment. Well, you know how it is—one thing led to another, and here I am." "Now, don't you lie to me, you horrible creature!" screamed the wife. "I know you've been out all night playing poker with the boys!"

1335. A woman noticed that a man was following her and stopped to ask him why.

"Because I have fallen in love with you," he said.

"My sister, who is coming after me, is much prettier than I," she said. "Go back and make love to her."

The man went back, but the next woman was very ugly. Angry, he hastened after the first woman and asked:

"Why should you tell me a lie?"

"Neither did you tell me the truth," she answered, "for if you were in love with me, why did you go back looking for another woman?"

VERACITY

1336. The captain of a ship once wrote in his log, "Mate was drunk today." When the mate became normal, he was terribly chagrined and angry; he pleaded with the captain to strike out the record; he declared that he had never been drunk before; that he would never drink again. But the captain said, "In this log we write the exact truth."

The next week the mate kept the log, and in it he wrote, "Captain was sober today."

1337. A New Yorker, pointing to a hillside field, complimented the New Englander on his corn.

"How do you plow that field? It looks pretty steep."

"Don't plow it; when the spring thaws come, the rocks rolling down hill tear it up."

"That so? How do you plant it?"

"Don't plant it really. Just stand in my back door and shoot the seed in with a shotgun."

"Is that the truth?" asked the New Yorker.

"Hell, no. That's conversation."

1338. *Bus driver* (to little girl): "You're only six? When will you be eleven?"

Little girl: "When I get off the bus."

1339. It was 2:30 a.m. when little Sally woke up.

"Tell me a story, mama," she pleaded.

"Hush, dear," replied the wife. "Daddy ought to be along pretty soon now, and he'll tell us both one."

1340. "What is the defendant's reputation for veracity?" asked the judge.

"Your Honor," said the witness, "I have known him to admit that he had been fishing all day and hadn't gotten a single bite."

1341. "Does your husband always lie to you?"

"No, some nights I'm too tired to ask questions."

1342. *Caller:* "I want to see the boss."

Office girl: "Sorry, but he's in conference with the vice-president and general manager."

Caller: "Let me in. I know a funny story too."

244

1343. Heywood Broun was listening with disbelief to a speaker at a political rally who was giving his own version of the facts.

"How does he get away with it?" whispered a fellow reporter to Broun. "He's murdering the truth."

Broun shook his head in disagreement. "He'll never get close enough to it to do it bodily harm," he said.

1344. One day, while President Grant was sitting in his bedroom in the White House where he had retired to write a message to Congress, a card was brought in by a servant.

An officer on duty at the time, seeing that the President did not want to be disturbed, remarked to the servant, "Say the President is not in."

General Grant overheard the remark, turned around suddenly in his chair, and cried out to the servant:

"Tell him no such thing! I don't lie myself, and don't want anyone to lie for me!"

War

1345. A German was the guest of a Frenchman who asked him how they distinguish between an optimist and a pessimist in Germany.

"It is very simple," replied the German. "The optimists are learning English and the pessimists are learning Russian."

1346. "Who are those people who are cheering?" asked the recruit as the soldiers marched toward the train.

"Those," replied the veteran, "are the people who are not going."

1347. A war was going on, and one day, the papers being full of the grim details of a bloody battle, a woman said to her husband:

"This slaughter is shocking. It's fiendish. Can nothing be done to stop it?"

"I'm afraid not," her husband answered.

"Why don't both sides get together and arbitrate?" she asked.

"They did," said he. "They did several months ago. That's how the whole thing got started."

Wealth

1348. Money still talks; but with the dollar so depreciated, it no longer talks common cents.

1349. To show their contempt for wealth ("Who steals my gold steals trash"), the original owners of the Venetian Palazzo Rezzonico, after giving great banquets, used to throw the gold plate into the side canal. However, a net had first been placed in the canal, and, after the departure of all the guests, it was hauled in and the gold plate replaced in its repository.

1350. A multimillionaire was being interviewed about his self-made fortune. "I never hesitate," he said, "to give full credit to my wife for her assistance."

"And just how did she help?" asked a reporter.

"Frankly," said the millionaire, "I was curious to see if there was any income she couldn't live beyond."

1351. Years ago, when Ernie Pyle was on the Washington *News* as a $30-a-week copyreader, he tagged a story with the headline: "Man Inherits Huge Fortune of $15,000."

"Where do you get the idea that $15,000 is a huge fortune?" his executive editor asked.

"If you were earning the same dough I am," Ernie replied, "you'd think so, too."

1352. *She:* "Which is more satisfied, a man with a million dollars or a man with six children?"

He: "A man with six children."

She: "Can you prove it?"

He: "Yes, a man with a million dollars wants more."

1353. One day a farmer came to pay his rent to a man whose love of money was very great. After settling the account, the farmer said, "I will give you a shilling if you will let me go down to the vault and have a look at your money."

The farmer was permitted to see the piles of gold and silver in the miser's big chest. After gazing for a while the farmer said, "Now I am as well off as you are."

"How can that be?" asked the man.

"Why, sir," said the farmer, "you never use any of this money. All you do with it is look at it. I have looked at it, too, so I am just as rich as you are."

1354. A young father, proudly holding his infant son in his arms, was lost in thought as his mind trailed off into a daydream of happy anticipation of a successful future. Suddenly he turned to his wife and said, "You know, dear, I'm going to work hard, and some day we are going to be rich."

His wife quickly replied, "We are already rich, dear. We have each other. Some day maybe we'll have money."

Woman-Women

1355. Confusion is one woman plus one left turn; excitement is two women plus one secret; bedlam is three women plus one bargain; chaos is four women plus one luncheon check.

1356. There is only one way to handle a woman. The trouble is, nobody knows what it is.

1357. Women are a lot like ships. If kept in good shape and painted occasionally, they will stay see-worthy.

1358. "But, Captain, why do they always call a ship 'she'?"
"You wouldn't ask that, Miss, if you'd ever tried to steer one."

1359. "Ma," said the small boy, "why are the women in this country always so tired?"

"What makes you ask such a question?"

"Well, most every place we go, I see a place marked 'Ladies' Rest Room.' "

1360. *Life Insurance Actuary:* "At the age of 75, there are 18 per cent more women than men."

Agent: "At 75, who cares?"

1361. A woman is like a newspaper because:
(1) they both have forms;
(2) back numbers are not in demand;
(3) they're well worth looking over;

(4) they have a good deal of influence;

(5) there's small demand for the bold-faced type;

(6) you can't believe all they say;

(7) they always have the last word; and

(8) every man should have one of his own and not go borrowing his neighbor's.

1362. The trouble with being a woman these days is that you've got to look like a girl, dress like a boy, think like a man, and work like a dog.

1363. "I love women," the famous lecturer told his feminine audience, "whether they are charming or beautiful."

"What's the difference?" came a voice from the enraptured audience.

"There is quite a difference, dear lady. You see, a beautiful woman is one *you* notice, while a charming one is one who notices you."

DEFINITIONS

SECTION

A

Ability: a poor man's worth.

Abstainer: a weak person who yields to the temptation of denying himself a pleasure.

Absurdity: a statement of belief manifestly inconsistent with one's own opinion.

Accident: 1. a condition of affairs in which presence of mind is good, but absence of body is better. 2. a head-on collision between two stationary cars parked on their own sides of the road.

Accordion: an instrument invented by the man who couldn't decide how big the one was that got away.

Accordion music: noise that comes from playing both ends against the middle.

Acquaintance: 1. a degree of friendship called slight when its object is poor or obscure, and intimate when he is rich or famous. 2. a person we know who falls short of being a friend, either because he isn't well-to-do enough, or because he won't let us borrow from him. 3. a person whom we know well enough to borrow from, but not well enough to lend to.

Actor: 1. a guy who, if you ain't talking about him, he ain't listening. 2. a man who tries to be everything but himself. 3. a man with an infinite capacity for taking praise. 4. a person who makes $50,000 a year some weeks.

Actor's agent: a guy who sometimes bites the ham who feeds him.

Adherent: a follower who has not yet obtained all that he expects to get.

Admiration: our polite recognition of another's resemblance to ourselves.

251

DEFINITIONS

Adolescence: 1. an independent state, highly taxing yet often insolvent; located just beyond comprehension. 2. a period in which girls try to make little boys stop asking questions, and big boys begin. 3. a period in which children begin to question the answers. 4. that period when a boy refuses to believe that someday he'll be as dumb as his father. 5. that period when children feel their parents should be told the facts of life. 6. the period in which the young suddenly begin to feel a great responsibility about answering the phone. 7. the period when a girl begins to powder and a boy begins to puff. 8. when a boy has reached the state when he knows why a strapless gown must be held up, but doesn't understand how. 9. when boys begin to notice that girls notice boys who notice girls. 10. when children start bringing up their parents.

Adolescent: 1. a person old enough to stay up for the late programs on TV and young enough to enjoy them. 2. a teen-ager who acts like a baby when you don't treat him like an adult.

Adore: to venerate expectantly.

Adult: one who has stopped growing except in the middle.

Adversity: 1. the only diet that will reduce a fat head. 2. the state in which a man most easily becomes acquainted with himself, being especially free from admirers then.

Advertising: that which makes you think you've longed all your life for something you never even heard of.

Advertising agency: eighty-five percent confusion and fifteen percent commission.

Advertising man: yessir, nosir, ulcer.

Advice: 1. something which we give by the bushel but take by the grain. 2. that which the wise don't need and fools won't take. 3. the one thing which it is "more blessed to give than receive." 4. the worst vice. 5. you never know whether it's good or not until you no longer need it.

After-dinner speaker: 1. a fellow who rises to the occasion—and then stands too long. 2. a man who knows exactly what not to say, but not when to quit saying it. 3. a person who only has a few words to say, but seldom stops when he has said them. 4. the guy who starts the bull rolling.

After-dinner speeches: though boresome, they give us the low-down on a lot of people we used to consider bright.

Age: that which makes wine worth more and women less.

Airflow: condition of a car created by putting the wife in the back seat.

Airplanes: one of those things that's of no earthly use.

Air travel: seeing less and less of more and more.

Alarm clock: that which scares the daylights out of you.

Alas: early Victorian for—oh, hell.

Alcohol: 1. a liquid good for preserving almost everything except secrets. 2. something which often puts the wreck in recreation. 3. the only known substance that will make a woman beautiful when taken internally—by her escort.

Alibi: slip cover.

Alimony: 1. a man's cash surrender value. 2. another war debt a lot of husbands would like to see canceled. 3. a one-man war debt. 4. a splitting headache. 5. bounty on the mutiny. 6. giving comfort to the enemy. 7. man's best proof that you have to pay for your mistakes. 8. one more form of the guaranteed annual wage. 9. the high cost of leaving. 10. the high cost of loving. 11. the method some women use for taking the drudgery out of housework. 12. the stuff that makes separations look like reparations. 13. when a bride continues to get wedding gifts after the divorce.

Alliance: in international politics, the union of two thieves who have their hands so deeply inserted in each other's pockets that they cannot separately plunder a third.

Amateur photographer: a person who takes a dim view of things.

Ambition: 1. a boy's future; a man's past. 2. an itching sensation caused by inflammation of the wishbone. 3. the last refuge of the failure. 4. what it takes to get where you'll wish you hadn't bothered.

DEFINITIONS

America: 1. a nation that conceives many odd inventions for getting somewhere, but can think of nothing to do when it gets there. 2. a place where they lock up juries and let defendants out. 3. a land of untold wealth. 4. the country where you buy a lifetime supply of aspirin for one dollar, and use it up in two weeks. 5. the land where in one generation a family can rise from a plain cabin to a cabin plane. 6. the wonderful land where it's trashy to sit on the back stoop in your undershirt, but gracious living if you've got nothing on but your shorts.

American: 1. a person who isn't afraid to bawl out the President, but who is always polite to a politician. 2. a person who yells for the government to balance the budget and borrows five dollars 'til payday. 3. one who doesn't know the words to "The Star-Spangled Banner."

American history: the replacement of the red Indian by red tape.

American idealism: being willing to make any sacrifice that won't hurt business.

Americanism: 1. trying to make hotels more like homes; trying to make homes more like hotels. 2. voting to set the speed limit at 45 and demanding a car which will do 90.

Americans: those who think they are as good as anybody, and those who think they are better.

Anatomy: something that everyone has, but it looks better on a girl.

Ancestral pride: going forward by backing up.

Ant: a small insect that, though always at work, still finds time to go to picnics.

Anthologist: a lazy fellow who likes to spend a quiet evening at home "raiding a good book."

Antique: 1. an object that has made a round trip to the attic. 2. something no one would be seen with if there were more of them. 3. something too old to be anything but too expensive.

Any business man: one who could have made more money with less trouble in an easier line.

254

Apology: 1. egotism wrong side out. 2. laying the foundation for a future offence. 3. politeness too late. 4. the attempt to escape punishment for a mistake.

Appeaser: one who feeds a crocodile—hoping it will eat him last.

Appendicitis: a modern pain, costing about $200 more than the old-fashioned stomach ache.

Appendix girl: the kind that gets taken out.

Archaeology: a science that proves you can't keep a good man down.

Arch criminal: one who robs shoe stores.

Architects: people who now have to measure their patrons for the breakfast nook.

Argument: where two people are trying to get the last word in first.

Army captain: a uniform with two chips on each shoulder.

Arson: fire caused by friction between the insurance policy and the mortgage.

Artichoke: 1. strip tease with mayonnaise. 2. the only vegetable you have more of when you finish eating it, than you had when you started.

Artistic temperament: seldom recognized until it's too old to spank.

Art school: a place for young girls to pass the time between high school and marriage.

Artist's model: a girl unsuited for her work.

Ash tray: something for a cigarette butt when there is no floor.

Assistant: a fellow that can't get off.

Atheist: 1. a man who doesn't care who wins the Notre Dame-S.M.U. football game. 2. a man who has no invisible means of support. 3. a man who looks through a telescope and tries to explain all that he can't see.

DEFINITIONS

Athlete: a dignified bunch of muscles, unable to split wood or sift ashes.

Auction: a place where, if you aren't careful, you'll get something for nodding.

Auctioneer: the man who proclaims with a hammer that he has picked a pocket with his tongue.

August: the month you can't open the bus window which you couldn't close in December.

Author: a fool who, not content with having bored those who have lived with him, insists on boring future generations.

Autobiography: fiction written by someone who knows the facts.

Auto driver: a person who speeds up to get in front of you so he can slow down.

Automation: the science of doing it with machines at the plant so that men can have more time to do it themselves at home.

Automobile: 1. a guided missile. 2. a vehicle which is rapidly dividing mankind into two classes, the quick and the dead.

Average husband: one who isn't as good as she thought he was before she married him, nor as bad as she thinks he is afterward.

Average man: 1. a person who doesn't want much, and usually gets a little less than that. 2. one who thinks he isn't. 3. the fellow who gets mad when you refer to him as the average man.

Average person: one who thinks someone else is the average person.

Awkward age: when girls are too old to count on their fingers and too young to count on their legs.

Axiom: a thing that is so visible that it is not necessary to see it.

B

Babble: a feminine noise, somewhat resembling the sound of a brook, but with less meaning.

Babies: 1. angels whose wings grow shorter as their legs grow longer. 2. little rivets in the bonds of matrimony.

Baby: 1. alimentary canal with a loud voice at one end and no responsibility at the other. 2. an inhabitant of Lapland. 3. a nocturnal animal to which everyone in a sleeping car is eager to give a wide berth. 4. a tiny feather from the wing of love dropped into the sacred lap of motherhood. 5. morning caller, noonday crawler, midnight bawler. 6. something that gets you down in the daytime and up at night.

Baby sitter: 1. one who accepts hush money. 2. what too many women in slacks definitely don't have.

Baby sitters: girls you hire to watch your television sets.

Bachelor: 1. a chap who believes it's much better to have loved and lost than to have to get up for the 2 A.M. feeding. 2. a fellow who hasn't anyone to share the troubles he doesn't have. 3. a fellow who has only himself to blame. 4. a fellow who usually wants one single thing in life—himself. 5. a guy with just a single thought: staying that way. 6. a guy who is footloose and fiancée-free. 7. a man who can be miss-led only so far. 8. a man who can get out of bed from either side. 9. a man who can have a girl on his knees without having her on his hands. 10. a man who can keep both a checking account and a savings account. 11. a man who can pull on his socks from either end. 12. a man who can take a nap on top of the bedspread. 13. a man who does not want to play troth or consequences. 14. a man who'd rather have a woman on his mind than on his neck. 15. a man who hasn't yet come face-to-face with a feminine roadblock. 16. a man who hasn't made the same mistake once. 17. a man who looks, but does not leap. 18. a man who plays the field without ever fielding the play. 19. a man who refuses to run the risk of ob-

257

DEFINITIONS

taining a master's degree. 20. a man who tries to avoid the issue. 21. a man who, when he accomplishes something, gets all the credit himself. 22. a man who will get married as soon as he can find a girl who will love him as much as he does. 23. a man who wouldn't take yes for an answer. 24. a man who would rather cook his own goose. 25. a man who would rather wash a pair of socks than a sink full of dishes. 26. a man with enough confidence in his judgment of women to act upon it. 27. an eligible mass of obstinacy entirely surrounded by suspicion. 28. an unmarried man who has been singularly lucky in his love affairs. 29. a selfish, callous, undeserving man who has cheated some worthy woman out of a divorce. 30. a guy who didn't have a car when he was young. 31. one who knows when he receives a Christmas present he won't have to pay for it later. 32. the most miss-informed man in town. 33. the only species of big game for which the license is taken out after the safari.

Bachelor girl: a girl who is still looking for a bachelor.

Bachelors: married men may have better halves, but bachelors have better quarters.

Bachelor's life: just one undarned thing after another.

Backward nation: one that hasn't tried to borrow money from the U.S.A.

Bad girl: nothing but a good girl found out.

Bad husband: the only thing that beats a good wife.

Bad luck: to have thirteen people seated at the table when you're paying for the drinks.

Bad times: a period when people worry about the business outlook instead of being on the lookout for business.

Bagdad: what mother did when she met father.

Balanced diet: what you eat at buffet suppers.

Bald-headed man: one who, when expecting callers, has only to straighten his necktie.

Baldness: hair today and gone tomorrow.

258

DEFINITIONS

Bank: 1. an institution that has a hard time getting all its vice-presidents to attend a directors' meeting without giving the public the impression of a run on the bank. 2. an institution that will gladly lend you money provided you can prove you are already so well off that you really don't need it.

Banker: a man who offers you an umbrella when the sun is shining, then wants it back when it starts to rain.

Bankruptcy: a legal proceeding in which you put your money in your pants pocket and give your coat to your creditors.

Banquet: 1. a fifty-cent dinner served in sufficient number to enable a caterer to charge five dollars for it. 2. an affair where you eat a lot of food you don't want before talking about something you don't understand to a crowd of people who don't want to hear you. 3. a plate of cold chicken and anaemic green peas completely surrounded by dreary speakers and appeals for donations.

Barber: a brilliant conversationalist, who occasionally shaves and cuts hair.

Bargain: 1. a disease common to women, caught in the Sunday papers and developed in department stores on Mondays. 2. a transaction in which each party thinks he has cheated the other. 3. something you can't use, at a price you can't resist.

Bargain hunter: one who is often led astray by false profits.

Bargain sale: where a woman can ruin one dress while she buys another.

Barometer: an ingenious instrument which indicates what kind of weather we are having.

Baseball: 1. a game in which the young man who bravely strikes out for himself receives no praise for it. 2. a game many enjoy more than football because they don't need a college education to get tickets.

Baseball fan: a spectator sitting 500 feet from the plate who can see better than an umpire standing five feet away.

Bathing beauty: 1. a girl who has a lovely profile all the way down. 2. a girl who is worth wading for.

DEFINITIONS

Bathing suit: 1. a garment with no hooks but plenty of eyes on it. 2. the little bit that isn't bare.

Bathing suit, modern: two bandannas and a worried look.

Beach: a place where people lie upon the sand about how rich they are in town.

Beauty: a pretty, effective substitute for brains.

Beauty contest: lass roundup.

Beauty parlor: 1. a place where women can let their hair down while it's being put up. 2. where the talk alone is enough to curl your hair.

Beauty shop: where men are rare and women well done.

Benefactor: one who makes two smiles grow where one grew before.

Best people: the ones your wife knew before she married you.

Bigamist: 1. a man who keeps two himself. 2. a man who makes the same mistake twice. 3. a person who took one too many. 4. one who marries twice in a wifetime.

Bigamy: 1. when a fellow loves not wisely—but two well. 2. having one husband too many and monogamy is frequently the same thing. 3. when one loves not wisely, but too well. 4. two rites that make a wrong. 5. when a man marries a beautiful girl and a good cook. 6. when a man marries a beautiful girl and a good housewife.

Big gun: frequently an individual of small calibre and immense bore.

Bigot: one who is obstinately and zealously attached to an opinion that you do not entertain.

Big shots: only little shots who keep shooting.

Bill collector: 1. a man who doesn't believe in putting off until tomorrow what can be dunned today. 2. a man whom few care to see but many ask to call again.

Birth control: evasion of the issue.

260

Birthday: anniversary of one's birth. Observed only by men and children.

Blind date: when you expect to meet a vision and she turns out to be a sight.

Blonde: an established bleachhead.

Blotter: something you spend time looking for while the ink is drying.

Blunderbuss: kissing the wrong girl in the dark.

Blunt person: one who says what he thinks without thinking.

Bonds of matrimony: worthless unless the interest is kept up.

Book censor: a person who reads so much he gets asterisks in front of his eyes.

Book ends: the part of a book many girls read first.

Book jacket: fable of contents.

Bookworm: a person who would rather read than eat, or a worm that would rather eat than read.

Bore: 1. a fellow who can change the subject to his topic of conversation faster than you can change it back to yours. 2. a fellow who opens his mouth and puts his feats in it. 3. a guy who is here today and here tomorrow. 4. a guy who keeps the conversation ho-humming. 5. a guy with a one crack mind. 6. a man who deprives you of solitude without providing you with company. 7. a person who has flat feats. 8. a person who knows the same stories you do. 9. one who insists upon talking about himself when you want to talk about yourself. 10. one who is interesting to a point—the point of departure. 11. one whose shortcoming is his long-staying. 12. the kind of man who, when you ask him how he is, tells you. 13. the one on your invitation list who never has a previous engagement.

Borrower: 1. a man who tries to live within your means. 2. one who exchanges hot air for cold cash.

Boss: the man who is early when you are late, and late when you are early.

261

DEFINITIONS

Boss of the family: whoever can spend ten dollars without thinking it necessary to say anything about it.

Bostonian: an American, broadly speaking.

Bowling alley: a quiet place of amusement where you can hear a pin drop.

Boy: 1. a noise with some dirt on it. 2. a pain in the neck when he is around; a pain in the heart when he isn't.

Braggart: a person who starts out telling white lies and soon grows color blind.

Brain: the apparatus with which we think we think.

Brains: 1. what a man looks for in a wife, after not using any in selecting one. 2. what a man looks for in a woman after he's looked at everything else.

Brat: a child who displays his pest manners.

Breeding: the quality that enables a person to wait in well-mannered silence while the loudmouth gets the service.

Brevity: words that cover more ground than they occupy.

Bridegroom: a wolf who paid too much for his whistle.

Bridge: 1. a card game in which a good deal depends on a good deal. 2. a game which gives women something to try to think about while they are talking.

Bridge partner: a person who is undesirable if he has a one-trick mind.

Brilliant epigram: a solemn platitude gone to a masquerade ball.

Broad-mindedness: 1. the ability to smile when you suddenly discover that your roommate and your girl are both missing from the dance floor. 2. high-mindedness which has been flattened by experience.

Broadway: 1. America's hardened artery. 2. a place where people spend money they haven't earned to buy things they don't need to impress people they don't like.

262

Budget: 1. a bunch of figures that prove you shouldn't have gotten married in the first place. 2. a mathematical confirmation of our suspicions. 3. a method of worrying before you spend, instead of afterward. 4. an attempt to live below your yearnings. 5. an orderly system of living beyond your means. 6. telling your money where to go instead of wondering where it went. 7. what you can't do to a woman's mind once it's made up.

Budgeting: the most orderly way of going into debt.

Bulldozing: going to sleep during a political speech.

Bum: 1. a chap who is jugged by the company he keeps. 2. a man who has lived down to his own ideals.

Bus: 1. a vehicle that has empty seats when going in the opposite direction. 2. where a man will stand for anything but a woman.

Business: the only thing which can be dead and still have a chance to revive.

Business man: one who talks golf all morning at the office, and business all afternoon on the links.

Busy body: one born with an interferiority complex.

C

Caddie: 1. a boy who stands behind a golfer, and who didn't see where it went either. 2. a golfing expert who loses balls for you in one round, so that he can find them for himself in the next. 3. a small boy employed at a liberal stipend to lose balls for others and find them for himself. 4. one of those little things that count.

Calamity: a more than commonly plain and unmistakable reminder that the affairs of this life are not of our own ordering. Calamities are of two kinds: misfortune to ourselves and good fortune to others.

California patriot: a man who derives a certain amount of satisfaction from getting almost killed by a Florida hurricane.

DEFINITIONS

Camel: an animal that looks as though it had been put together by a committee.

Camp: where parents spend $1,000 for eight weeks to teach their son to make a 25-cent ash tray.

Canapés: a sandwich cut into 24 pieces.

Candidate: one who talks about public opinion until he's defeated, then about herd ignorance.

Cannibal chief: one who gets fed up with people.

Capitalism: the system by which one lives on the wealth of brains —his father's or his own.

Capitalist: one who thinks he must choose between being held up by native labor or being blown up by imported labor.

Capital punishment: 1. most Washington cocktail parties. 2. the income tax. 3. what a woman gets for marrying a congressman.

Career girl: 1. one who gets a man's pay by working for it. 2. one who is more interested in plots and plans than in pots and pans.

Career woman: one who goes out and earns a man's salary instead of sitting at home and taking it away from him.

Caricature: the tribute that mediocrity pays to genius.

Carpet: a floor-covering that is bought by the yard and worn by the foot.

Car sickness: that feeling you get every month when the payment falls due.

Casserole: a method used by ingenious cooks to get rid of left-over leftovers.

Cauliflower: a cabbage with a college education.

Cavity: empty space ready to be stuffed with dentist's bills.

Celebrity: 1. a man who works all his life to become famous enough to be recognized—then goes around in dark glasses so no one will know who he is. 2. a person who is very much in the public's eye and often gets in the public's hair. 3. a person whose name is in everything but the telephone book.

Censor: a man who knows more than he thinks you ought to know.

Censure: the tax a man pays to the public for being eminent.

Ceremony: the invention of wise men to keep fools at a distance.

Chairmaning: the art of being one up on the lecturer.

Chamber of Commerce Executive: a man who will never admit he has seen better days.

Champagne: a beverage that makes you see double and feel single.

Chance: a pseudonym that God uses when he doesn't want to seem responsible.

Chance remark: anything a man chances to say when two women are talking.

Chaos: three women discussing the two sides of an issue.

Chaperone: one who is too old to get into the game, but still tries to intercept the passes.

Character: 1. that which one is called if one doesn't have any. 2. what a man is in the dark. 3. what you have left when you've lost everything you can lose.

Charity: the sterilized milk of human kindness.

Charm: 1. that indefinable something possessed by girls with stunning figures. 2. the ability to make someone else think that both of you are pretty wonderful. 3. what one is told he has until he begins to rely on it.

Chauffeur: a man who is smart enough to operate an automobile, but clever enough not to own one.

Checkmate: the gal you marry for her money.

Cheesecake: a magazine with a beautiful girl on the cover—and no cover on the girl.

Chef: a man with a big enough vocabulary to give the soup a different name every day.

DEFINITIONS

Chemical warfare: the eternal conflict between blondes and brunettes.

Child: a thing that stands halfway between an adult and a television set.

Childhood: a happy period when nightmares occur only during sleep.

Childish games: those at which your wife beats you.

Child psychology: the art of applying a soft pedal instead of a hard paddle.

Children: small people who are not permitted to act as their parents did at that age.

Chiropodist: a man who makes money hand over foot.

Chivalry: 1. a man's inclination to defend a woman against every man but himself. 2. the attitude of a man toward somebody else's wife. 3. the attitude of a man toward a strange woman.

Chorus girl: one who never worries about getting ahead because she doesn't need one.

Chow line: the men behind the men . . . behind the men . . . behind the men.

Christmas: 1. a time for exchanging a lot of things you can't afford for a lot of things you don't want. 2. a widely observed holiday on which neither the past nor the future is of so much interest as the present. 3. the season when we get the children something for their father to play with. 4. when the radios keep you awake till three in the morning playing "Silent Night."

Christmas shopping: a time when we must get the children something for their father to play with.

Chronic grumbler: one who, when opportunity knocks, complains about the noise.

Church: 1. an institution supported by the husbands of the members. 2. a place in which gentlemen who have never been to Heaven brag about it to persons who will never get there. 3. the place where we encounter nodding acquaintances.

266

DEFINITIONS

Cigarette lighter: where the spirit is willing but the flash is weak.

Cinder: one of the first things to catch your eye in traveling.

Cinemascope: a wider scope of sin.

Cinerama: a new movie process that will make Katherine Hepburn look like Jane Russell.

Circus: a group that carries on where Congress leaves off.

City life: millions of people being lonesome together.

City paving: something always on the up and up.

Civilization: 1. a process whereby one generation finds the questions to the previous generation's answers. 2. a scheme devised by women to get men to work for them. 3. a system under which a man pays a quarter to park his car so he won't be fined a dollar while eating a fifteen cent meal. 4. just a slow process of getting rid of our prejudices. 5. the advancement from shoeless toes to toeless shoes.

Civil service: a commodity formerly obtainable in restaurants.

Classic: a book everyone wants to have read, but no one wants to read.

Class reunion: a gathering where you come to the conclusion that most of the people your own age are a lot older than you are.

Clergyman: 1. a man who undertakes the management of our spiritual affairs as a method of bettering his temporal ones. 2. a ticket speculator outside the gates of Heaven.

Clever investment: the one you failed to make.

Clichés: fixtures of speech.

Clouds: the traveling mountains of the sky.

Cloverleaf: crossroads puzzle.

Coach: a fellow who will gladly lay down your life for the school.

Cocktail: an ice cube with an alcohol rub.

Cocktail lounge: a half-lit roomful of half-lit people.

267

DEFINITIONS

Cocktail party: 1. a gathering where you spear olives and stab friends. 2. a place where they serve whisky on the knocks. 3. a place where you meet a lot of old friends you never saw before. 4. where a handful gather a snootful and earful. 5. where they cut sandwiches and friends into little pieces. 6. where two and two make a bore.

Coed: 1. a girl who also goes to college. 2. a girl who didn't get her man in high school. 3. a moron with less on.

Coffee break: about the only break some workers feel they get.

Coiffure: a French word meaning "you'll keep coming to us because you'll never be able to do it this way yourself."

Colleague: someone who is called in at the last moment to share the blame.

Collection: a church function in which many take but a passing interest.

College: 1. a fountain of knowledge where students gather to drink. 2. just a place to keep warm between high school and early marriage.

College boy: 1. a young man who likes to be treated with kindness by his parents, but not with unremitting kindness. 2. one who gets up at five every day all summer to carry milk, but can't make an eight o'clock class all winter.

College bred: a four-year loaf requiring a fearful amount of dough and seldom self-raising.

College dean: a man who doesn't know enough to be a professor, but who is too smart to be a president.

College education: a four-year plan for confusing a young mind methodically.

College graduate: a person who had a chance to get an education.

Colleges: institutions which sometimes lower entrance requirements with an end in view—not to mention promising tackles and backs.

268

College years: the only vacation a boy gets between his mother and his wife.

Comic books: illiterature.

Comic relief: when the life of the party goes home.

Comic strip: an eight-column diagram of an old joke.

Commercial: the din you love to shush.

Committee: 1. a body that keeps minutes and wastes hours. 2. a group of the unfit, appointed by the unwilling, to do the unnecessary. 3. a group which succeeds in getting something done only when it consists of three members, one of whom happens to be sick and the other absent. 4. a noun of multitude, signifying many, but not signifying much. 5. something which consists of three people who are unfit, being appointed by someone unwilling to do a job which, in the last analysis, happens to be unnecessary.

Committee-of-five: consists of a man who does all the work, three others to pat him on the back, and one to bring in a minority report.

Communist: 1. a fellow who has given up all hope of ever becoming a capitalist. 2. a fellow who will gladly divide his hunger and thirst with you if you'll divide your beer and salami with him. 3. a guy who borrows your pot to cook your goose. 4. a guy who says everything is perfect in Russia, but stays here because he likes to rough it. 5. one who has yearnings for equal division of unequal earnings.

Community chest: an organization that puts all its begs in one ask it.

Commuter: a traveling man who pays short visits to his home and office.

Compliment: 1. something which you say to another which he and you know is not true. 2. the applause that refreshes.

Compromise: a deal in which two people get what neither of them wanted.

Conceit: 1. a disease that makes everyone sick but the one who has it. 2. a form of I-strain. 3. God's gift to little men.

DEFINITIONS

Concrete opinions: those that are thoroughly mixed and permanently set.

Cones: ice cream you can walk with.

Coney Island: where the surf is one third water and two thirds people.

Conference: 1. a big business term for swapping stories in somebody's private office. 2. a group of men who individually can do nothing, but as a group can meet and decide that nothing can be done. 3. a meeting at which people talk about what they should already be doing. 4. a place where conversation is substituted for the dreariness of labor and the loneliness of thought. 5. an organized way of postponing a decision. 6. coffee-break with real napkins. 7. the confusion of the loudest talking character multiplied by the number present.

Confidence: the cocky feeling you have just before you know better.

Confirmed bachelor: one who thinks that the only thoroughly justified marriage was the one that produced him.

Congressman: a man who votes for all appropriations and against all taxes.

Conscience: 1. a device that doesn't keep you from doing anything; just keeps you from enjoying it. 2. a guilt-edged knife. 3. an inner voice that warns us somebody is looking. 4. a walkie-talkie set by which God speaks to us. 5. something that feels terrible when everything else feels swell. 6. that sixth sense that comes to our aid when we are doing wrong and tells us that we are about to get caught. 7. the still small voice that makes you feel still smaller. 8. the voice that tells you not to do something after you have done it. 9. what makes you tell your wife before someone else does.

Conscientious woman: one who never breaks a confidence without first imposing the strictest secrecy.

Conservative: 1. a man who acts impulsively after thinking for a long time. 2. a man who is too cowardly to fight and too fat to run. 3. a man who just sits and thinks, mostly sits. 4. a statesman who is enamored of existing evils, as distinguished from the liberal, who

270

wishes to replace them with others. 5. one who does not think that anything should be done for the first time.

Consult: to seek another's approval of a course already decided upon.

Contempt: the feeling of a prudent man for an enemy who is too formidable safely to be opposed.

Contortionist: a guy who can still make both ends meet these days.

Convalescent: a patient who is still alive.

Convention: an excuse for doing the unconventional.

Conventional: not necessarily the way a man acts at a convention.

Conventions: what the road to Hell is paved with.

Convict: the only person who likes to be stopped in the middle of a sentence.

Convictions: what an employee has after he knows what the boss thinks.

Coordinator: 1. a man who brings organized chaos out of regimented confusion. 2. a man who has a desk between two expediters.

Coquette: a woman without a heart, who makes a fool of a man who has no head.

Corn-on-the-cob: the stuff you eat like you play a mouth organ.

Corporal: as high as you can go and still have friends.

Corporation: an ingenious device for obtaining individual profit without individual responsibility.

Co-respondent: the right man in the wrong place.

Corset: like love; something which binds us together and makes us better than we are by nature.

Cost of living: the difference between your net income and your gross habits.

DEFINITIONS

Counterfeiter: a guy who gets into trouble by following a good example.

Counter-irritant: the woman who shops all day and buys nothing.

Courage: fear that has said its prayers.

Courtesy: the quality that keeps a woman smiling when a departing guest stands at the open screen door and lets the flies in.

Courtship: 1. a man pursuing a woman until she catches him. 2. a period during which a girl decides whether or not she can do better. 3. the period during which a man spends so much on his girl friend that he finally marries her for his money. 4. when a fellow and a girl are always trying to show how smart he is. 5. when a fellow gets so wrapped up in a girl that it's easy to tie the knot.

Coward: one who in a perilous emergency thinks with his legs.

Credit: 1. a commodity that becomes better the less it is used. 2. a person who can't pay, gets another person who can't pay, to guarantee that he can pay.

Creditor: a man who has a better memory than a debtor.

Crew cut: furry with a singe on top.

Criminal: one who gets caught.

Critic: 1. a legless man who teaches running. 2. a wet blanket that soaks everything it touches. 3. one quick-on-the-flaw.

Criticism: 1. a study by which men grow important and formidable at very little expense. 2. something you can avoid by saying nothing, doing nothing, and being nothing.

Critics: people who go places and boo things.

Crooning: a continuous hollow sound, as of cattle in pain.

Cupid: one who when he hits the mark usually Mrs. it.

Curve: something which may wreck your car . . . if you hug it at the wrong time.

Curved line: the loveliest distance between two points.

272

Cynic: 1. a blackguard whose faulty vision sees things as they are, not as they ought to be. 2. a man who knows the price of everything and the value of nothing; a sentimentalist is one who values everything and knows the price of nothing. 3. a man who looks at the world with a monocle in his mind's eye. 4. a man who looks both ways before crossing a one-way street. 5. a man who, when he smells flowers, looks around for a coffin. 6. one who looks down on those above him.

D

Dancing: the art of pulling your feet away faster than your partner can step on them.

Dandruff: chips off the old block.

Dark glasses: a device to make the obscure feel important.

Death: 1. Patrick Henry's second choice. 2. to stop sinning suddenly.

Debt: 1. a trap which a man sets and baits himself, and then deliberately gets into. 2. the only thing that expands in proportion as it is contracted.

Debts: the certain outcome of an uncertain income.

Debutante: 1. a bareback with greenbacks. 2. a young girl with bride ideas. 3. girl who goes out a vision and comes in a sight. 4. one who comes out at eighteen and gets up at twelve. 5. one who lives a date-to-date existence.

Decency: indeceny's conspiracy of silence.

Delegate-at-large: a man at a convention whose wife didn't accompany him.

Delinquent children: those who have reached the age where they want to do what mama and papa are doing.

Delta: a river with its mouth full of mud.

DEFINITIONS

Demagogue: a man who can rock the boat himself and persuade everybody else that there is a terrible storm at sea.

Democracy: 1. a country where you can say what you think without thinking. 2. a form of religion; the worship of jackals by jackasses. 3. a land where you are free to choose your own form of government —blonde, brunette, or redhead. 4. a place where you can say what you please, but don't have to listen unless you want to. 5. a small hard core of common agreement, surrounded by a rich variety of individual difference. 6. a state of mind in which every man is as good as every other man, provided he really is. 7. a system whereby the person who never votes can cuss out the man the other people elected. 8. that form of society, no matter what its political classification, in which every man has a chance and knows that he has it.

Dental parlor: a drawing room.

Dentist: 1. a collector of old magazines. 2. a man who lives from hand to mouth. 3. a man who runs a filling station. 4. a prestidigitator who, putting metal in your mouth, pulls coins out of your pocket.

Department store detective: counter spy.

Depression: a period during which we have to get along without the things our grandparents never dreamed of.

Desertion: the poor man's method of divorce.

Desire: the thing that is so often nipped in the budget.

Desk: wastebasket with drawers.

Detour: 1. something that lengthens your mileage, diminishes your gas, and strengthens your vocabulary. 2. the roughest distance between two points.

Diamond: 1. a bright gem, the sparkle of which sometimes renders a woman stone-blind to the defects of the man proffering it. 2. a stepping stone in every girl's life. 3. a woman's idea of a stepping stone to success. 4. nothing harder except making the payments on one.

Diamond cutter: one who mows the grass at the ball park.

Diamonds: chunks of coal that stuck to their job.

DEFINITIONS

Diaphragm: a muscular partition separating disorders of the chest from disorders of the bowels.

Dictator: one who thinks he can take it—no matter to whom it belongs.

Dictatorship: 1. a place where public opinion can't even be expressed privately. 2. a system of government where everything that isn't forbidden is obligatory.

Diet: 1. a short period of starvation preceding a gain of five pounds. 2. something to take the starch out of you. 3. something you keep putting off while you keep putting on.

Dieting: 1. the penalty for exceeding the feed limit. 2. the triumph of mind over platter.

Difficult: that which can be done immediately; impossible: that which takes a little longer.

Dignity: 1. something that can't be preserved in alcohol. 2. the capacity to hold back on the tongue what never should have been on the mind in the first place.

Dilemma: a politician trying to save both his faces at once.

Dilettante: a philanderer who seduces the several arts and deserts each in turn for another.

Dime: a dollar with all the taxes taken out.

Diner: a chew-chew car.

Dining room: the place where the family eats while painters are doing over the kitchen.

Diplomacy: 1. a peaceful substitute for shooting. 2. cutting the other fellow's throat without using a knife. 3. lying in state. 4. the ability to take something and make the other fellow believe he is giving it away. 5. the art of handling a porcupine without disturbing the quills. 6. the art of laying down the law gently enough to keep it from being broken. 7. the art of letting someone else have your own way. 8. the art of saying "Nice doggie!" until you can find a rock. 9. the art of skating on thin ice without getting into deep water. 10. the art of turning a dropped stitch into a loophole.

DEFINITIONS

Diplomat: 1. a fellow who prefers ironing out his differences to flattening his opponent. 2. a gent who thinks twice before he says nothing. 3. a man who convinces his wife that a woman looks stout in a fur coat. 4. a man who has learned that you can't bend a nail by hitting it squarely on the head. 5. a man who remembers a woman's birthday but forgets her age. 6. a man who tries to settle problems created by other diplomats. 7. a person who can be disarming even though his country isn't. 8. a person who can juggle a hot potato long enough for it to become a cold issue. 9. a person who can keep a civil tongue in his cheek. 10. a person who does not think it necessary to understand things in order to argue about them. 11. a person who says, "I will take the matter under advisement," instead of "no." 12. if you have the advantage over someone, and you lead him to think that he has the advantage over you, without giving him the chance to take advantage of you. 13. one who can bring home the bacon without spilling the beans.

Director: the one who always faces the music.

Disc jockey: one who earns his living by putting on airs.

Discount: something often sold in place of goods.

Discouragement: seeing the secretary yawn over one of your snappy salesmanship letters.

Discretion: 1. a comb that experience hands us after we have lost our hair. 2. a sense that comes to a man too late to do him any good. 3. closing your eyes to a situation before someone closes them for you.

Discussion: a method of confirming others in their errors.

Distance: that which lends enchantment to the view, but not when you run out of gas.

District of Columbia: a territory hounded on all sides by the United States of America.

Divorce: 1. going through a change of wife. 2. hash made from domestic scraps. 3. what results when the bonds of matrimony no longer bear interest.

Divorcee: a woman who gets richer by decrees.

Doctor: 1. a guy who tells you if you don't cut out something he'll cut something out of you. 2. a man who keeps telling children to eat more and parents to eat less. 3. a man who suffers from good health. 4. one who kills you today to prevent you from dying tomorrow.

Doctor's prescription: something written on a subway train with a post office pen.

Dogmatism: puppyism come to its full growth.

Dollar: the jack of all trades.

Dollar sign: an S that's been double-crossed.

Domestic argument: one after which the husband either goes to his club or reaches for it.

Doorman: a genius who can open the door of your car with one hand, help you in with the other, and still have one left for the tip.

Dots: symbols which, in the modern novel, mean proceed at your own risque.

Double jeopardy: when your doctor calls in a consulting physician.

Draft board: where young men are weighed and found wanted.

Drama critic: a person who surprises the playwright by informing him what he meant.

Dramatic critic: one who gives the best jeers of his life to the theater.

Dreamer: one who waits for something to turn up—whereas a doer turns up something while waiting.

Drinking: act which does not drown your sorrows—only irrigates them.

Drive-in theater: 1. sparking place. 2. where a guy goes to shut off his ignition so he can try out his clutch.

Drug store: 1. a telephone with a business attached. 2. the poor man's country club.

Drunkard: 1. a man who knows his capacity but gets drunk be-

DEFINITIONS

fore he reaches it. 2. human prune, the more he is soaked, the more he swells.

Duel: pistols for two; breakfast for one.

Durable goods: those that last longer than the time payments.

Duty: 1. that which sternly impels us in the direction of profit, along the line of desire. 2. what one expects from others, not what one does oneself. 3. what the normal man looks forward to with distaste, does with reluctance, and boasts about forever after.

Dyspeptic: a man that can eat his cake and have it too.

E

Early rising: triumph of mind over mattress.

Earth: a solid substance, much desired by the seasick.

Easter millinery: hatrocities.

Easy chair: the hardest one to find empty.

Easy payments: the ones that are easier said than done.

Eccentric: one who minds his own business.

Echo: 1. no sooner said than said. 2. the only thing that can cheat a woman out of the last word.

Economic depression: when the tenth word of a telegram is "please" instead of "love."

Economics: college professor talk for "What happened to the money in the cookie jar?"

Economist: 1. a man who knows more about money than the people who have it now. 2. a man who tells you what to do with your money after you have done something else with it. 3. one who takes a lot of unwarranted assumptions and reaches a foregone conclusion.

Economy: 1. a way to spend money without getting any fun out of it. 2. denying ourselves a necessity today in order to buy a luxury

278

tomorrow. 3. living within your means even if you have to borrow money to do so.

Editor: the fellow who makes a long story short.

Educate: to render harmless by cultivation.

Educated man: one who has finally discovered that there are some questions to which nobody has the answers.

Educated person: one who voluntarily does more thinking than is necessary for his own survival.

Education: 1. a debt due from present to future generations. 2. forcing abstract ideas into concrete heads. 3. that mysterious process whereby information passes from the lecture notes of the professor through the fountain pen and onto the notebook. 4. that which discloses to the wise and disguises from the foolish their lack of understanding. 5. what a father gets when he sits in on a conversation with a group of teen-agers. 6. what's left over after you've gotten the facts.

Efficiency: 1. the ability to do a job well, plus the desire to do it better. 2. the knack of getting somebody to do a job you don't like.

Efficiency expert: 1. a man smart enough to tell you how to run your business and too smart to start his own. 2. a man who knows less about your business than you do and gets paid more for telling you how to run it than you could possibly make out of it, even if you ran it right instead of the way he told you to. 3. a man who walks in his sleep so that he can get his rest and his exercise at the same time. 4. one who always has to make up a foursome before passing through a revolving door.

Ego: 1. some spark within us which leads us to believe that we are better than we are, and which is often instrumental in proving it. 2. the only thing that can keep on growing without nourishment.

Egotism: 1. an anaesthetic that nature gives to a man to deaden the pain of being a darn fool. 2. self-confidence looking for trouble. 3. something that enables the man in a rut to think he's in the groove. 4. usually just a case of mistaken non-entity.

Egotist: 1. a conceited ass who thinks he knows as much as you do. 2. a fellow who certainly knows a good thing when he says it.

DEFINITIONS

3. a man who thinks that a woman will marry him for himself alone. 4. a person of low taste, more interested in himself than in me. 5. a person who persists in telling you things about himself that you had planned on telling him about yourself. 6. one who is always me-deep in conversation. 7. one who thinks that if he hadn't been born, people would wonder why. 8. one whose eyes look in instead of out. 9. someone who thinks all the world is a stooge.

Eiffel Tower: the Empire State Building after taxes.

Elderly wolf: Jill collector with jack.

Electoral College: institute of higher yearning.

Eloquence: logic on fire.

Engagement: 1. a period in which a girl is placed in solitaire confinement. 2. a period of urge on the verge of a merge. 3. the time a girl takes until she finds out if she can do any better.

Enthusiast: one who preaches four times as much as he believes, and believes four times as much as a sane man ought to.

Epigram: 1. a half-truth so stated as to irritate the person who believes the other half. 2. a wise crack that's played in Carnegie Hall. 3. truth on a "binge."

Epitaph: 1. a belated advertisement for a line of goods that has been permanently discontinued. 2. a statement that lies above the one that lies beneath.

Eskimos: people who, after a few months of work, call it a day.

Estates: acreage in the country owned by people who have "gone to town."

Etc.: a sign; when used makes others believe you know more than you do.

Eternal struggle: keeping your earning capacity up to your wife's yearning capacity.

Etiquette: 1. a convenient code of conduct which makes lying a virtue and snobbishness a righteous deed. 2. learning to yawn with your mouth closed. 3. the noise you don't make when you eat soup.

Eulogy: praise that's too much and too late.

Eve: the first chicken to ruin a man's garden.

Evening dress: more gone than gown.

Evil: that which one believes of others. It is a sin to believe evil of others, but it is seldom a mistake.

Exclamation point: a period that has blown its top.

Executive: 1. a big gun—that hasn't been fired yet. 2. a fellow who goes out and finds something that needs to be done; then finds someone willing to pay for it; then hires somebody to do it. 3. a man who can take two hours off for lunch without hindering production. 4. a man who goes around with a worried look on the face of his assistant. 5. a man who talks to visitors so the other employees can get their work done. 6. one who makes an immediate decision and is sometimes right.

Executive ability: the art of getting the credit for all the hard work that somebody else does.

Experience: 1. a form of knowledge acquired only two ways—by doing and being done. 2. a name given to our mistakes. 3. a revelation in the light of which we renounce our errors of youth for those of age. 4. the name an older man gives to his mistakes. 5. not what happens to me, but what a man does with what happens to him. 6. the mistakes we like to remember. 7. what you get from being inexperienced. 8. what you get when you're expecting something else. 9. what causes a person to make new mistakes instead of the same old ones.

Expert: 1. a fellow who has made a lot of good guesses. 2. a man from another city, and the farther away that city is, the greater the expert. 3. a man wearing a tie and an important look on his face who knows how to complicate simplicity. 4. a man who avoids the small errors as he sweeps on to the grand fallacy. 5. a man who is seldom in doubt, but often in error. 6. an ordinary man away from home. 7. any person who has tried and failed—and can tell you why. 8. a person who not only knows all the answers but can think up problems to fit them. 9. one who can take something you already knew and make it sound confusing. 10. one who knows more and more

DEFINITIONS

about less and less. 11. one who tells you to do something exactly the way you decided to do it before you asked him.

Extravagance: buying whatever is of no earthly value to your wife.

Extravagant girl: one who usually makes a poor mother and a bankrupt father.

F

Fad: something that goes in one era and out the other.

Failure: 1. the quickest method known for making money. 2. the line of least persistence.

Fairway (golf): the well-kept and seldom used portion of a golf course.

Faith: 1. belief without evidence in what is told by one who speaks without knowledge of things without parallel. 2. illogical belief in the occurrence of the improbable.

False economy: using only 30 candles on her 40th birthday cake.

Falsies: 1. a helpful aid to any girl in acquiring a disappointed husband. 2. a sort of hope chest.

Fame: 1. chiefly a matter of dying at the right moment. 2. the advantage of being known to those who do not know us. 3. the best way to rise to its dizzy heights is to stay on the level.

Family tree: the only tree whose branches seek the shelter of its roots.

Fanatic: 1. one who can't change his opinion and won't change the subject. 2. one who is highly enthusiastic about something in which you are not even remotely interested. 3. one who redoubles his efforts after he has forgotten his objectives.

Farm: what a city man dreams of at 5 p.m., never at 5 a.m.

Farmer: a handy man with a sense of humus.

282

Farmers: men successful only if they sell their farms to golf clubs.

Fashion: 1. a despot whom the wise riducule and obey. 2. something that goes out of style as soon as most people have one.

Father: one who gives the lover his daughter's hand and hopes he takes the one she's had in his pocket all this time.

Father's Day: the annual day in June set aside so merchants can get rid of their leftover Christmas ties and shaving lotion.

Fat man: 1. one who knows where his cigar ashes are going to land. 2. one who leans heavily against his belt.

Federal aid: a system of making money taken from the people look like a gift when handed back.

Female friends: women mad at the same person.

Feminine wile: keeping a man at arm's length by a hair's breadth.

Fern: a plant that you're supposed to water once a day, and when you don't it dies, but if you do it dies anyway, only not so soon.

Fiction: something that can't hold a scandal to biography.

Fiddler: a violinist before he becomes the virtuoso who refuses to play a real tune.

Fidelity: a virtue peculiar to those who are about to be betrayed.

Filing cabinet: a place where you can lose things systematically.

Finance company: an outfit that lives on the flat of the land.

Financial wizard: a husband who can pay the last of last month's bills out of next month's salary.

Financier: a pawnbroker with imagination.

Firmness: the admirable quality in ourselves that is detestable stubbornness in others.

First grade teacher: one who knows how to make little things count.

First love: a little foolishness and a lot of curiosity.

DEFINITIONS

Fish: 1. an animal that grows fastest between the time it is caught and the time a fisherman describes it to his friends. 2. a creature that goes on vacation about the time most fishermen do.

Fishing: 1. a delusion entirely surrounded by liars in old clothes. 2. a heroic treatment tried by some laymen to avoid falling to sleep in church on Sunday.

Flashlight: a case in which to carry dead batteries.

Flatterer: one who says things to your face that he wouldn't say behind your back.

Flattery: 1. a commodity that makes everybody sick except those who swallow it. 2. a sort of verbal peroxide that turns a woman's head. 3. cologne water, to be smelled of but not swallowed. 4. soft soap; and soft soap is 90% lye. 5. the art of pretending you like the girl more than you like the kiss.

Flirt: 1. a girl who got the boy you wanted. 2. a woman who believes it's every man for herself.

Flirtation: 1. a spoon with nothing in it. 2. paying attention without intention.

Flood: a river too big for its bridges.

Fly paper: stationery they use in airplanes.

Fool: one whom bigger fools believe to be a man of merit.

Football: a clever subterfuge for carrying on prize fights under the guise of a reputable game.

Football fan: one who knows the nationality of every man on the All-American team.

Football season: 1. the only time of the year when a man can walk down the street with a blonde on one arm and a blanket on the other without encountering raised eyebrows. 2. the time of the year when girls whistle at men in sweaters.

Forecaster: a person skilled in the art of drawing useful conclusions from inadequate premises.

Forger: 1. a man who made a name for himself. 2. the fellow who gives a check a bad name.

284

Forgiveness: the fragrance the violet sheds on the heel that has crushed it.

Forty: the age when a woman stops patting herself on the back and begins under the chin.

Fox: a wolf that sends flowers.

Frankage: the only known method of sending hot air through the mails.

Freckles: a nice sun tan—if they'd only get together.

Freedom: being able to do what you please without considering anyone but the wife, police, boss, life insurance company, state, federal, and city authorities, and the neighbors.

Friend: 1. one before whom one may think aloud. 2. one who has the same enemies you have. 3. one who knows all about you and still loves you just the same.

Friends: 1. people who borrow my books and set wet glasses on them. 2. persons who stick together until debt do them part. 3. what you think you have oodles of, until you happen to be badly in need of just one.

Futile remark: the one a man makes for the purpose of changing the subject when the wife complains because he has forgotten their wedding anniversary.

G

Gambling: a way of getting nothing for something.

Garden: 1. a place where some of the bulbs seem to think they're buried instead of planted. 2. a thing of beauty and a job forever. 3. something most men prefer to turn over in their minds. 4. something that dies if you don't water it, and rots if you do.

Gardener: someone who thinks that what goes down must come up.

DEFINITIONS

Gardening: 1. a matter of enthusiasm holding up until your back gets used to it. 2. man's effort to improve his lot.

Gastric ulcer: something you get mountain-climbing over mole-hills.

Genealogy: 1. an account of one's descent from an ancestor who did not particularly care to trace his own. 2. tracing yourself back to people better than you are.

Genius: 1. a capacity for making somebody else take infinite pains. 2. a crackpot who made a screwball idea work. 3. any other woman's husband. 4. one percent inspiration and ninety-nine percent perspiration. 5. one who can do almost anything except make a living. 6. the infinite capacity not only for taking pains, but for giving them.

Genius (in Washington): the infinite capacity for taking trains.

Gentility: eating meat with a silver fork, neither being paid for.

Gentleman: 1. a gardener who can call a spade a spade without adding any qualifying adjectives. 2. a man who doesn't pretend to be anything that he isn't. 3. a man who holds the door open for his wife while she carries in a load of groceries. 4. a man who is always as nice as he sometimes is. 5. a man who never makes passes at girls; to him they're overtures. 6. a man who remembers a girl's birthday but forgets her age. 7. a man who will step aside for a lady in a crowd, so she can make a pathway for him. 8. a man with more hay in the bank than in the barn. 9. any man a girl hasn't been out with yet. 10. a worn-out wolf. 11. nothing but a wolf with his ears pinned back. 12. one who doesn't care whether he is one or not. 13. one who has never heard the story before. 14. one who never hurts another's feelings unintentionally. 15. one who never strikes a woman without provocation. 16. something made by three generations or one darn good guess on the stock market.

Getting ahead: a process which implies that one must have one to start with.

Gift necktie: the tie that blinds.

Gift shop: a place where you can see all the things you hope your friends won't send you for Christmas.

DEFINITIONS

Girdle: 1. accessory after the fat. 2. a device that a woman uses to make a waist out of her waste. 3. an article which prevents a lot of loose walk. 4. the difference between fact and figure.

Girl: always one of three things; hungry, thirsty, or both.

Girls: 1. creatures who are fond of pretty clothes but are not wrapped up in them. 2. creatures who can make up their faces more easily than their minds.

Glamour girl: one who has what it takes to take what you have.

Glutton: a man who eats dessert before the echo of his soup has stopped.

Goat: a lamb who has kidded himself into believing that he knows Wall Street.

Gold digger: 1. a fund-loving girl. 2. a girl who breaks dates by going out with them. 3. a girl who forgets all about the past and the future and simply enjoys the present. 4. a girl who will date any man that can pass the asset test. 5. a girl with a gift for grab. 6. a human gimme pig. 7. a woman after all. 8. a young woman who likes to go buy-buy.

Gold tooth: flash in the pan.

Golf: 1. a game in which a ball one and a half inches in diameter is placed on a ball 8000 miles in diameter, the object being to hit the small ball but not the large. 2. a game that is played by a lot of men to keep from falling asleep in church on Sunday mornings. 3. a game where the ball usually lies poorly and the player well. 4. just a lot of walking broken up by disappointment and bad arithmetic.

Golfer: 1. a guy who can walk several miles toting 25 miles of equipment, but who has Junior bring him an ash tray. 2. a man who hits and tells.

Good breeding: an expedient to make fools and wise men equal.

Good citizen: one who behaves as if there were no laws.

Good diplomat: someone who can lose all the points and still win the game.

DEFINITIONS

Good husband: 1. one who feels in his pockets every time he passes a mail box. 2. one who will wash up when asked and dry up when told.

Good line: the shortest distance between dates.

Good neighbor: 1. a fellow who smiles at you over the back fence, but doesn't climb it. 2. one who doesn't borrow his garden hose back too often. 3. one who gives you the benefit of the dirt.

Good old days: 1. what people fifty years hence will be calling the present time. 2. when a juvenile delinquent was a kid who owed a few cents on an overdue library book. 3. when a man looked for money in his pockets before having a suit cleaned. 4. when a teen-ager went into the garage and came out with a lawn mower. 5. when the prisoner, not the sentence, was suspended. 6. when you got the landlord to fix anything by just threatening to move.

Good speech: a beginning and a conclusion placed not too far apart.

Good sport: one who will always let you have your own way.

Good storyteller: a person who has a good memory and hopes other people haven't.

Good talker: one who learns to listen.

Good teacher: one who makes himself progressively unnecessary.

Good times: 1. the period when you accumulate those debts that you're unable to pay in bad times. 2. those in which people who have money contrive to get a little more.

Good wife: one you can propose to on the front porch, and then still love in the kitchen.

Gossip: 1. a newscaster without a sponsor. 2. anything that goes in one ear and over the back fence. 3. a person who puts two and two together—whether they are or are not. 4. a person who will never tell a lie if the truth will do as much damage. 5. a person who syndicates his conversation. 6. letting the chat out of the bag. 7. conversation without thought. 8. one who pumps to a conclusion. 9. one who takes people at deface value. 10. one with a keen sense of rumor. 11. ped-

288

dling meddling. 12. sharing deride. 13. sociologists on a mean and petty scale. 14. somebody who knows how to add to . . . and to. 15. something negative that is developed and then enlarged. 16. talling the story. 17. the art of saying nothing in a way which leaves nothing unsaid. 18. when one just can't leave bad enough alone. 19. when someone puts two and two together and gets whee!

Gossip columnist: 1. a guy who finds out things people don't want known, and tells them to others to whom it doesn't make any difference. 2. one who keeps us posted on how the other half lives it up. 3. the spies of life.

Government bureau: where the taxpayer's shirt is kept.

Grandfather: a grandchild's press agent.

Grandmother: an old lady who keeps your mother from spanking you.

Grand jury: one that says "not guilty."

Grass: the green stuff that wilts in the yard and flourishes in the garden.

Grass widow: the angel a man loved, the human being he married, and the devil he divorced.

Gratitude: 1. an idiotic word; it is put in the dictionary, but it does not exist in the human heart where it belongs. 2. a secret hope of greater favors.

Great American: what speakers call a man when they can't think of anything specifically complimentary to say.

Great Dane: the kind of puppy that has the house broken before he is.

Great timesaver: love at first sight.

Growing old: a process hard to do gracefully with modern furniture.

Guest: a person for whom you lay out a special towel, which both of you know won't be used.

Gum chewer's mouth: that which goes without saying.

DEFINITIONS

H

Habits: 1. cobwebs that become cables. 2. trait jackets.

Halter: something grooms get at the altar.

Handicap (golf): a device for "collective bargaining" on the first tee.

Hangover: 1. something to occupy a head that wasn't used the night before. 2. the moaning after the night before. 3. toot ache.

Hangover (champagne): the wrath of grapes.

Happiness: 1. a delicate balance between what one is and what one has. 2. a way station between too little and too much. 3. good health and a poor memory. 4. perfume you cannot pour on others without getting a few drops on yourself. 5. that peculiar sensation you acquire when you are too busy to be miserable. 6. the perpetual possession of being well-deceived.

Happy marriage: a long conversation that always seems too short.

Hard times: when all we can pay is compliments.

Hard work: an accumulation of easy things you didn't do when you should have.

Harp: a piano in the nude.

Has-been: one who lives on the reputation of his reputation.

Hash: enthusiastic food—the cook puts all she has into it.

Hat: 1. a woman's clowning glory. 2. something the average man covers his head with, the beggar passes around, the statesman throws into the ring, and the politician talks through.

Hay: grass à la mowed.

Health: the thing that makes you feel that now is the best time of the year.

290

DEFINITIONS

Hearse: a handsome vehicle in which the man who has always been a tail-ender is finally permitted to lead the procession.

Heckler: a guy who ribs you the wrong way.

Heirloom: some old thing nobody liked well enough to wear out.

Helicopter: an egg beater with ambition.

Helpmate: a wife, or bitter half.

Heredity: the bad traits a child gets from the other side of the family.

Hick: a person who looks both ways before crossing a one-way street.

Hicks: people who come to town at intervals to provide the gay night-life of the city.

Hick town: 1. one where, if you see a girl dining with a man old enough to be her father, he is. 2. one where there is no place to go where you shouldn't be.

Highboy: a form of greeting.

Highbrow: 1. a man who has found something more interesting than women. 2. a person who has the patience to sit through something that would make him a lowbrow if he didn't. 3. one who likes a thing so long as he's sure you don't like it too. 4. one whose learning has outstripped his intelligence. 5. the kind of person who looks at a sausage and thinks of Picasso.

High heels: the invention of a woman who had been kissed on the forehead.

Hire education: when an athlete is given financial inducements to attend a certain college.

Historian: a prophet looking backwards.

Historical novel: a fictitious tale covering up a stern reality.

History: an account mostly false, of events unimportant, which are brought about by rulers mostly knaves, and soldiers mostly fools.

Hitler: the greatest seizer of them all.

DEFINITIONS

Hobby: 1. hard work you wouldn't do for a living. 2. something you do to have fun whether you enjoy it or not.

Holding company: a thing where you hand an accomplice the goods while the policeman searches you.

Hole-in-one (golf): a stroke of genius.

Hollywood: a place where people from Iowa mistake each other for movie stars.

Hollywood aristocrat: anyone who can trace his ancestry back to his father.

Hollywood marriage: much "I do" about nothing.

Hollywood pal: someone who is always around when he needs you.

Hollywood wedding: one where they take each other for better or worse—but not for long.

Home: 1. a place in which we are treated the best and grumble the most. 2. a place where a man is free to say anything he pleases because no one pays any attention to him. 3. there's no place like it if you haven't got the money to go out. 4. where part of the family waits until the rest of them bring back the car.

Home cooking: what more women should be.

Home town: where they wonder how you ever got as far as you did.

Honest: that which a man gets credit for being when he's merely doing business with folks that never give him a chance to be anything else.

Honesty: the fear of getting caught.

Honeymoon: 1. a short period of doting between dating and debting. 2. coo-existence. 3. the period between "I do" and "You'd better." 4. the thrill of a wife-time. 5. the time during which the bride believes the bridegroom's word of honor. 6. the vacation a man takes before starting to work for a new boss.

Honeymoon sandwich: just lettuce alone.

292

DEFINITIONS

Hope: a pathological belief in the occurrence of the impossible.

Horsepower: a power which has put the horse out of business.

Horse sense: 1. a degree of wisdom that keeps one from betting on the races. 2. stable thinking coupled with the ability to say nay (neigh). 3. that inestimable quality in a horse that keeps it from betting on a man. 4. when a fellow knows enough to stay away from a nag.

Hospital: 1. a place where people who are run down wind up. 2. a place where they wake you up to give you a sleeping pill.

Hospitality: the virtue which induces us to feed and lodge certain persons who are not in need of food and lodging.

Hot dog: the only animal that feeds the hand that bites it.

Hotel: a place where you give up good dollars for bad quarters.

Housewarming: the last call for wedding presents.

Housework: something you do that nobody notices unless you don't do it.

Howling success: the baby that gets picked up.

Hug: 1. a roundabout way of expressing affection. 2. energy gone to waist.

Hula dancer: a shake in the grass.

Human being: an ingenious assembly of portable plumbing.

Human brain: like a freight car—guaranteed a certain capacity, but always running empty.

Humiliation: an emotion caused by suddenly shrinking to one's normal proportions.

Humorist: a writer who shows us the faults of human nature in such a way that we recognize our failings and smile—and our neighbors' and laugh.

Hunch: what you call an idea that you're afraid is wrong.

293

DEFINITIONS

Husband: 1. a gay dog who is spousebroken. 2. a man who exchanges a bushel of fun for a peck of trouble. 3. a man who, if given enough rope, will be tied up at the office. 4. a man who knows that his wife's reasoning is largely sound. 5. a man who lost his liberty in the pursuit of happiness. 6. an experienced domestic creature who can guess what his wife is going to say before she repeats it. 7. a polygamous animal in a monogamous strait-jacket. 8. one who lays down the law to his wife, and then accepts all her amendments. 9. one who stands by you in troubles you wouldn't have had if you hadn't married him. 10. one who thinks twice before saying nothing. 11. the next thing to a wife. 12. what's left of a sweetheart after the nerve has been killed.

Hypochondria: a disease without a disease.

Hypochondriac: 1. a person with infinite capacity for faking pains. 2. one who can't leave well-enough alone.

Hypocrisy: the homage which vice pays to virtue.

Hypocrite: 1. a man who sets good examples when he has an audience. 2. one who pretends to be burying the hatchet when he's only digging up dirt. 3. one who talks on principles and acts on interest.

I

Idealist: 1. a person who helps other people to be prosperous. 2. one who tries to keep politics out of politics.

Ideals: funny little things that don't work unless you do.

Ideal summer resort: a place where fish bite and mosquitoes don't.

Ideal wife: any woman who has an ideal husband.

Igloo: an icicle built for two.

Ignorance: when you don't know something and somebody finds it out.

Illegibility: a doctor's prescription written with a post-office pen in the rumble seat of a second-hand car.

Imagination: something that sits up with a woman when her husband comes home late.

Immorality: the morality of those who are having a better time.

Impatience (a child's definition): waiting in a hurry.

Impossible: (see difficult.)

Income: 1. in these days, something you cannot live without nor within. 2. the sum of money which it costs more than to live.

Income tax: 1. a fine imposed for reckless thriving. 2. guaranteed annual rage.

Income-tax expert: someone whose fee is the amount he saves you in making out your tax return.

Income tax return: something that if you make out honestly you go to the poorhouse; or if you make it out dishonestly—you go to jail.

Incongruous: where our laws are made and how they appear.

Indian summer: that period between World Series drawings and football pools.

Indigestion: the failure of a round stomach to adjust to a square meal.

Infant prodigies: young people with highly imaginative parents.

Inflation: 1. a fate worse than debt. 2. a national headache caused by asset indigestion. 3. a period when two can live as steep as one. 4. a state of affairs where you never had it so good, or parted with it so fast. 5. just a drop in the buck. 6. the art of cutting a dollar bill in half without touching the paper. 7. when dollars to doughnuts becomes an even bet. 8. when nobody has enough money because everybody has too much.

Influence: something you think you have until you try to use it.

Innocent bystander: a person so simple-minded he doesn't know enough to get out of the way.

DEFINITIONS

Insincerity: a method by which we can multiply our personalities.

Insomnia: 1. a contagious disease often transmitted from babies to parents. 2. what a person has when he lies awake all night for an hour.

Installment paying: a condition which makes the months shorter and the years longer.

Instinct: the faculty which tells a woman whether a man needs inducement or encouragement.

Integrity: the thing that keeps you from looking ahead to see how the story ends.

Intellectual: 1. a fellow who is willing to discuss the preceding night's television programs, but makes it clear he only happened to be watching because the children turned the set on. 2. a man who hears the name of Monroe and thinks of the fifth President. 3. someone who knows when to quote what some bright fellow once said.

Intelligent girl: 1. one who knows how to refuse a kiss without being deprived of it. 2. one who knows less than the man with whom she happens to be talking at the moment.

Intelligent minority: a group which doesn't stay that way after it becomes a majority.

Interior decorator: a man who does things to your house he wouldn't dream of doing to his own.

Intoxication: to feel sophisticated and not be able to pronounce it.

Intuition: 1. suspicion in skirts. 2. that which enables a woman to put two and two together and get your number. 3. the ability women have to read between the lines on a blank page. 4. the sixth sense that allows a woman five wrong guesses. 5. the strange instinct that tells a woman she is right whether she is or not. 6. woman's ability to read between men's lyings.

Inveterate smoker: one who can shave without getting lather on his cigarette.

296

J

Jade: a semi-precious stone or a semi-precious woman.

Janitor: the only man who makes a quick clean-up in Wall Street and gets away with it.

Jay walker: a person who bets two legs against four wheels and usually loses.

Jealousy: 1. the friendship one woman has for another. 2. the theory that some other fellow has just as little taste.

Jeep: 1. a cocktail shaker with three speeds. 2. a man's most nearly successful effort to produce a mechanical mule.

Jewelers: men who ought to keep abreast of the times and rent wedding rings.

Joint account: an account where one person does the depositing and the other the withdrawing—usually husband and wife.

Joint checking account: a device to allow the wife to beat her husband to the draw.

Journalist: a person who works harder than any other lazy person in the world.

Joy of motherhood: what a woman experiences when all the kids are in bed.

Judge: 1. a law student who marks his own examination papers. 2. a lawyer who once knew a politician. 3. a man in a trying position.

Jukebox: a device for inflicting your musical taste on people who wouldn't give a plugged nickel for it.

June: the month when unmarried girls like to be well-groomed.

Junk: something you keep ten years and then throw away two weeks before you need it.

Jury: 1. a body of twelve men selected to decide which of the contestants has the better lawyer. 2. a group of twelve people of average ignorance.

Justice: 1. the insurance which we have on our lives and property; to which may be added, and obedience is the premium which we pay for it. 2. what we get when the decision is in our favor.

Juvenile delinquency: modern term for what we did as kids.

Juvenile delinquents: other people's children.

K

Keepsake: something given us by someone we've forgotten.

Kibitzer: a guy with an interferiority complex.

Kidnapping: the short snatches of rest a parent gets when baby sleeps.

Kindness: something you can't give away since it always comes back.

Kindred: fear that relatives are coming to stay.

Kiss: 1. a contraction of the mouth due to an enlargement of the heart. 2. a course of procedure, cunningly devised, for the mutual stoppage of speech at a moment when words are superfluous. 3. a mutual interchange of salivary bacteria. 4. an indescribable something that is of no value to anyone but is much prized by the right two. 5. a noun; though often used as a conjunction it is never declined; it is more common than proper, is used in the plural, and agrees with all genders. 6. nothing divided by two; meaning persecution for the infant, ecstasy for the youth, fidelity for the middle-aged, and homage for the old. 7. the anatomical juxtaposition of two orbicularis oris muscles in a state of contraction. 8. the shortest distance between two. 9. two divided by nothing. 10. what the child gets free, the young man steals, and the old man buys.

Kissing: a means of shortening single life.

Knickerbockers: a long name for short pants.

298

Knitting: an occupation that gives women something to think about while talking.

Knocker: a fellow who gets caught on the losing side.

L

Labor: a group which, in working for the five-day week, looks longingly for a five-day week end.

Ladies' sewing circle: where more husbands are darned than socks.

Lady: 1. a woman who always remembers others, and never forgets herself. 2. a woman who has enough willpower to resist a man's advances and enough wile power to block his retreat. 3. a woman who makes it easy for a man to be a gentleman. 4. one who never shows her underwear unintentionally.

Landed gentry: men who are either married or engaged.

Las Vegas: 1. just wheels and wails. 2. the land of the spree and the home of the knave.

Laughter: the sound you hear when you chase your hat down the street.

Laundry: 1. a business with clothes competition. 2. a place where clothes are mangled.

Law: the kind of ban that men forget.

Lawsuit: 1. a machine which you go into as a pig and come out of as a sausage. 2. generally a matter of expense and suspense. 3. something which nobody likes to have and nobody likes to lose.

Lawyer: 1. a fellow who is willing to go out and spend your last cent to prove he's right. 2. a learned gentleman who rescues your estate from your enemies and keeps it himself. 3. a man who induces two other men to strip for a fight, and then runs off with their clothes. 4. a person who helps you get what's coming to him. 5. he who is summoned when a felon needs a friend. 6. one who protects us against rob-

DEFINITIONS

bery by taking away temptation. 7. the only man in whom ignorance of the law is not punished.

Leadership: the art of getting somebody else to do something you want done because he wants to do it.

Learned fool: one who has read everything, and simply remembered it.

Lecture: 1. an entertainment at which it costs but little to look intelligent. 2. an occasion when you numb one end to benefit the other. 3. a process by which the notes of the professor become the notes of the student, without passing through the minds of either.

Lecturer: one with his hand in your pocket, his tongue in your ear, and his faith in your patience.

Lecturers: traveling men who express themselves collect.

Legend: a lie that has attained the dignity of age.

Leisure: the two minutes' rest a man gets while his wife thinks up something for him to do.

Letter: a form of composition opening with an excuse for not opening sooner and closing with an excuse for not closing later.

Level-headed person: one who doesn't get dizzy from doing good turns.

Liar: 1. one who tells an unpleasant truth. 2. one with no partition between his imagination and his information.

Liberal: 1. a man who is willing to spend somebody else's money. 2. a man with his mind open at both ends. 3. one who has both feet firmly planted in the air.

Liberty: 1. consists in giving everyone full right to mind everyone else's business. 2. preserved in some countries—canned in others. 3. the privilege of being free from the things we don't like in order to be slaves of things we do like.

Lie: 1. a very poor substitute for the truth, but the only one discovered up to date. 2. ever-present help in time of trouble. 3. man's worst liability. 4. something that fell from the truth in climbing towards it.

300

DEFINITIONS

Lie (golf): position of a ball; also proclivity of a golfer.

Lieutenant commander: the wife of a lieutenant.

Life: 1. a hospital in which every patient is possessed by a desire to change his bed. 2. a predicament which precedes death. 3. a span of time of which the first half is ruined by our parents and the second half by our children. 4. living expensively to impress people who live expensively to impress us. 5. made up of trials, appeals, reversals, but few convictions. 6. school tablets; aspirin tablets; stone tablets.

Life insurance: a contract that keeps you poor all your life so you can die rich.

Lisp: calling a spade a thpade.

Loafer: 1. a person who tries to make both weekends meet. 2. one who continues to live even though he complains that he can't exist on the wages he turns down.

Lobster-Newburg: a dish ordered at hotels by those who usually get beans at home.

Local bus: a device that makes mountains out of molehills.

Logic: an organized procedure for going wrong with confidence and certainty.

Logrolling: an aye for an aye.

Lorgnette: a dirty look you can hold in one hand.

Los Angeles: six suburbs in search of a city.

Love: 1. a conflict between reflexes and reflections. 2. a form of insanity which makes a girl marry her boss and work for him for the rest of her life without salary. 3. a form of self-government under a two-party system. 4. a lot of dame foolishness. 5. a man's insane desire to become a woman's meal ticket. 6. an insane desire on the part of a chump to pay a woman's board-bill for life. 7. it may be blind but the neighbors are not. 8. like a cigar—the brighter it burns, the quicker it's ashes. 9. oceans of emotions surrounded by expanses of expenses. 10. the delusion that one girl differs from another. 11. the triumph of imagination over intelligence. 12. the feeling that makes a woman make a man make a fool of himself. 13. the only game which two can play and both win.

DEFINITIONS

Love song: a caress set to music.

Lowbrow: a person who can't appreciate something he doesn't like.

Low neckline: something you can approve of and look down on at the same time.

Luck: 1. the thing that draws us for jury duty, but never for the sweepstakes. 2. what happens when effort and opportunity meet.

Luxury: 1. a necessity when it is found that you can make the down payment on it. 2. any bare necessity—with the taxes added. 3. anything a husband needs.

Luxury resort: one where a waiter expects a 25 cent tip when he presents a 60 cent bill for serving a 35 cent bottle of beer.

M

Majority: a large number of people who have gotten tired thinking for themselves and have decided to accept somebody else's opinion.

Mal de mer: French for "You can't take it with you."

Man: 1. a creature of superior intelligence who elects creatures of inferior intelligence to govern him. 2. a creature who is trying to make something for himself rather than something of himself. 3. a creature whom God made little lower than angels, and who has been getting lower ever since. 4. a large irrational creature who is always looking for home atmosphere in a hotel and hotel service around a home. 5. one who wishes he were as wise as he thinks his wife thinks he is.

Mandate: an appointment with the boy friend.

Manicurist: a girl who makes money hand over fist.

Manuscript: something submitted in haste and returned at leisure.

Marriage: 1. a book in which the first chapter is written in poetry and the remaining chapters in prose. 2. a ceremony in which rings are put on the finger of the lady and through the nose of the gentleman. 3. a feast where the grace is sometimes better than the dinner. 4. a hit-or-miss proposition—if you don't make a hit you remain a miss. 5. a mutual partnership with the husband as the mute. 6. an arrangement like the block-booking of motion pictures, in which a number of less desirable features must be accepted in order to obtain one or two of major attraction. 7. an institution that changes a woman from an attraction to a distraction. 8. a process of finding out what sort of guy your wife would have preferred. 9. a souvenir of love. 10. a state where a woman is no longer hoping—just expecting. 11. a woman's hair net tangled in a man's spectacles on top of the bedroom dresser. 12. before it, he talks and she listens; during the honeymoon, she talks and he listens; later, they both talk and the neighbors listen. 13. one long conversation, checkered by disputes. 14. the alliance of two people, one of whom never remembers birthdays and the other never forgets them. 15. the difference between painting the town and painting the back porch. 16. the first union to defy management. 17. the miracle that transforms a kiss from a pleasure into a duty and a life from a luxury into a necessity. 18. the only known example of the happy meeting of the immovable object and the irresistible force. 19. the only life sentence that is suspended by bad behavior. 20. the state or condition of a community consisting of a master, a mistress, and two slaves, making, in all, two. 21. when a woman turns an old rake into a lawn mower.

Marriage proposal: a speech often made on the purr of the moment.

Married couple: 1. two minds without a single thought. 2. two people who sit in the balcony at a movie because they want to smoke.

Married man: a fellow who used to think that being lonesome was man's worst fate.

Married woman: one who gives up the romantic attention of several men for the phlegmatic attention of just one.

Martini: an olive with an alcohol rub.

Martyrdom: 1. telling your wife the exact truth and then having her refuse to believe a word of it. 2. the only way in which a man can become famous without ability.

303

DEFINITIONS

Mason-Dixon line: a geographical division between "you all" and "youse guys."

Mass psychology: doing it the herd way.

Maternity hospital: an heirport.

Maternity ward: the only place in the world where there isn't a chance of dodging the issue.

Matrimony: 1. a knot tied by a preacher and untied by a lawyer. 2. an institution of learning in which a man loses his bachelor's degree without acquiring a master's. 3. it isn't a word, it's a sentence. 4. like making a call. You go to adore, you ring a belle, you give your name to a maid . . . and then you are taken in. 5. something that the bachelor misses and the widower escapes.

Maturity: the time of life when, if you had the time, you'd have the time of your life.

Me: the objectionable case of I.

Mealtime: when youngsters sit down to continue eating.

Medicine cabinet: a thing which looks like a drugstore only there are no sandwiches.

Meek: they inherit the earth and it's just as well—no one else would pay the inheritance taxes.

Memory: the feeling that steals over one as he listens to a friend's original stories.

Men: 1. often in the back yard looking for four-leaf clovers when opportunity knocks at the front door. 2. some dislike women without any reason while others like them that way.

Menace: a fellow on the dance floor with a rhumba mind and a waltz technique.

Meteorologist: a man who can look into a girl's eyes and tell whether.

Meteorology: the science of being up in the air and all at sea.

304

Microphone: some are metal discs and broadcast exactly what you say—others use rouge and lipstick and don't.

Middle age: 1. a man who remembers when corn-cure ads showed only the toes. 2. a time of life when our tripping becomes less light and more fantastic. 3. a time of life when winking at a girl is closing one eye to reality. 4. a time when you want to look fit as a fiddle, but bulge like a bass. 5. that period in a man's life when he'd rather not have a good time than have to get over it. 6. that period in life when you can't decide which there is more of—age or middle. 7. that period when a man begins to shed his hair, his teeth, and his illusions. 8. that period when a woman's life appears to be all bleaches and cream. 9. that time in a man's life when the elasticity lost from his sinews seems to settle in his conscience. 10. that time in life when we begin to develop scales resistance. 11. that time of life when you're reduced to reducing. 12. the time of life that affects us in the middle. 13. the time of life when a man can get exhausted simply by wrestling with his conscience. 14. the time when a man is always thinking that in a week or two he will feel as good as ever. 15. the time when you'll do anything to feel better, except give up what's hurting you. 16. when a man says he is going to begin saving next month. 17. when a man starts complaining that the cleaners are shrinking his suits. 18. when a man stops wondering if he can escape temptations and begins to wonder if he's missing any. 19. when a woman takes her high school annual out of the bookcase and hides it where the children can't find it. 20. when greener grass is something that just has to be mowed more often. 21. when many women consider mending their weighs. 22. when the girl you smile at thinks you are one of her father's friends. 23. when the girl you whistle at thinks you must be calling a dog. 24. when you are sitting at home on Saturday night and the telephone rings and you hope it isn't for you. 25. when you begin to exchange your emotions for symptoms. 26. when you can do as much as before, but don't. 27. when you don't care how long you stay out if you're home by 9:00 P.M. 28. when you go all-out and end up all-in. 29. when you laugh at pictures that you once prized. 30. when you look forward to a dull evening. 31. when you no longer care where your wife wants to go—so long as you don't have to go with her. 32. when you're as young as ever, but it takes a lot more effort. 33. when you're grounded for several days after flying high for one night. 34. when you start eating

DEFINITIONS

what is good for you instead of what you like. 35. when you step on a scale and the balance is no longer in your favor. 36. when you still have the old spark, but it takes more puffing. 37. when you stop setting-up exercises and start setting over buttons. 38. when you've met so many people that every new person you meet reminds you of someone else.

Military expert: one who tells you what's going to happen tomorrow—then tells you why it didn't.

Military science: that remarkable art in which the lessons learned in winning one war, if strictly followed, lose the next.

Millinery secret: one that should be kept under your hat.

Millionaire: 1. a billionaire after he pays his taxes. 2. a man who travels between his air-conditioned home and air-conditioned office in an air-conditioned car, then pays $50 to go over to the steam room at the club and sweat.

Minor operation: one performed on someone else.

Miracle: an event described by those to whom it was told by men who did not see it.

Miser: one who's perfectly content to let the rest of the world go buy.

Mistake: proof that somebody tried anyhow.

Mixed company: what you are in when you think of a story you can't tell there.

Mixed emotions: to see your mother-in-law go over the cliff in your brand new Cadillac.

Model husband: one who thinks his wife's headache is as important as his own rheumatism.

Modern age: when girls wear less on the street than their grandmothers did in bed.

Modern country: one which can ban fireworks and produce H-bombs.

Modern employer: one who is looking for men between the ages of 25 and 30 with 40 years' experience.

Modern girl: 1. one who believes in marrying a man to find out if she can live without him. 2. one who'd rather be well formed than well informed. 3. one who sticks to the spinning wheel—until her chips give out.

Modern home: 1. one in which a switch regulates everything but the children. 2. where the dwellers would speedily become bored, idle, cold, hungry, dirty, and unkempt if the electric current were cut off.

Modern male: one who will stand for anything but a woman on a streetcar.

Modern mother: one who worries if her daughter gets in too early.

Modern parent: one who puts the cat out at night by shutting off the hi-fi.

Modern party: one where there's always rum for one more.

Modern pioneer: the mother who manages to get through a rainy Saturday with the television set out of order.

Modern plays: most of them have to be sin to be appreciated.

Modern thrift: when we take care of the down payments and let the installments take care of themselves.

Modern wisdom: an open mind and a closed mouth.

Modesty: 1. the art of encouraging people to find out for themselves how important you are. 2. the art of imperfectly concealing your talents. 3. the feeling that others will surely discover in a little while just how wonderful you are. 4. the gentle art of enhancing your charm by pretending not to be aware of it.

Monday: in Christian countries, the day after the baseball game.

Money: the mint makes it first and it's up to us to make it last.

Money-grabber: anybody who grabs more money than you can grab.

Monologue: a conversation between a husband and his wife.

DEFINITIONS

Monopolist: a guy who keeps an elbow on each arm of his theatre chair.

Monsoon: a typhoon that's going steady with a tornado.

Moon: a heavenly body which sways the tide, and the untied, too.

Moose: an animal that has a head and horns on one end and a living-room wall on the other.

Moral indignation: jealousy with a halo.

Morality: the attitude we adopt towards people whom we personally dislike.

Moratorium: that which results when an implacable creditor meets an unpayable debt.

Morning after: when getting up gets you down.

Moron: something which in the wintertime girls wouldn't have so many colds if they put.

Mortgage: a house with a guilty conscience.

Mosquito: a small insect designed by God to make us think better of flies.

Moth: a perverse creature that spends the summer in a fur coat and the winter in a bathing suit.

Mother-in-law: 1. a referee with an interest in one of the fighters. 2. a talkie that has come to stay. 3. a woman who is never outspoken.

Mother-in-law sandwich: cold shoulder and tongue.

Mother's life: one darned stocking after the other.

Motion-picture preview: a place where four or five men, each making $5000 or $6000 a week, go to watch an adolescent kid write "It smells" on a card.

Motorist: 1. a person who, after seeing a wreck, drives carefully for several blocks. 2. a person who forgets that he used to be a pedestrian.

Motorists: people in such a hurry to get into the next county that they often get into the next world.

308

Mouth: the grocer's friend, the orator's pride, the fool's trap, the dentist's salvation.

Movie actor's salary: the haul of fame.

Movie hero: one who sits through the average double bill.

Mugwump: a man who sits on a fence with his mug on one side and his wump on the other.

Mule: 1. an animal that is stubbornly backward about going forward. 2. an animal who boasts that his ancestors were horses.

Music: the only language in which you cannot say a mean or sarcastic thing.

Musical comedy: where all good jokes go just before they die.

N

Nag: a woman with no horse sense.

Nagging woman: one who keeps a swivel tongue in her head.

Necessity: almost any luxury you see in the home of a neighbor.

Neck: something which, if you don't stick out, you won't get into trouble up to.

Needle: formerly hard to find in a haystack; now hard to find in a woman's hand.

Neighbor: one whom we are commanded to love as ourselves, and who does all he can to make us disobedient.

Nepotism: putting on heirs.

Network: a pattern, reticulated and decussated at equal intervals with interstices between the intersections.

Neurasthenic: a person who is always on pills and needles.

Neurotic: 1. a person who has discovered the secret of perpetual emotion. 2. a person who, when you ask how she is, tells you. 3. a woman who calls a doctor when all she wants is an audience. 4. one who believes the world owes him a loving.

New baby: an event similar to an opera—full of grand marches and loud cries for the author every night.

New hairdo: a way to get your husband to appreciate the old one.

News: the same thing happening today that happened yesterday, but to different people.

Newspaper: 1. a circulating library with high blood pressure. 2. a portable screen behind which man hides from the woman who is standing up in a streetcar. 3. a publication that condemns gambling on the editorial page and prints racing tips on the sports page.

New Yorker: one who gets acquainted with his neighbor by meeting him down in Florida.

Night club: 1. a place where the tables are reserved and the guests are not. 2. a place where they get away with murder and you face the charges. 3. a place where they take the rest out of restaurant and put the din in dinner.

Night clubs: where people with nothing to remember go to forget.

No-account: the man without a bank account.

Nonchalance: the ability to look like an owl when you have behaved like an ass.

Nostalgia: longing for the place you wouldn't move back to.

Nudism: 1. a back to the form movement. 2. a person who goes coatless and vestless, and wears trousers to match. 3. one suffering from clothestrophobia. 4. the only person with less pocket space than a sailor.

Nursery: bawlroom.

O

Oats: a grain, which in England is generally given to horses, but in Scotland supports the people.

Obesity: a surplus gone to waist.

Ocean: huge body of water surrounded entirely by rumors of ever-lasting peace.

Old age: 1. when you find yourself using one bend-over to pick up two things. 2. when all girls look good to you.

Old-fashioned girl: 1. one who has never been kissed—and admits it. 2. one who says, "I don't intend to be married till I'm thirty," while her modern sister says, "I don't intend to be thirty until I'm married."

Old maid: 1. a debutante who overdid it. 2. a girl who has been looked over and then overlooked. 3. a girl who knows all the answers but is never asked the questions. 4. a girl who regrets she had so much sense when she was young. 5. a girl who spends too much time chinning and not enough time necking. 6. a "yes" girl who never had a chance to talk. 7. slipping beauty.

Oldster: one who remembers when child guidance was something parents were expected to administer, not submit to.

Old-timer: 1. a fellow who remembers when rockets were just part of a fireworks celebration. 2. a man who can remember when a careless driver, out with his girl, let the horse stop to graze. 3. a man whose summer vacation was one day at the county fair. 4. a man who turned out the gas while courting, instead of stepping on it. 5. a person who can remember when he could remember. 6. a real old-timer can remember when Sunday drivers let off steam by shaking their buggy whips at each other. 7. one who can recall when a bureau was a piece of furniture. 8. one who can recall when a shoemaker stuck to his last, and wives stuck to their first. 9. one who can remember when callers rang the door-bell instead of blowing the horn. 10. one who can remember when folks sat down at the dinner table and counted their blessings instead of calories. 11. one who can remember when grand-pap wore his suspenders the way modern gals wear a one-strap evening dress. 12. one who can remember when the woman he left behind stayed there. 13. one who can remember when there were no deductions in his pay until he got home. 14. one who can remember when there were no gags beginning "An oldtimer is one who can remember . . ." 15. one who can remember when women had no figures to speak of. 16. one who can remember when

311

DEFINITIONS

you couldn't eat a dollar's worth at a cafeteria. 17. one who has never been able to figure out why women still take as much time to dress as they did when they wore clothes. 18. one who remembers when a baby sitter was called a mother. 19. one who remembers when a child had more brothers and sisters than fathers. 20. one who remembers a housewife putting food into cans, instead of taking it out. 21. one who remembers when a dishwashing machine had to be married, not bought. 22. one who remembers when a man did his own withholding on his take-home pay. 23. one who remembers when charity was a virtue and not an organization. 24. one who remembers when dancing was done with the feet. 25. one who remembers when he could buy a pound of steak for a dime, but forgets he had to work an hour to earn the dime. 26. one who remembers when, if a woman told how many quarts and pints she had on the shelf, she meant canned fruit. 27. one who remembers when it cost more to run a car than to park it. 28. one who remembers when marriage problems were solved, not dissolved. 29. one who remembers when modern meant being up to the minute, instead of years and years ahead. 30. one who remembers when only fighting men died with their boots on. 31. one who remembers when people were more intelligent than machines. 32. one who remembers when people who wore blue jeans worked. 33. one who remembers when the medicine man used to come to town on a wagon instead of a television signal. 34. one who remembers when the only people who paid income taxes were those who could afford to. 35. one who remembers when the only problem about parking was to get the girl to agree to it. 36. one who remembers when we just laughed at the fellow who thought he was going to set the world on fire. 37. you're an old-timer if you can remember when any man who washed dishes worked in a restaurant.

Oleomargarine: the food of people who haven't seen butter days.

Open mind: 1. a mind in which convictions go out as fast as they come in. 2. one that is too porous to hold a conviction.

Opera: where a guy gets stabbed in the back and instead of bleeding he sings.

Operation: a surgical job taking minutes to do and years to describe.

312

DEFINITIONS

Opinionated people: little rotund islands of complacency anchored in a sea of prejudices.

Opportunist: 1. a person who, finding himself in hot water, decides he needs a bath anyway. 2. one who meets the wolf at the door and appears the next day in a fur coat.

Opportunity: a favorable occasion for grasping a disappointment.

Optimism: 1. a cheerful frame-of-mind that enables a tea kettle to sing though in hot water up to its nose. 2. the noble temptation to see too much in everything. 3. waiting for a ship to come in when you haven't sent one out.

Optimist: 1. a fellow who believes a housefly is looking for a way to get out. 2. a fellow who goes into a hotel without baggage and asks to have his check cashed. 3. a fellow who is always talking about what a fool he *used* to be. 4. a girl who mistakes a bulge for a curve. 5. a guy who starts putting on his shoes when the speaker says, "And now, in conclusion . . .". 6. a happychondriac. 7. a hope addict. 8. a man who is just starting to shovel out a long driveway. Pessimist: one who has been working at it for five minutes. 9. a man who marries his secretary—thinking he'll continue to dictate to her. 10. a man who thinks a woman in a phone booth will be right out when he hears her starting to say good-by. 11. a man who thinks his wife has stopped smoking cigarettes when he finds cigar butts around the house. 12. a man who, while waiting for a woman, keeps his motor running. 13. a middle-aged man who believes that the cleaners have been shrinking the waistband of his pants. 14. a person who puts a 3¢ stamp on a letter and marks it "rush". 15. a single man contemplating marriage. Pessimist: a married man contemplating it. 16. a woman who leaves the dinner dishes because she will feel more like washing them in the morning. 17. one who already has his bad breaks relined. 18. one who calls a spade two spades. 19. one who doesn't care what happens—so long as it doesn't happen to him. 20. one who makes the best of conditions, after making the conditions the best possible. 21. one who says his glass is half-full, while the pessimist says his is half-empty. 22. one who thinks humorists will some day run out of definitions of an optimist. 23. someone

DEFINITIONS

who tells you to cheer up when things are going his way. 24. someone who thinks he has a new definition of one. 25. the man who thinks his wife has given up when she has given in. 26. the sort of man who marries his sister's best friend.

Oration: a flood of words and a drought of reason.

Orator: a man who's willing to lay down your life for his country.

Oratoreador: an orator who specializes in throwing the bull.

Oratory: 1. eloquence accompanied by a Prince Albert. 2. the art of making deep noises from the chest sound like important messages from the brain.

Originality: undetected imitation.

Osteopath: a man who works his fingers to your bones.

Our national air: carbon monoxide.

Outlaws: a menace to society, but in-laws are worse.

Over-optimistic news commentator: Pollyanalist.

P

Pacifist: a fellow who could attend a peace conference without getting into a fight.

Panic: a sudden desertion of us, and a going-over to the enemy of our imagination.

Paper napkin: its only ambition is to get down off your lap and play on the floor.

Par (golf): mathematical perfection, usually attained with a soft pencil and a softer conscience.

Paragon: the model man a woman regrets she gave up for the one she mistakenly married.

Parasite: one who goes through a revolving door on another's push.

314

Paratrooper: 1. a soldier who climbs down trees he never climbed up. 2. the only man who gets up in the world by falling down on the job.

Parent: 1. a person who believes the words "progeny" and "prodigy" are interchangeable. 2. (collegiate definition) the kin you love to touch.

Parents: 1. one of the hardships of a minor's life. 2. persons who spend half their time worrying how a child will turn out, and the rest of the time wondering when a child will turn in.

Parking meter: a snitching post.

Parking space: 1. an unfilled opening in an unending line of cars near an unapproachable fire plug. 2. an unoccupied area along the curb on the other side of the street. 3. something you see when you haven't got your car. 4. that area that disappears while you are making a U-turn.

Passport photo: a way to see yourself as others see you.

Past: something often forgotten for a present.

Patience: 1. a minor form of despair, disguised as a virtue. 2. the ability to idle your motor when you feel like stripping your gears. 3. the ability to stand something as long as it happens to the other fellow. 4. the quality that is needed most just as it is exhausted.

Patient man: one who can put up with himself.

Patriot: 1. man who loves his country, and wants to make as much out of it as possible. 2. one who is sorry because he has only one income to give to his country. 3. one who loves his country's flag and robs his countrymen.

Patriotic American: one who never orders from a menu anything he can't pronounce.

Patriotism: 1. realization that this is a nation and not a denomination. 2. your conviction that this country is superior to all others because you were born in it.

Patron: commonly a wretch who supports with insolence and is paid with flattery.

DEFINITIONS

Peace: 1. a period in which men toil to meet the expense of the wars preceding and succeeding. 2. a short pause between wars for enemy identification. 3. in international affairs, a period of cheating between two periods of fighting.

Peace conference: a meeting to find out who won't win the next war.

Pedestrian: 1. a car owner who has found a parking space. 2. a fellow whose wife beats him to the garage. 3. a guy who counted on his wife to put some gas in the car. 4. a guy with three good tires. 5. a man who falls by the wayside. 6. a man who thought there still were a couple of gallons of gas left in the tank. 7. a man with a son in high school and only one car in the family. 8. streetwalking object invisible to the motorist. 9. the most approachable chap in the world.

Peeping Tom: one who climbs the ladder of success stare by stare.

Pen-pal: the fellow who signs your paycheck.

Pension: in England, understood to mean pay given to a state hireling for treason to his country.

Perfect bridge lamp: light enough to see by, too heavy to throw.

Perfect gentleman: a man of high principle and no interest.

Perfectionist: one who takes infinite pains, and often gives them to other people.

Perfect man: a wife's first husband.

Perfume: 1. any smell that is used to drown a worse one. 2. chemical warfare.

Perpetual motion: the family upstairs.

Perseverance: a lowly virtue whereby mediocrity achieves an inglorious success.

Personality: the name we give to our own little collection of funny habits.

Pessimist: 1. a man to whom an optimist owes money. 2. an optimist on the way home from the horse races. 3. an optimist who

316

endeavored to practice what he preached. 4. a woman driver who's sure she can't park her car in a tight place. Optimist: a man who thinks she won't try. 5. one who blows out the light to see how dark it is. 6. one who feels bad when he feels good for fear he'll feel worse when he feels better. 7. one who is always building dungeons in the air. 8. one who, of two evils, chooses them both. 9. one who sizes himself up and then gets sore about it. 10. one who thinks everybody as nasty as himself, and hates them for it.

Petition: a list of people who didn't have the nerve to say "no."

Philanderer: a man who considers himself too good to be true.

Philanthropist: 1. a man who atones openly for the wrong which he has done secretly. 2. one who gives away what he should be giving back. 3. one who returns to the people publicly what he steals from them privately. 4. a rich old gentleman who has trained himself to grin while his conscience is picking his pocket.

Philosopher: 1. a fellow who always knows what to do until it happens to him. 2. a man who can get the "fun" out of "defunct." 3. a person wearing a blindfold, in a dark room, looking for a black cat—which wasn't there. 4. a person who says he doesn't care which side his bread is buttered on, because he eats both sides anyway. 5. one who, instead of crying over spilt milk, consoles himself with the thought that it was over four-fifths water.

Philosophers: people who talk about something they don't understand, and make you think it's your fault.

Philosophy: 1. a route of many roads leading from nowhere to nothing. 2. a study which enables man to be unhappy more intelligently. 3. something that enables the rich to say there is no disgrace in being poor. 4. unintelligible answers to insoluble problems.

Phony: a guy who tries to cut his throat with an electric razor.

Photograph albums: the strange views people take of things.

Photographer: one who can make an ugly girl as pretty as a picture.

DEFINITIONS

Physician: a man who pours drugs of which he knows little into a body of which he knows less.

Pink elephant: a beast of bourbon.

Pink tea: giggle, gabble, gobble, git.

Pipe: a thing that makes a man think—he thinks it's lit when it isn't.

Planned economy: where everything is included in the plans except economy.

Platitude: 1. a truth we are tired of hearing. 2. a dull old saw that everyone borrows, but no one sharpens. 3. an old saw that has lost its teeth.

Platonic friendship: play for him and tonic for her.

Platonic love: 1. all of the pleasures with none of the responsibilities. 2. the gun you didn't know was loaded.

Platonic lover: a man who holds the eggshells while somebody else eats the omelette.

Playboy: 1. a man who summers in the Alps, winters in Miami, and springs at blondes. 2. one who is very good at being no good.

Pleasingly plump: a girl with a shape like a figure ate.

Pleasure trip: any trip that your wife can put in the memory book—and you can put on the expense account.

Poise: 1. an acquired characteristic which enables father to buy a new pair of shoes at the same time he is ignoring a hole in his sock. 2. the ability to keep talking while somebody else picks up the check. 3. the ability to remain calm and at ease in a barber chair, with your mouth full of lather, while the porter tries to give your new hat to another fellow. 4. the act of raising the eyebrows instead of the roof.

Poker: when it's darkest just before you've drawn.

Politeness: 1. the art of choosing among your thoughts. 2. the most acceptable hypocrisy.

Political campaign: a matter of mud, threats, and smears.

318

DEFINITIONS

Political economy: two words that should be divorced on grounds of incompatibility.

Political machine: a united minority working against a divided majority.

Political platform: a platform like that on the front of a street-car—not meant to stand on, just to get in on.

Political war: one in which everyone shoots from the lip.

Politician: 1. a career that's most promising. 2. a fellow who borrows your pot in which to cook your goose. 3. a fellow who's got what it takes to take what you've got. 4. a man who divides his time between running for office and running for cover. 5. a man who shakes your hand in the hope of shaking your purse. 6. a man who spends half his time making laws, and the other half helping friends evade them. 7. a man who stands for what he thinks others will fall for. 8. a person who can talk in circles while standing foursquare. 9. one who promises the people a car in every garage when he runs for office, and after he is elected proceeds to erect parking meters. 10. one who, when he comes to the parting of the ways, goes both ways.

Politicians: 1. people who get in the public eye by getting in the public chest. 2. something like poor relatives; you only see them when they need help.

Politics: 1. a simple matter of either passing the buck or passing the doe. 2. be sure you're in right, then go ahead. 3. one party trying to get into office and the other party trying to stay in. 4. the art of looking for trouble, finding it everywhere, diagnosing it incorrectly, and applying the wrong remedies. 5. the art of obtaining money from the rich and votes from the poor on the pretext of protecting each from the other. 6. the only profession for which no preparation is thought necessary. 7. where people work hard to get a job and do nothing after they get it.

Polls: places where you stand in line for a place to decide who will spend your money.

Poor man: a man who has nothing but money.

Popularity: to be gifted with the virtue of knowing a whole lot of uninteresting people.

319

DEFINITIONS

Positive: being mistaken at the top of one's voice.

Posterity: what the founding fathers would not have talked about so glowingly if they had known we were going to be it.

Potomac fever: that hideous disease which causes one to swell without growing.

Poverty: a state of mind sometimes induced by a neighbor's new car.

Powder: something that may cause an explosion if found on the lapel.

Power: to know, and to know that you know.

Practical nurse: one who marries her rich patient.

Practical politician: a man who shakes your hand before election and your acquaintance afterwards.

Praise: what you receive when you are no longer alive.

Prejudice: 1. a lazy man's substitute for thinking. 2. a vagrant opinion without visible means of support. 3. being down on something you're not up on. 4. merely bad manners raised to an intolerable degree. 5. the dislike of the unlike. 6. weighing the facts with your thumb on the scale.

Press agent: one who has hitched his braggin' to a star.

Prodigy: a child who plays the piano when he ought to be asleep in bed.

Producer: a man who stands in the back of the theatre on opening night and wishes he were dead.

Professor: 1. a man whose job it is to tell students how to solve the problems of life which he himself has tried to avoid by becoming a professor. 2. a textbook wired for sound. 3. one who talks in someone else's sleep.

Professor emeritus: a teacher who has had it.

Professors: those who go to college and never get out.

Progress: 1. a state of human development where a man pays a laundry for destroying his shirts and collars. 2. something that's achieved by man's innate desire to live beyond his means. 3. swapping old troubles for new. 4. the slow business of falling in line with the schemes of minorities. 5. what an inactive committee always reports.

Promoter: a man who will furnish the ocean if you will furnish the ships.

Propaganda: 1. baloney disguised as food for thought. 2. the other side's case put so convincingly that it annoys you.

Proposal: 1. a figure of speech ending in a sentence. 2. a girl listening faster than a man can talk.

Prosperity: 1. being able to pay a little more for things we shouldn't buy anyway. 2. something the businessmen created for the politicians to take credit for. 3. that short period between the final installment and the next purchase. 4. the sweet buy and buy.

Proverbs: 1. the wisdom of many and the wit of one. 2. short sentences drawn from long experiences.

Prune: a plum that has seen better days.

Psychiatrist: 1. a fellow who goes to a burlesque show to watch the audience. 2. a guy who makes you squeal on yourself. 3. a man who doesn't have to worry as long as other people do. 4. a mind sweeper. 5. one who tries to find out whether an infant has more fun in infancy than an adult in adultery.

Psychologist: a man who, when a good-looking girl enters a room, watches everybody else.

Psychology: the science that tells you what you already know in words you can't understand.

Public interest: a term used by every politician to support his ideas.

Public opinion: 1. private gossip which has reached the proportions and virulence of an epidemic. 2. what people think other people are thinking.

DEFINITIONS

Public relations: the letter you don't write when you're mad and the nice letter you write to the so-and-so the next day, after you've regained your sense of humor.

Public speaking: the art of diluting a two-minute idea with a two-hour vocabulary.

Pugilist: a person who believes that it is better to give than to receive.

Pun: the lowest form of humor—when you don't think of it first.

Punctuality: 1. a grandstand play in an empty ball park. 2. the art of guessing how late the other fellow is going to be. 3. the art of wasting only your own time. 4. waiting around for other people.

Puncture: a little hole in a tire found a great distance from a garage or gas station.

Puppy: a little waggin' without wheels.

Puppy love: the beginning of a dog's life.

Puritan: a person who pours righteous indignation into the wrong things.

Puttering: woman's word for man's work.

Putting green: great oaths from little acorns grow.

Q

Quartet: 1. four guys who think the other three sing off-key. 2. the sum of two pints.

Question: a thing with two sides so long as it does not concern us personally.

R

Race horse: a fast means of redistributing wealth.

Racetrack: 1. a place where a man is washed up as soon as he loses his shirt. 2. a place where windows clean people. 3. where thousands of people can go for a ride on the same horse.

Radical: 1. a conservative out of a job. 2. anyone whose opinion differs from ours.

Radio announcer: a man who talks until you have a headache, then tries to sell you something to relieve it.

Radio City: the tower of babble.

Radio commercial: the pause that depresses.

Raise: the increase in pay you get just before going into debt a little further.

Raisin: a worried grape.

Rare volume: a borrowed book that comes back.

Rationing: less and less of more and more oftener and oftener.

Reactionary: a somnambulist walking backward.

Reading: thinking with someone else's head instead of one's own.

Recess: teacher's coffee break.

Recession: a period in which you tighten your belt. Depression: a period in which you have no belt to tighten.

Red light: the place where you catch up with the motorist who passed you at 60 m.p.h. a mile back.

Redskins: people on the American bathing beaches.

Reducing: wishful shrinking.

Reformer: 1. a man who rides through a sewer in a glass-bottomed boat. 2. one who insists upon his conscience being your guide. 3. one who, when he smells a rat, is eager to let the cat out of the bag.

Regret: insight that comes a day too late.

Relations: 1. a tedious pack of people who haven't the remotest knowledge of how to live nor the smallest instinct about when to die. 2. people who come to visit you when the weather is too hot to cook their own meals.

323

DEFINITIONS

Reno: 1. large inland seaport in America with the tied running in and the untied running out. 2. residence of the bitter half. 3. the land of the free and the grave of the home.

Reno cocktail: marriage on the rocks.

Reno-vated: divorced in Nevada.

Repartee: 1. an insult with its dress-suit on. 2. knowing what to say after you've just missed your chance to say it. 3. what a person thinks of after he becomes a departee. 4. what you wish you had said.

Repentance: to be sorry enough to quit.

Reputation: 1. a bubble which man bursts when he tries to blow it for himself. 2. a personal possession, frequently not discovered until lost.

Resort: 1. a place where the tired grow more tired. 2. a place where they charge you enough to make up for the nine months you are not there.

Respectability: the offspring of a liaison between a bald head and a bank account.

Restaurant: an eating place that does not sell drugs.

Restricted: a piece of inside news you get from a civilian.

Reticence: knowing what you're talking about but keeping your mouth shut.

Revolution (in politics): an abrupt change in the form of mis-government.

Rhumba: a fox trot with the backfield in motion.

Riches: a burden on those who have them and a greater burden on those who haven't them.

Rich man: one who isn't afraid to ask the clerk to show him something cheaper.

Rich relatives: the kin we love to touch.

Righteous indignation: your own wrath, as opposed to the shocking bad temper of others.

324

Rising generation: a generation which is fond of sitting.

Roadhog: a fellow who meets you more than half way.

Road map: a book of etiquette showing motorists which fork to use.

Roulette: a wheel that seldom takes a turn for the bettor.

Rumble seat: a breakfast nook on wheels.

Rummage sale: where you buy stuff from somebody else's attic to store in your own.

Rush hour: when traffic is at a standstill.

Rye: grain for sowing wild oats.

S

Sailor: a man who makes his living on water but never touches it on shore.

Saint: a dead sinner, revised and edited.

Salary: 1. an unearned income. 2. a stipend, part of which is withheld biweekly, the balance returnable on April 15. 3. a thing you can't bank on nowadays.

Salesman: one who often needs the wind taken out of his sales.

Salesmanship: transferring a conviction by a seller to a buyer.

Salesmen: people with both feet on the ground who take orders from people with both feet on the desk.

Sales resistance: the triumph of mind over patter.

Salmon: a fish that lurks in a can and only comes out when unexpected company arrives.

Sandwich: an unsuccessful attempt to make both ends meat.

Saxophone: an ill wind that blows no good.

DEFINITIONS

Scandalmonger: 1. a prattlesnake. 2. one who puts who and who together and gets whew!

Science: an orderly arrangement of what, at the moment, seems to be the facts.

Screen door: something the kids get a bang out of.

Sculptor: a poor unfortunate who makes faces and busts.

Seasickness: traveling across the ocean by rail.

Seasoned troops: soldiers that are mustered by the officers and peppered by the enemy.

Second marriage: the triumph of hope over experience.

Second wind: what a public speaker acquires when he says, "And, in conclusion."

Secret: 1. something a woman can keep with a telling effect. 2. something that is hushed about from place to place.

Secretary: 1. an office worker who is obliged to look like a girl, think like a man, and work like a horse. 2. (undesirable) one that is clock-eyed.

Secrets: things we give to others to keep for us.

Self-control: when a woman checks out of a market with nothing more than she had on her shopping list.

Self-importance: a feeling that is momentarily removed by a walk through the cemetery.

Selfishness: that detestable vice which no one will forgive in others and no one is without in himself.

Self-made man: a horrible example of unskilled labor.

Self-respect: the secure feeling that no one, as yet, is suspicious.

Self-restraint: feeling your oats without sowing them.

Sense of humor: being able to laugh at your friends' misfortunes.

Service station: a place where you fill the car and drain the family.

Sewing circle: where friendship hangs by a thread.

Shakespeare: a dramatist of note who lived by writing things for other people to quote.

Shape: what a bathing suit takes when a girl's in it.

Shipboard: where four bells means three cocktails.

Shooting script: a letter from a blonde that your wife finds in your pocket.

Short vacation: half a loaf.

Shoulder strap: a device for keeping an attraction from becoming a sensation.

Silence: 1. the only successful substitute for brains. 2. unbearable repartee.

Silent film: one where no one in the audience bought popcorn.

Sinner: a stupid person who gets found out.

Skeleton: a person with the inside out and the outside off.

Skiing (Indian's definition): Whoosh! Then walk a mile.

Skunk: a streamlined cat with a 2-tone finish and a fluid drive.

Slang: 1. language that takes off its coat, spits on its hands, and goes to work. 2. the speech of him who robs the literary garbage cans on their way to the dump.

Small town: 1. a place where everybody knows the troubles you've seen. 2. a place where everybody knows whose check is good. 3. where everybody is interested in what the Joneses will name the latest baby, while a big city is where they worry about what the zoo will call the new elephant.

Smart bride: one who quits playing ball after she makes a good catch.

Smart man: one who hasn't let a woman pin anything on him since he was a baby.

Smart girl: 1. one who can get her way without half crying.

DEFINITIONS

2. one who can tell the difference between being bitten by a love bug and a louse.

Smog: the air apparent.

Smokers: people who claim the more they fume, the less they fret.

Snack: the pause that refleshes.

Snob: 1. one who, in climbing the ladder of success, kisses the feet of the one ahead of him and kicks the head of the one following him. 2. one who talks as though he had begotten his own ancestors.

Snoring: sheet music.

Snuff maker: a man who puts his business in someone else's nose.

Social success: the infinite capacity for being bored.

Social tact: the ability to make your guests feel at home where you wish they were.

Society: 1. that which some folks are born in, others are taken in, but most folks pay to get in. 2. where every woman wants to enlarge her sphere but not her circumference.

Solemnity: a trick of the body to hide the faults of the mind.

Song: the licensed medium for bawling in public things too silly or sacred to be uttered in ordinary speech.

Sophistication: knowing enough to keep your feet out of the crack of the theatre seat in front of you.

Sorority: a group of girls living in one house, with a single purpose . . . to get more girls to live in one house, with a single purpose.

Spanking: a process which takes less time than reasoning and penetrates sooner to the seat of memory.

Specialist: a doctor whose patients are expected to confine their ailments to office hours.

Speculator: a man who observes the future and acts before it occurs.

DEFINITIONS

Spendthrift: one who grows poor by seeming rich.

Spinster: 1. a lady in waiting. 2. a lady frequently guilty of contempt of courting.

Spring: 1. the season of balls—golf, tennis, base, and moth. 2. the time of the year when farmers and golfers start their spring plowing. 3. the time of year when motorists drain the anti-freeze from their radiators two weeks too soon. 4. when a young man's fancy lightly turns to what the girl has been thinking about all winter. 5. when boys begin to feel gallant and girls begin to feel buoyant.

Stagnation: a country without women.

Stalemate: a husband with one joke.

Statesman: 1. an ex-politician who has mastered the art of holding his tongue. 2. a politician who is held upright by equal pressure from all directions.

Static: Nature's way of protecting us from certain radio programs.

Station wagon: something a city person uses when he moves to the country so the country people will know he's from the city.

Statistician: a man who draws a mathematically precise line from an unwarranted assumption to a foregone conclusion.

Statistics: mendacious truths.

Stockbroker: a man who can take a bankroll and run it into a shoestring.

Stomach: a bowl-shaped cavity containing the organs of indigestion.

Stooge: a guy who lives by the wrong side of the cracks.

Stork: a bird with many things charged against it which should have been blamed on the lark.

Strapless gown: 1. when a woman won't shoulder the responsibility. 2. a compromise between the law of decency and the law of gravity.

Strategy: usually darn poor judgment that happens to work out all right.

DEFINITIONS

Stucco: what a lot of house hunters are getting these days.

Subtlety: the art of saying what you think and getting out of range before it is understood.

Substitute: the right article made of the wrong material.

Suburb: a place where, by the time you've finished paying for your home there, the suburbs have moved 20 miles out.

Suburbanite: a man who hires someone to mow his lawn so he can play golf for exercise.

Suburbs: where the station wagons are bigger than the stations.

Success: 1. failure with a fresh coat of paint. 2. getting what you want. Happiness—wanting what you get. 3. making more money to meet obligations you wouldn't have if you didn't make so much money. 4. self-expression at a profit. 5. the ability to hitch your wagon to a star while keeping your feet on the ground. 6. the art of making your mistakes when nobody is looking. 7. the one unpardonable sin committed against one's fellows. 8. the degree to which other people envy you.

Successful gossip columnist: top man on the quote 'em pole.

Successful man: 1. a man who so lives that when he dies even the undertaker is sorry. 2. one who earns more than his wife can spend.

Successful marriage: where the wife is the boss and doesn't know it.

Successful woman: one who finds such a man.

Sugar daddy: a form of crystallized sap.

Suicide blonde: one who dyed by her own hand.

Suitcase: something you sit on while waiting for the train.

Summer: 1. the season when children slam the doors they left open all winter. 2. the time of year when the highway authorities close the regular roads and open up the detours. 3. when the four-color pictures in the seed catalog turn into four-hour backaches in the garden.

330

Summer camps: those places where little boys go for mother's vacation.

Sunbather: a fry in the ointment.

Sunburn: 1. getting what you basked for. 2. the red menace.

Sunday drive: creeping up with the Joneses.

Sunday school: a prison in which children do penance for the evil conscience of their parents.

Superiority: the feeling you get when riding on an express train and pass a local.

Super-salesman: one who can sell a double-breasted suit to a man with a Phi Beta Kappa key.

Superstition: the error of putting faith in the wrong things.

Surprise: opening your laundry to see what you get.

Swearing apparel: a stuck zipper.

Sweater: a garment worn by a child when his mother feels chilly.

Swell-head: nature's frantic effort to fill a vacuum.

Swimming pool: a crowd of people with water in it.

Sympathizer: a fellow that's for you as long as it doesn't cost anything.

Sympathy: what one girl offers another in exchange for details.

Syncopation: a lively movement from bar to bar.

Synonym: a word you use when you can't spell the other one.

T

Tabloid: a newspaper with a permanent crime wave.

Tabloids: fast reading for the slow-thinking.

Tact: 1. the ability to arrive at conclusions without expressing them. 2. the ability to change a porcupine into a possum. 3. the ability to describe others as they see themselves. 4. the ability to give a person a shot in the arm without letting him feel the needle. 5. the ability to hammer home a point without hitting the other fellow on the head. 6. the ability to make your guests feel at home when you wish they were. 7. the ability to put your best foot forward without stepping on anybody's toes. 8. the ability to shut your mouth before someone else does. 9. the art of knowing how far one may go too far. 10. the knack of making a point without making an enemy. 11. the unsaid part of what you think. 12. to lie about others as you would have them lie about you.

Tainted money: tain't yours and tain't mine.

Take-home pay: a 19th century custom, now outmoded by the tax laws.

Tangerine: a loose-leaf orange.

Tarnished lady: one that is not bright.

Taxation: the process by which money is collected from the people to pay the salaries of the men who do the collecting. The surplus is used to pay the salaries of the men the people elect to decide how much shall be collected from them.

Taxidermist: a man who knows his stuff.

Taxpayer: 1. a government worker with no vocation, no sick leave, and no holidays. 2. a person who has the government on his payroll. 3. incomepooped.

Teacher: a person who swore she would starve before teaching, and who has been doing both ever since.

Teen-agers: 1. people who express a burning drive to be different by dressing alike. 2. people who get hungry again before the dishes are even washed.

Teen-age talk: idol gossip.

Telegram: a form of correspondence sent by a man in a hurry and delivered by a boy in sleep.

Telephone: 1. a contrivance for letting us talk to people whom we don't want to meet. 2. an invention of the devil which abrogates some of the advantages of making a disagreeable person keep his distance.

Television: 1. a kind of radio which lets people at home see what the studio audience is not laughing at. 2. a means of getting a baby-sitter so Mom and Dad can get out to the movies. 3. a medium of entertainment that permits a female singer wide-range—from high C to low V. 4. radio with eyestrain. 5. something to put on a radio so that folks can see things are really as bad as they heard they were. 6. summer stock in an iron lung. 7. vidiot's delight. 8. where the law of the jingle prevails.

Temperament: temper that is too old to spank.

Temperamental: 1. easy glum, easy glow. 2. ninety percent temper, ten percent mental.

Temptation: 1. an irresistible force at work on a movable body. 2. something which, when resisted, gives happiness and which, when yielded to, gives even greater happiness.

Ticket scalper: a man who enables you to see one football game for the price of five.

Tightwad: one who has an impediment in his reach.

Time: 1. the arbitrary division of eternity. 2. the only money that cannot be counterfeited. 3. the stuff between paydays.

Tips: wages we pay other people's help.

Toastmaster: 1. a gentleman who introduces a gentleman who needs no introduction. 2. a man who eats a meal he doesn't want so he can get up and tell a lot of stories he doesn't remember to people who have already heard them. 3. the man at a banquet whose duty it is to inform you that the best part of the entertainment is over. 4. the punk that starts things off.

Tobacco: found in many southern states and in some cigarettes.

Today: the tomorrow you worried about yesterday.

Tolerance: 1. another word for indifference. 2. something parents have to teach a child in the first ten years—so he'll be able to put up with them for the next ten. 3. that uncomfortable feeling that the other fellow might be right after all.

Tongue twister: a phrase that gets your tang all tongueled up.

Torch singer: a woman who lights a fire that the customers put out with liquor.

Totalitarian state: a place where the people in jail are better than the people who put them there.

Toupee: top secret.

Tourist: a person who stops at filling stations for free air, free water, free crankcase service, free information, and to blame the attendant for the condition of the roads.

Tourists: people who travel thousands of miles to get a picture of themselves standing by the car.

Trade secrets: what women do.

Tradition: what a town gets when its residents don't want to build new buildings.

Traffic: a lot of cars moving fast until your car joins them.

Traffic light: 1. a little green light that changes to red as your car approaches. 2. a trick to get pedestrians halfway across the street safely. 3. a device for luring pedestrians out where cars can get at them.

Traffic ticket: finale of the policeman's bawl.

Tragedy: getting what one wants—or not getting it.

Train announcer: a misunderstood man.

Travel: people travel for the same reason as they collect works of art; because the best people do it.

Traveler: one who usually returns brag and baggage.

Travel folder: a trip teaser.

Tree: an object that will stand in one place for years, then jump in front of a lady driver.

Trim figures: what women do when they tell their age.

Triumph: umph added to try.

Trouble: 1. opportunity in work clothes. 2. something that many are looking for but no one wants.

Truck driver: a man who has the opportunity to run into so many nice people.

True musician: when one hears a lady singing in the bath, he puts his ear to the keyhole.

Truly happy marriage: one in which a woman gives the best years of her life to the man who made them the best.

Typewriter: a machine used by stenographers and which can't spell, either.

U

Ukulele: a so-called musical instrument which, when listened to, you cannot tell whether one is playing on it or just monkeying with it.

Umbrella: 1. a shelter for one and a shower bath for two. 2. something to put away for a rainy day.

Unaware: what you put on first and take off last.

Uncanny: the way our grandmothers prepared meals.

Under separate cover: twin beds.

Unimportance: the sensation that comes when you make a mistake and nobody notices it.

United States: where under the Constitution every man may make a fool of himself as he sees fit.

Untold wealth: that which does not appear on income tax returns.

Upper berth: where you rise to retire and get down to get up.

Upper crust: a bunch of crumbs stuck together with their own dough.

335

DEFINITIONS

Used car: 1. a car in first crash condition. 2. not what it's jacked up to be.

Usher: 1. a guy who can really put you in your place. 2. one who takes a leading part in a theater.

Utopia: conditions that will prevail when Americans enjoy 1958 wages, 1926 dividends, 1932 prices, and 1910 taxes.

V

Vacation: 1. a period during which people find out where to stay away from next year. 2. a sunburn at premium prices. 3. a trip to put you in the pink—and leave you in the red!

Vacation menace: sabotourists.

Vacation time: that period when the flowers in the home garden are at their best and only the neighbors are around to enjoy them.

Vegetable: a substance used to ballast a child's plate while it's carried to and from the table.

Violinist: a man who is always up to his chin in music.

Virtue: 1. insufficient temptation. 2. in the female, lack of temptation—in the male, lack of opportunity.

Virus: 1. a Latin word used by doctors to mean "your guess is as good as mine." 2. a word coined by someone who couldn't spell pneumonia.

Voting: a process of standing in line for the opportunity to help decide which party will spend your money.

Vulgarity: the conduct of others.

W

Waiter: a man who thinks money grows on trays.

War: a monster which will destroy us unless we destroy it.

336

Wartime travel: the most uncomfortable distance between two points.

Washington: hubbub of the universe.

Waterworks: a woman's tears.

Wealth: a curse when the neighbors have it.

Wedding: 1. a ceremony at which a man loses complete control of himself. 2. a ceremony where the bridegroom starts kissing the bride and the other fellows stop. 3. a funeral where you smell your own flowers. 4. the point at which a man stops toasting a woman and begins roasting her.

Wedding license: a certificate that gives a woman the legal right to drive a man.

Wedding ring: the smallest hand cuff in the world.

Weed: a plant whose virtues have not been discovered.

Welcome: something that can't be reconditioned after it's worn out.

Well-informed woman: one who's on a party line.

White collar worker: one who carries his lunch in a brief case instead of a pail.

Wickedness: a myth invented by good people to account for the singular attractiveness of others.

Wife: 1. a dish jockey. 2. a former sweetheart. 3. a person who can look into the top drawer of a dresser and find a man's handkerchief that isn't there. 4. a person who may suffer in silence but who usually has a lot to say about it later. 5. a woman who sticks with her husband through all the troubles he never would have had if he hadn't married her.

Will power: 1. the ability, after you have used three-fourths of a can of paint and finished the job, to close the can and clean the brush, instead of painting something else that really doesn't need it. 2. the ability to eat *one* salted peanut. 3. the ability to stick to a diet for two days in a row.

DEFINITIONS

Window screen: a device to prevent the escape of insects.

Winter: the season when we try to keep the house as hot as it was in the summer, when we complained about the heat.

Wisdom: 1. common sense in an uncommon degree. 2. knowing when to speak your mind and when to mind your speech.

Wise husband: one who buys his wife such fine china she won't trust him to wash the dishes.

Wise man: 1. one who is smarter than he thinks he is. 2. one who thinks all he says. Fool: one who says all he thinks.

Wolf: 1. a fellow who wants his hands on a girl, but doesn't want a girl on his hands. 2. a guy who strikes while the eyein' is hot. 3. a man with a community chest. 4. a wild animal on two legs, with a pair of eyes on two other legs. 5. frequently a fine fellow once you get to no him. 6. one who enjoys life, liberty, and the happiness of pursuit.

Woman: 1. a creature who dresses for men's eyes and women's eyebrows. 2. a creature whom God made beautiful that man might love her; and unreasonable that she might love man. 3. a person who can hurry through a drug store aisle 18 inches wide without brushing against the piled up tinware, and then drive home and still knock off one of the doors of a 12-foot garage. 4. a person who can't change her opinion and won't change the subject. 5. a person who goes to a football game to look at mink coats. 6. a person who needs a shoe larger inside than outside. 7. a person who's always ready to take what's becoming her. 8. a person who stands 20 minutes talking at a door because she hasn't time to come in. 9. a person who tells what somebody said about somebody without even pausing every fifteen minutes for station announcements. 10. a person who will spend $20 on a beautiful slip and then be annoyed if it shows. 11. one who, generally speaking, is generally speaking. 12. someone who reaches for a chair when answering the telephone. 13. the only one who can skin a wolf and get a mink. 14. the opposition sex; the weeper sex; a species of creatures known for untold ages.

Woman driver: 1. a person who drives the same way a man does —only she gets blamed for it. 2. one who doesn't let her right hand know what her left hand has signaled.

338

Woman motorist: one who, when she holds her hand out, you can be certain is either going to turn to the right, turn to the left, or stop.

Woman's club: 1. a place where they knock *after* they enter. 2. a room full of loose tongues and tight girdles.

Woman shopper: one who returns an article for credit, buys something that costs twice as much, and figures she has saved half the amount.

Women: 1. people who are biased—"buy us this" and "buy us that." 2. people who need a shoe larger inside than outside. 3. the sex that believes that if you charge it, it's not spending, and if you add a cherry to it, it's not intoxicating. 4. the weeper sex.

Women's clothes: go to extremes, but seldom to extremities.

Wood: that remarkable material which burns so easily in a forest and with such difficulty in a fireplace.

Word: something you must keep after giving it to another.

Work: a tonic which contains no habit-forming drugs.

Work days: an unfortunate lapse of time occurring somewhere between paid holidays and sick and annual leave.

Working girl: one who quit her job to get married.

World: 1. a big ball which revolves on its own taxes. 2. a place so full of a number of things, and they all seem piled on our desk.

Worry: 1. interest paid on trouble before it falls due. 2. putting today's sun under tomorrow's cloud.

Wrinkle: the nick of time.

Y

Yawn: 1. a silent shout. 2. the only time some married men ever get to open their mouths.

DEFINITIONS

Yes-man: 1. a yes-sir who has been promoted. 2. one who stoops to concur.

Yes-men: fellows who hang around the man whom nobody noes.

Younger generation: a group that is alike in many disrespects.

Young man: one whose hardest problem is to find a girl attractive enough to like, but dumb enough to like him.

Youth: 1. that brief period, as distinguished from childhood or middle age, when the sexes talk to each other at a party. 2. the first fifty years of your life; the first twenty of anyone else's.

Youthful figure: something you get when you ask a woman her age.

Z

Zeal: a certain nervous disorder afflicting the young and inexperienced.

Zoo: a place devised for animals to study the habits of human beings.

340

GENERAL INDEX

*(Numbers in the index refer to selections
in the text, not to page numbers.)*

A

Abbreviation, 628
Academic, 147
Acceleration, 324
Accident, 267, 631, 1299
Accident, automobile, 581, 593, 770,
821, 1289, 1305
Accident, streetcar, 680
Accidental, 841
Acclaim, 973
Accompanist, 845
Accomplishment, 1149
Accord, 1040
Accordion, 302
Accuracy, 651
Acknowledgment, 63, 1350
Acquaintance—Acquaintances, 705, 1088,
1294
Acquiescence, 782
Act—Acting, 751, 964
Actor, 415, 751, 964, 1048, 1257
Actress, 423, 1143, 1301
Actuary, life insurance, 1360
Adam, 216, 834, 932
Adams, Sam, 860
Address, 1097
Adhesive tape, 104, 356
Adjuster, insurance, 581
Adjustment, 58, 1144
Admiration, 131
Admission against interest, 954
Advancement, 1224
Advance payment, 252
Advantage, 16, 114, 779
Advertisement, 2, 4, 196, 726, 1252
Advertising, *1-11*, 1126
Advice, *12-17*, 64, 74, 156, 160, 358,
421, 457, 572, 868, 893, 1181
Advice, free, 684
Advice, legal, 679, 1101
Adviser, vocational, 395
Affection, 480
Affluence, 775, 1113

Africa, 233, 545, 691
African chieftain, 674
After-dinner speaker, 1019
Age, *18-28*, 80, 1008, 1250, 1338
Age, Old. See Old Age
Age disparity, 855
Aggressiveness, 763
Aging, *29-34*, 84, 206, 1067, 1183, 1271,
1338
Agony, 692
Agreement, 979, 1040
Agriculture, scientific, 419
Ailment, 831
Air-conditioning, 1059
Airplane, 897, 942, 1309, 1327
Airplane hostess, 942, 968
Aisle—Aisles, 729
Alarm, 1081
Alarm clock, 910, 1033
Albany, N. Y., 548
Album, family, 84, 765
Alcohol, 347
Alcoholic liquor, 129, 134, 201, 298, 347,
692, 938, 1154
Alibi, 967
Alienist. See also Psychiatry, 1007
Alimony, 684
All-purpose, 1325
Allergy, 320
Allowance, 184
Alma Mater, 1017
Alphabet, 203
Altar, 236, 705, 1098
Alteration, 517, 713
Alternate, 323
Alternative, 56, 68, 125, 1105
Alumni, college, 214
Alumni dinner, 464
Alumni reunion, 214
Ambassador, 916
Ambition, 156, 376, 739, 1192, 1212
America, 217, 218, 878, 892
American, 995, 1244, 1287, 1321
American jurisprudence, 655

341

GENERAL INDEX

GENERAL INDEX

Convertible automobile, 1165
Conveyance, public, 583
Convict, 256, 401
Convincing, 723, 900, 1115
Convocation, Religious, 942
Cook—Cooking—Cooks, 243, 545, 643, 734, 743, 946, 952
Cook book, 806
Coolidge, Calvin, 1182
Coonskin cap, 590
Cooperation, 64
Copper plate, 890
Copper production, 913
Copyreader, 1351
Cordiality, 407
Cork, 339, 441
Corn, 1337
Cornfield, 1306
Coroner, 911
Corporal, 784
Correction, 10, 45, 1144
Correspondence, 138, 290
Correspondence school, 1058
Cosmetics, 108
Costliness. See also Expensive, 9, 201
Cottage, 903
Couch, 1000
Couch, psychiatrist's, 1008
Cough drop, 962
Counterbalance, 807
Counterfeit money, 114
Country club, 81, 489
Country doctor, 1181
County jail, 924
Courage, *233, 234*
Court, 1263
Court, contempt of, 1270
Court hearing, 1297
Court record, 446
Courtesy, 334, 1289, 1302
Courtroom, 339, 678
Courtship, *235-240,* 528, 582, 1064
Courtyard, 1187
Cover-up, 36, *241-244*
Cow—Cows, 49, 93, 422, 1021
Cow, Black, 1010
Cow shed, 903
Coward, 287
Cowardice, 181
Cowpuncher, 631, 690
Crayon, 1010
Creation, 572
Credit, 132, 212, *245-249,* 647
Credit buying. See also Installment purchase, *621-627*
Credit terms, 621
Creditor, 99, 160, *250-253,* 273, 317, 969
Creeping inflation, 614
Cremation, 835, 1018
Crew, 1314
Crime, 629

Crime and Punishment, *254-257,* 634
Criminal—Criminals, 254, 255, 912
Crisis, Marital, 767
Critic, 260, 1137
Critic, art, 47, 55
Criticism, 66, 69, *258-262,* 457, 750, 845, 1137
Crop, 39
Cross-country driver, 585
Cross-examination, 1263
Cross-eyed, 1006
Crouse, Russel, 69
Crow, 628
Cruelty, 1084
Cruise, lake, 851
Cruise, world, 1314
Crutches, 680
Cry—Crying, 28, 120, 619
Curbstone, 338
Cure, 33, 298, 317, 322
Curiosity, 88, 153, *263-266,* 546, 556, 820, 1065
Currency, 994, 1200
Currency, paper, 402
Cussing, 960
Custom, 850, 1255
Customer, 21, 1127
Customs declaration, 1319
Customs officer, 1319

D

Dance—Dancing, 81, 239, *267-270,* 718, 830, 844, 1099
Dance hall, 35
Dance ticket, 1055
Dancer, 38
Dancing school, 268
Danger, 1303
Darkness, 667
Darwin, Charles, 598
Darwinian theory, 37
Dating, 206, 358
Daughter, 1256
Daydreaming, 1354
Deacon, 804
Dead, 1225
Deaf—Deafness, 238, 267, 760, 1297
Dean of women, 202
Death, 32, 192, *271, 272,* 316, 322, 462, 641, 685, 974, 1077, 1205
Death, natural, 314
Death, proof of, 995
Death notice, 45
Deathbed, 1228
Debonair, 1085
Debt—Debts, 248, 249, *273-278,* 564, 621, 622, 761, 969, 1200, 1328
Debussy, Claude Achille, 602
Deceased, 1191
Decency, 424

348

349

GENERAL INDEX

GENERAL INDEX

F

GENERAL INDEX

GENERAL INDEX

GENERAL INDEX

Milwaukee, Wis., 123
Mind, 147, 310, 601
Mind, change of, 161, 182
Mind, peace of, 5
Mind, presence of, *798-803*, 1044
Mind reader, 160
Minerva, 732
Miniature, 669
Minister. See also Preacher, 7, 110, 125, 180, 195, 242, 349, 462, 648, 695, 719, 726, 814, 833, 938, 944, 945, 947, 953, 954, 959, 960, 965, 984, 1040, 1061, 1070, 1132, 1171, 1269
Mink coat, 171
Minneapolis, Minn., 958
Minuet, 270
Miracle, 492, 637
Mirror, 356, 408, 862, 1324
Miser, 470, 875, 1353
Miserliness, 358
Misfire, 21
Misinterpretation, *804-806*
Missing persons, 836
Missionary, 175, 1120
Mississippi, State of, 394
Mississippi River, 394
Missile, Space, 887
Mistake—Mistakes, 10, 133, 243, 280, 497, 678, 742, 793, *807-820*, 858, 962, 972, 1118, 1144, 1240
Mistaken identity, 898
Mistress, 593
Misunderstanding, 514, *821-826*
Model, 572, 594, 665
Modesty, 81, 973
Money, 97, 109, 152, 332, 358, 390, 518, 566, 575, 613, 619, 688, 694, 710, 745, 747, 761, 775, *827-829*, 854, 862, 920, 986, 1089, 1090, 1093, 1199, 1200, 1202, 1231, 1348, 1353
Money, counterfeit, 114
Money, spending, 617
Money order, 994
Money-saving, 746
Money value, 617
Monkey, 132
Monopoly, 224
Monosyllable, 1182
Monroe, Marilyn, 898
Monument, 260, 896
Moody, Dwight L., 1061
Moral—Morals, 197, *691, 692*
Moral age, 27
Morris, Sir Lewis, 258
Mortgage, 246
Mortician, 591, 1229
Moscow, Russia, 219
Mother, 425, 588, 715, *830-832*, 952
Mother, expectant, 1054
Mother-in-law, 390, 397, 561, *832-842*, 1151, 1184

Mother-love, 335
Mother of the bride, 838
Motherhood, *830, 831*
Motion picture, 634, 790, 1268
Motion picture director, 1078
Motion picture producer, 1104
Motion picture studio, 423
Motive, *843, 844*
Motorboat, 1127
Motorcycle, 911
Motorcycle cop, 1296
Motorist, 367, 760, 800, 1166, 1262, 1267, 1279, 1287, 1292, 1304, 1305
Motto, 804
Mourner—Mourners, 963
Mourning, 734, 1068, 1213
Mouse—Mice, 562, 775
Mouth, 517
Move—Moving, 787
Movie, 790
Movie producer, 469, 852
Movie star, 1104
Mule, 59, 833, 931, 1132, 1267
Multimillionaire, 1350
Multitude, 907
Mumps, 1331
Murder, 262, 678, 776, 970
Murderer, 256
Muscatine, Ia., 914
Mushrooms, 256
Music, 10, 262, 267, 717, 721, *845-847*, 1131, 1185, 1187, 1326
Music composer, 846
Music composition, 992
Music lesson, 1216
Musical, 718
Musical comedy, 846
Musical concert, 1188
Musical instrument, 771, 1083, 1114, 1326
Musical performance, 1188
Musical score, 846
Musician, 260, 302
Mustache, 84
Mythology, Greek, 732

N

N.S.F., 95
Nag—Nagging, 747
Naiveté, 548, 1180
Nakedness, 325, 423
Name—Names, 255, 291, 322, *848-85*, 1013, 1054, 1060, 1072, 1097, 1104
Name, assumed, 162
Napkin, 666, 1176
Narrow escape, 785, 985
National Press Club, 1021
Nationality, 216
Native—Natives, 1287
Natural death, 314

GENERAL INDEX

GENERAL INDEX

Poverty, 648
Practicability, 469, *942, 943*
Practical joke, 1261
Practical joker, 1106
Practice, 467, 1115
Prairie, 1027
Praise, 1060
Prayer, 381, 649, *944-953*
Preacher. See also Minister, 7, 191, 192, 513, 958, 979, 1232
Preaching, 191, *954-965*, 1061
Precaution, 14, 245, 402, 633, 905, *966-971*
Preciseness, 962
Precocity, 364
Predecessor, 992
Preference, 495, 740, 942, 943, 1321
Prejudice, *972, 973*
Preliminary, 59
Premium, insurance, 995
Preparation, 555, 974
Preparedness, *974-976*
Prescription, 306, 312, 313, 320, 324, 327, 805, 809, 977, 978, 1181
Presence of mind, *798-803*
President of the United States, 674, 1250
Presidential message, 1344
Press interview, 931
Presumption of innocence, 655
Pretend, 619
Pretense, 1262
Pretext, 586
Prevarication, 1122
Preview, movie, 1334
Price—Prices, 44, 144, 420, 790, 794, 795, 954, 1066
Price reduction, 1234
Priceless, 984
Pride, 1215, 1243
Priest, 1109
Priest, Catholic, 1041
Priesthood, Catholic, 1109
Prima donna, 1334
Printer, 133, 209
Priority, 344
Prison, 146, 679, 940
Prison life, 257
Prison warden, 1057
Prisoner, 401, 1037, 1057, 1173
Private, army, 784
Private enterprise, 159
Private office, 1141
Prize, 396, 930, 1073
Prize fight—Prize fighting, 522, 1197
Pro and con, 900
Problem—Problems, 999, 1003, 1059
Problem, solution of, 999
Process, manufacturing, 212
Producer, motion picture, 469, 852, 1104, 1334
Production, 44

Profanity, 28, 509, 513, 577, 681, √38, 960, 1072, 1153, 1206
Profession, 116, 932, 965
Profession, medical, 591
Professional, golf, 498
Professional fees, 280, 304, 324, 332, 814, *979-994*, 1248
Professor, 63, 104, 141, 208, 209, 213, 278, 546, 601, 732, 818, 1179, 1212
Professor-Student, 278
Profit—Profits, 155, 473
Profit and loss, 53
Profit-sharing, 98
Prognosis, 330
Progress, 917
Progress chart, 333
Prohibition, 291
Projectile, rocket, 887
Projectile, thermonuclear, 364
Prolapsus, 989
Promise, 474, 1069, 1106
Promise, breach of, 778
Promise, campaign, 927
Promissory note, 96, 317
Promotion, 383, 1224
Promptness, 378, 1190
Proof, 24, 438, 446, 632, *995-998*, 1253, 1300
Proof of death, 995
Proposal, marriage, 193, 236, 238, 715, *740, 741*, 786, 1081, 1094, 1099, 1193, 1247
Proprietorship, 76
Propriety, 399
Prosecuting attorney, 1142
Prosecution, 655
Prosecutor, 254
Prospective purchaser, 626
Protective tariff, 930
Protestant, 1041, 1109
Prowler, 801
Pseudonym, 852
Psychiatrist, 317, 763
Psychiatry, 568, 701, *999-1011*
Psychoanalyst, 1005
Psychological age, 27
Psychologist, child, 184
Public, the, 522
Public conveyance, 583, 813
Public good, 937
Public official, 919, 924
Public opinion, 931
Public park, 830
Public speaking, 287, 646, 957, 973, *1012-1030*, 1274
Publicity, 641, 934
Publisher, 67, 343
Pulitzer, Joseph, 651
Pullman conductor, 1312
Pullman porter, 1239
Pulpit, 790, 950, 957, 1269

GENERAL INDEX

GENERAL INDEX

GENERAL INDEX

370

GENERAL INDEX

Underwater, 198, 959
Undisclosed, 603
Undress, 822
Uneducated, 359
Unenthusiastic, 270
Unexpected, the, 166
Unfairness, 570, 656, 682
Unfinished. See also Incomplete, 203
Uniformity, 503
Unimportance, 582
Union Station, Chicago, 123
United Nations, 217
United States Congress, 940
United States of America, 89, 222, 1197
University, 359, 1158
University of Chattanooga, 996
University of Chicago, 1041
University of Michigan, 362
Unmanageable, 1358
Unsteadiness, 345
Untruth, 372, 432, 443, 609, 934, 1008,
  1095, 1107, 1344
Unwelcome, 388
Uphill, 879
Upholstery, 76, 1116
Used car, 75
Usefulness, 68, *1325-1327*
Uselessness, 412, 1251
Usher, 838
Uxoricide, 574

V

Vacancy, 386
Vacancy, job, 373
Vacation, 50, 98, 107, 316, 370, 442,
  523, 532, 641, 805, 843, 1260, 1314,
  1328-1333
Vacuum cleaner, 266, 1115, 1175
Value, 259, 615, 616, 702, 984, 1084,
  1118, 1264
Value, money, 617
Valueless, 615, 616
Values, 198
Vanity, 408
Vase, 380, 470
Vault, 1353
Venice, Italy, 1349
Veracity. See also Truth, 332, 436, 482,
  755, 799, 934, 1008, 1082, 1095, 1266,
  1334-1344, 1361
Vermin, 539
Vermont, State of, 42, 962, 998, 1269
Vest, 223, 563
Veterinarian, 285, 1299
Veterinary doctor, 1299
Vice-presidency, bank, 1174
Vice-president, 93, 1342
Vice versa, 1122
Victory, 649, 928
Victuals, 404

Village, 57
Violation, law, 1166
Violin, 1185
Violinist, 288, 1187
Virtue, 232, 651
Visitor, 1044
Vital statistics, 24
Vocabulary, 213
Vocalist, 1186
Vocational adviser, 395
Vocational guidance, 1212
Voice, 845
Voluntariness, 221
Volunteer, 1145
Vote—Voter—Voting, 941, 998
Vote tabulation, 998
Vouch—Vouchsafe, 542
Voyage, 435
Voyage, ocean, 1317
Vulgarity, 1153

W

Wage increase, 780
Wager. See also Bet—Betting, 160, 1111,
  1169
Wages, 379, 380, 391, 807, 1192
Wagon, 909
Wahr's Book Store, 362
Waiter, 6, 177, 366, 520, 936, 1068,
  1241, 1242, 1257
Waitress, 388, 516, 1065, 1067
Waiver, 960
Walk—Walking, 338, 493
Wallet, 749, 1074, 1118, 1252
Wallpaper, 1235
Walton, Izaak, 441
Wanamaker, John, 4
Wanderlust, 519
War, 1251, *1345-1347*
Warden, game, 447, 799, 1019
Warden, penitentiary, 214, 256
Warden, prison, 1057
Wardrobe, 434
Warning, 77
Washday, 803
Washington, Booker T., 973
Washington, George, 41, 443, 609, 1226
Washington Biological Survey, 628
Washington, D.C., 366
Washington (D.C.) News, 1351
Waste of time, 1269
Watch, 484
Watch, pocket, 907
Watchman, night, 910
Water, 192, 692, 1028, 1169
Water carrier, 1236
Water supply, 966
Waves, 696
Waves, black, 1010
Weakness, 163, 957

Index
for
SPECIAL OCCASIONS

*(Numbers in the index refer to selections
in the text, not to page numbers.)*

SPECIAL OCCASIONS INDEX

1123, 1124, 1125, 1126, 1127, 1128, 1164, 1230

Scientific meeting, 37, 104, 138, 598, 818, 877, 887, 891, 892, 1014, 1016, 1059, 1172, 1179, 1230

Sermon, 143, 478, 521, 524, 649, 907, 908, 949, 953, 955, 956, 957, 958, 959, 960, 961, 962, 964, 965, 1014, 1040, 1043, 1072, 1153, 1232

Service Clubs, 159, 1014, 1016

Sisterhood meeting, 122, 1014, 1016

Sports, 406, 481, 482, 485, 492, 1016, 1100, 1155, 1156, 1157, 1158, 1159, 1160, 1161, 1197, 1200, 1268

Sunday School, 194, 616, 1213, 1218, 1293

T

Temperance meeting, 50, 120, 199, 692, 888, 938, 939, 1014, 1016

Testimonial Dinner, 12, 71, 110, 139, 383, 929, 1014, 1016, 1168

Toastmaster, 71, 104, 146, 359, 372, 543, 929, 1012, 1013, 1014, 1015, 1016, 1017, 1018, 1020, 1028, 1029

Tolerance, 972, 973, 1016

Trade Association, 16, 35, 622, 647, 900, 975, 1014, 1016

Trophies, presentation of, 15, 110, 387, 1016

V

V. J. Day—See Veterans Day

Veterans Day, 139, 456, 884, 902, 1014, 1016, 1049, 1063, 1345, 1347

Veterans of Foreign Wars, 139, 456, 784, 1014, 1051

W

Washington's Birthday, 443, 609, 1016

Wedding anniversary, 13, 19, 30, 43, 64, 108, 136, 140, 225, 237, 263, 292, 662, 714, 772, 984, 1016, 1056, 1064, 1077, 1078, 1087, 1178

Wedding party, 13, 78, 140, 235, 243, 263, 358, 442, 527, 582, 696, 706, 1064, 1078, 1081, 1213

Woman's Club, 22, 26, 1014, 1016, 1363

Y

Y.M.C.A., 291, 1014, 1016

Y.W.C.A., 22, 1014, 1016

Youth, 18, 27, 51, 124, 126, 157, 186, 203, 291, 808, 876, 947, 948, 1016, 1052, 1071, 1154, 1313

Youth Organization, 18, 25, 27, 124, 1014, 1016

Index
for
SPECIAL GROUPS

(Numbers in the index refer to selections in the text, not to page numbers.)

A

ccountants, 158, 975, 1062
dvertising, 1, 2, 7, 8, 123, 230, 900, 907, 975, 1016, 1126
gricultural, 35, 152, 157, 173, 1016
rchitects, 35, 42, 243, 383, 907, 975, 1016
rmed Forces, 139, 287, 456, 735, 884, 902, 966, 1016, 1051, 1055, 1063, 1345
rt, Artists, 47, 55, 56, 57, 290, 654, 665, 907, 982, 992, 1137, 1227
uctioneers, 61, 62, 707, 907, 1015, 1016, 1074
uthors, 66, 69, 73, 258, 259, 656, 894, 900, 1069
utomobiles, 75, 76, 94, 230, 360, 383, 469, 622, 626, 816, 907, 975, 1016, 1049, 1116

B

akers, 35, 230, 597, 610, 1016
ankers, 35, 83, 86, 87, 90, 91, 92, 93, 94, 95, 96, 118, 150, 154, 155, 158, 159, 160, 245, 246, 247, 250, 376, 383, 402, 411, 614, 617, 622, 656, 895, 900, 907, 975, 1014, 1016, 1174, 1264
ar Association, 35, 203, 247, 254, 275, 603, 655, 659, 661, 682, 802, 900, 907, 975, 987, 1014, 1016
arbers, 35, 83, 100, 101, 273, 975, 1016
eauticians, 24, 35, 38, 58, 79, 107, 108, 111, 898, 1016, 1129
ook club, 73, 85, 141, 142, 143, 1016
ook sellers, 35, 73, 85, 142, 143, 230, 362, 419, 654, 806, 1016
oy Scouts, 18, 127, 1016
oys' Club, 18, 1016

C

hamber of Commerce, 35, 44, 56, 92, 98, 113, 154, 155, 157, 160, 383, 900, 1014, 1016

Clothing, 81, 118, 128, 423, 424, 425, 477, 551, 1016
College Fraternity, 35, 83, 84, 106, 149, 151, 199, 201, 202, 205, 540, 905, 1014, 1016
College Sorority, 25, 26, 107, 108, 119, 128, 140, 200, 202, 540, 905, 1014, 1016

D

Dance Masters, 81, 267, 268, 270, 843, 1016, 1099
Daughters of the American Revolution, 39, 1016
Dentists, 35, 353, 1014, 1016
Doctors, 169, 212, 243, 281, 282, 286, 298, 299, 303, 306, 332, 591, 599, 637, 678, 719, 805, 831, 932, 965, 977, 978, 979, 980, 981, 983, 985, 986, 989, 993, 994, 1181, 1199, 1248
Druggists' Association, 35, 212, 230, 298, 305, 313, 320, 383, 615, 668, 809, 826, 978, 1016

E

Employer-Employe, 98, 780, 807, 924, 971, 975, 1031, 1033, 1039, 1101, 1102, 1104, 1125, 1146, 1148, 1150, 1152, 1192, 1194, 1266, 1351
Engineers, 35, 357, 505, 932, 975, 1016
Executives' Club, 17, 83, 92, 98, 138, 152, 155, 159, 160, 203, 373, 383, 466, 645, 739, 893, 895, 900, 907, 975, 1014, 1016, 1141, 1148, 1152, 1342

F

Family Circle, 18, 36, 62, 63, 74, 84, 136, 137, 185, 327, 416, 417, 465, 515, 519, 820, 821, 832, 836, 875, 889, 970, 1032, 1045, 1053, 1151, 1177, 1202, 1233, 1267, 1352

377

SPECIAL GROUPS INDEX